Research methods for students, academics and professionals

Information management and systems

Second edition

Kirsty Williamson

with

Amanda Bow
Frada Burstein
Peta Darke
Ross Harvey
Graeme Johanson
Sue McKemmish
Majola Oosthuizen
Solveiga Saule
Don Schauder
Graeme Shanks
Kerry Tanner

Topics in Australasian Library and Information Studies, Number 20

Centre for Information Studies
Charles Sturt University
Wagga Wagga New South Wales

ISBN 1 876938 42 0
ISSN: 1030-5009

National Library of Australia cataloguing-in-publication data

---

Williamson, Kirsty.
    Research methods for students, academics and professionals: information management and systems.

    2nd ed.
    Bibliography.
    Includes index.
    ISBN 1 876938 42 0.

    1. Documentation - Research - Australia - Methodology. 2. Library science - Research - Australia - Methodology. 3. Information science - Research - Australia - Methodology. I. Bow, Amanda. II. Charles Sturt University. Centre for Information Studies. III. Title. (Series : Topics in Australasian library and information studies ; no. 20).

020.7094

This edition published in 2002

Copy editors: P. Whitten, R. Salmond
Index: R. Salmond
Cover design: B. Bicket, Reprographics Unit, Charles Sturt University
Printed by: Quick Print, Wagga Wagga

Centre for Information Studies
Locked Bag 660
Wagga Wagga NSW 2678
Fax: 61 2 6933 2733
Email: cis@csu.edu.au

Contents

List of figures, tables and boxes

Acknowledgments

The inspiration for this book came from Professor Don Schauder, of Monash University, who first saw the possibilities of a text which would relate research methods to professional practice in information management and systems. At this time (1998) we had recently become part of a new School of Information Management and Systems (SIMS). I am indebted to Don, not only for this initial inspiration, but also for his unstinting encouragement and support throughout the writing of the book.

My thanks go to my colleagues whose names are listed on the title page, and who have contributed chapters to the book. I have very much appreciated their specialist knowledge, their diverse approaches, and their patience with the complex process of creating a book which aims to meet a range of research-related needs in our field.

My thanks also go to students in SIMS (Monash University), RMIT's School of Business Information Technology (through Kerry Tanner) and The University of Melbourne's Department of Information Systems (through Associate Professor Graeme Shanks). We received very helpful feedback from students who read and commented on the draft chapters during Semester 1 of 1999.

The process of finishing the book would have been much more difficult had Professor Ross Harvey not arrived at Charles Sturt University at the time that the writing of the book was reaching its conclusion. Ross read all the chapters and provided excellent feedback, as well as generous support in other ways. He was also able to use his knowledge of the book to write the introduction. I acknowledge his contribution with thanks.

Stuart Ferguson, of the Centre for Information Studies, provided valuable guidance throughout the writing and publishing process. The book's editor, Penny Whitten, must be acknowledged with great gratitude for her perceptive and conscientious work in bringing the book up to a high standard. I believe that we could not have had a better editor.

Finally, I thank my husband, Geoff, for his excellent proof-reading skills and for the many hours in which he applied them to the book. He has been an outstanding support in many ways, and is greatly appreciated

Kirsty Williamson
December 1999

Introduction

Ross Harvey

Why another book about research methods? The answer is simple. Research is such an important subject for information professionals – those who work in the field of information management and information systems – that there will always be a need for effective guides to it. Research skills are a prerequisite for those who want to work successfully in information environments, an essential set of tools which enable information *workers* to become information *professionals*. *Research methods for students, academics and professionals: Information management and systems* provides such skills and encourages the information professional to acquire critical and evaluative attitudes. It also has the merit of being Australian-focused, unique among research texts for information professionals. Also notable is its multi-disciplinary focus (of which more later).

Research and professional practice

The work of information professionals is being transformed. The information services we offer, the information products we develop and sell, the information systems we design and implement, are undergoing rapid change. So, too, is the society in which we operate. We have a continual need to determine what is happening, how it is changing, how it will affect our places of work, how it will alter the services we offer. Change and its ramifications is the most important reason why research is necessary, and why it is here to stay. If you don't know something about the tools of research and about how to use these tools, then you cannot be an effective information professional.

Research and *professional* practice are inextricably linked. Research can and does play a vital role in professional practice in the fields of information management and information systems, in corporate, government, educational and community sectors. The most obvious uses of research in these information environments are for problem solving, for development, evaluation and improvement of services and systems, and to provide information before introducing new systems or services (perhaps through the assessment of user needs). As Williamson notes in Chapter 1, research in professional practice is undertaken for many reasons:

- to assist in understanding the problems and issues which arise in the workplace;

- to add to knowledge in the field and/or provide solutions to problems;

- to maintain dynamic and appropriate services;

- to meet requirements of accountability;

- to maintain and improve professional status; and

- to provide a body of research findings and theory to inform practitioners.

The inescapable conclusion is that information professionals need to be – at the very least – *intelligent* and *critical consumers of research*. A quote in Chapter 1 emphasises this point clearly and emphatically:

> Research enables professionals to add value to their work and work practices ... [Its use] distinguishes between professionals who maintain the status quo without question and those who strive to develop their work practices through continual evaluation and investigation (Lowe 1999, p. 1).

The bottom line is that all information professionals must be able to read research reports properly, to understand their contents, and to ascertain whether or not the contents are appropriate to apply to their own work. Many (but perhaps not all) information professionals will also require the critical facility and practical skills to be able to conduct their own research to address workplace problems and issues, to improve practice, and/or to offer better services and products.

Research methods for students, academics and professionals: Information management and systems focuses on producing critical consumers of research. It also goes some way towards producing researchers in the fields of information management and systems.

A multi-disciplinary approach

Who are the information professionals at whom this book is directed? It is multi-disciplinary in its approach, with its authors being drawn from information management (librarianship, archives and recordkeeping) and information systems. Examples are drawn from these multiple disciplines. This reflects the growing realisation that information management (or information studies) is redefining itself as a discipline. Formerly discrete areas (librarianship, archives, records management, information systems as a computing sub-discipline), they are now coalescing – the impetus being information and communications technology. The authors come from SIMS (the School of Information Management and Systems) at Monash University, Melbourne. In this School, the amalgamation of different disciplinary groups, initially made for pragmatic reasons, has been the impetus for identifying and developing productive synergies – hence this book.

One of the outcomes of the multi-disciplinary approach is that this book provides stimulus for those of us who come from a discrete research tradition. Here the various traditions of research are clearly explained and developed within a spectrum model, with positivist traditions at one end, and interpretivist at the other. The information management and systems discipline, this book makes clear, deals with all of them in varying mixes.

Another outcome is the variety of views provided by the book's many contributors based in different disciplines and research traditions. Although the variety of contributors also contributes to stylistic variation within the book, the reader will find that any unevenness of style is well and truly overridden by the strengths this variety contributes – a heady mix of the theoretical and the practical, and the stimulation provided by the multi-disciplinary approach.

How to use this book

The structure of this book differs from the usual research methods texts in information studies (Busha and Harter 1980; Glazier and Powell 1992; Gorman and Clayton 1997; Powell 1997; Slater 1990). It distinguishes between research *methods* and research *techniques*, on the basis that a research technique for data gathering (for example, focus groups) can be used with a number of different methods. Typically books about research treat technique and method together, thereby implicitly limiting the use of a particular technique to a certain method, for example, questionnaires with surveys. The approach offered in this book also helps the reader and beginning researcher to avoid the tendency to concentrate on a single method or technique to the exclusion of other viable approaches. The research problem, the research question, has to be the starting point of the research, with the choice of method(s) and technique(s) consequent on this. One of this book's strengths is that it presents the palette of methods and techniques from which the researcher can identify those which are most appropriate to the research problem.

Williamson acknowledges that it is not always easy to differentiate research method from research technique. Here *research method* denotes a design for undertaking research, including the theoretical background to this design. *Research techniques* are used to describe the means by which data are gathered and samples selected. Chapter 1 explains this further.

The book has four sections. The first, consisting of Chapters 1 to 4, introduces the subject, provides a framework for thinking about research, notes major issues and typologies of research, and describes what is required to get started on a research project. Chapter 4, a new chapter in this edition, addresses ethics, accommodating the realisation in recent decades that the ethical implications of our research have to be taken seriously. The second section (Chapters 5 to 12) examines research methods: survey, case study, experimental design, system development in information systems research, action research, ethnography, historical research, and the Delphi method. The third section (Chapters 13 to 16) describes techniques used for data collection: questionnaire design, interviewing, focus groups, and ethnographic techniques, including observation. The final section (Chapters 17 and 18) deals with data analysis, and evaluation of published research. A Postscript poses questions which will encourage further thinking about the role and conduct of research in information management and systems.

What the book does not cover

Inevitably a book of this nature will have omissions. Not present are some of the techniques occasionally applied in research in information management and information systems. The most obvious of these are bibliometrics and its offspring citation analysis, and content analysis. *Bibliometrics* is a technique which counts and interprets data gathered from and about publications. (Currently a claim is being made to allow webometrics into the echelon of research techniques.) *Content analysis* is used to analyse a body of literature and deduce from this analysis some characteristics of the literature, such as identification of themes and how frequently they occur.

Warranty statement

Finally, a guarantee of quality. The contents of this book have been road-tested with students and academics from several disciplines at several universities. Their input has been helpful, gratefully received, and incorporated into the text of the book. In research terms, the contents have been refereed and found to be authoritative!

References for Introduction

Busha, Charles H. and Harter, Stephen P. (1980). *Research methods in librarianship: Techniques and interpretations.* Academic Press: Orlando, NY.

Glazier, J.D. and Powell, R.R. (1992). *Qualitative research in information management.* Libraries Unlimited: Englewood, Co.

Gorman, G.E. and Clayton, Peter. (1997). *Qualitative research for the information professional: A practical handbook.* Library Association Publishing: London.

Lowe, D. (1999). Introduction to research in relation to professional practice. Unpublished paper. School of Information Management and Systems, Monash University, Caulfield, Vic., p. 1.

Powell, Ronald. (1997). *Basic research methods for librarians.* 3rd edn. Ablex: Norwood, NJ.

Slater, M. (ed.). (1990). *Research methods in library and information studies*. Library Association: London.

Section 1: Introduction to research methods

Introduction

The introductory section, Chapters 1 to 4, introduces the subject of research methods, provides a framework for thinking about research, discusses major philosophies and typologies, and describes the preliminaries required for a research project. The role of research in professional practice is highlighted in Chapter 1.

CHAPTER 1

Introduction to research in relation to professional practice
Kirsty Williamson with Frada Burstein and Sue McKemmish

Objectives

At the end of this chapter you will be able to:

- understand how research is defined;

- have begun to learn some of the specific terminology used by researchers;

- understand the major elements of a research project and how they are covered in this book;

- be aware of the roles which research can play and should play in professional practice; and

- understand the kinds of workplace issues which might warrant research.

Introduction

This introductory chapter considers how research is defined, both in general and more specific ways. This will lead to the roles which research can and should play in professional practice, particularly in the field of information management and systems – in corporate, government, educational and community sectors.

For many of you, some of the terminology used to describe research methodology will be new. A glossary of terms describing various aspects of research, is included at the end of the book. It would be a good idea to check it over now, and then be sure to refer to it as you meet an unfamiliar term along the way.

What is research?

The need to know, to interpret the environment or the world, is basic to us all. There is a sense in which research is simply one of the fundamental activities of human beings. The main difference between our everyday activity and formal research is the rigour and discipline with which the latter is carried out and the making of that process highly self-conscious. Below are a number of different definitions, not all from the 'information' field. The first two are very simple; the second two a lot more complex.

> Research is any conscious premeditated inquiry – any investigation which seems to increase one's knowledge of a given situation (Goldhor 1972, p. 7).

> Research is a systematic investigation to find answers to a problem (Burns 1990, p. 1).

> Research ... [is] an organised, systematic, data-based, critical, scientific inquiry or investigation into a specific problem, undertaken with the objective of finding answers or solutions to it (Sekeran 1992, p. 4).

> For the social scientist or researcher in applied fields, research is a process of trying to gain a better understanding of human interactions. Through systematic means, the researcher gathers information about actions and interactions, reflects on their meaning, arrives at and evaluates conclusions, and eventually puts forward an interpretation (Marshall and Rossman 1995, p. 15).

The third of these definitions emerges from the *positivist* tradition of research, which sees links between the ways in which the natural sciences and social sciences should be investigated. The emphasis in this tradition has been on the collection of *quantitative* data, which are data in the form of numbers collected by techniques such as questionnaires and other instruments of measurement. The fourth comes from the *interpretivist* approach, which emphasises meanings created by people and data which are *qualitative* (or in the form of words), collected by techniques such as interviews and observation. However, at least some of the time, both types of data and data collection are used by both types of researchers. The two different traditions are described in Chapter 2.

A fifth definition comes from Hernon (1991). It encompasses all styles of research and is said to cover the types of research in library and information studies:

> Research is an inquiry process that has clearly defined parameters and has as its aim, the:
>
> * Discovery or creation of knowledge, or theory building;
> * Testing, confirmation, revision, refutation of knowledge and theory; and/or
> * Investigation of a problem for local decision making (Hernon 1991, pp. 3-4).

In professional practice in information environments, the most obvious uses of research are for problem solving, for development, evaluation and improvement of services and systems, or to provide information before introducing new systems or services (probably through the assessment of user needs). This should not rule out 'theory building', which provides an important underpinning for all professions. The role of theory will be discussed in Chapter 3.

Research is often described as a linear, organised process. In fact, it is a good idea to realise that usually the process is less under control than the text books indicate. Figure 1.1 (The island of research) is provided with 'tongue in cheek', but contains more than an element of truth! As Marshall and Rossman (1995, p. 15) say: 'real research is often confusing, messy, intensely frustrating, and fundamentally nonlinear'.

Basic versus applied research

There are many ways of categorising and discussing research. As already mentioned, in Chapter 2 we shall explore the two major traditions of research. For now, the discussion concerns the categories of basic and applied research.

Basic research, also referred to as pure, fundamental or theoretical research, is primarily concerned with deriving new knowledge and is only indirectly involved (if at all) with how that knowledge will be applied to specific, practical problems. Basic research tends to focus on theory building and/or hypothesis testing. It extends horizons in a general, fundamental way. (See Box 1.1 for examples of basic research.)

Applied research is concerned with solving specific problems in real life situations. It is much more pragmatic and emphasises information which is immediately usable in the solution of actual problems. It is more likely to be the type of research which is applicable to information environments and in business. In terms of information environments, an example might be the evaluation of whether an innovative system of electronic recordkeeping is meeting the needs of users. In the business environment, an organisation contemplating a paperless office and a networking system for the company's personal computers, may conduct research to learn the amount of time its employees spend at personal computers in an average week (Zikmund 1994, p. 7).

In fact, the distinction between basic and applied research is not clear-cut. Many of the same techniques are used in both. Research can be practical (applied) and still generate new theory and make a contribution to fundamental knowledge. Conversely, the findings of basic or pure research will often have practical applications in the long term. (See Box 1.2 for an example of basic research with 'applied' elements.)

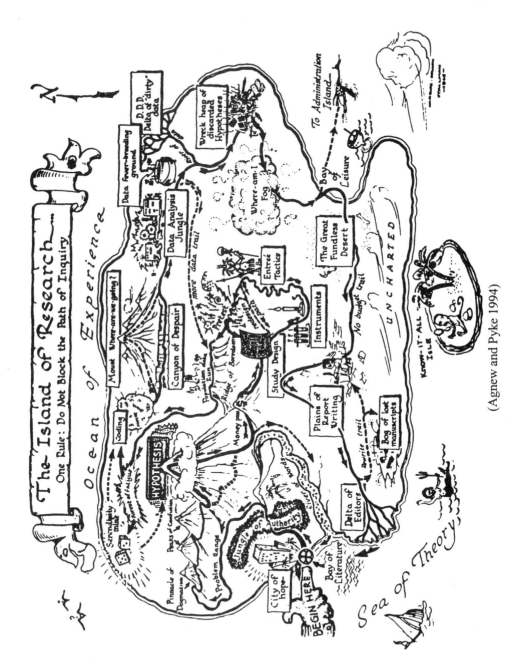

(Agnew and Pyke 1994)

Figure 1.1: The island of research

Box 1.1: Examples of basic research

1. A study (Williamson 1995) investigated the information, communication and telecommunications needs of older adults, aged sixty and over, along with the behaviours associated with these. This included a fundamental examination of the ways in which older people communicate: how they establish and maintain relationships which are important to their lives and how they seek and/or acquire information which they need for everyday living. Also included was the involvement of the telephone in information seeking and communication. There was no specific problem to solve, but a wealth of detail, helpful in understanding communication and information-seeking behaviour, emerged from the study. There was also a contribution to the theory of information-seeking and communication behaviours.

2. Another example of basic research is from the information systems field (Paranagama and Burstein 1996). This research established the influence of the personality types of managers. It looked at the ways personality types influenced preferences when managers make decisions with multiple evaluation criteria.

Box 1.2: Example of basic research with 'applied elements'

Returning to the first research example in Box 1.1 above, it was found that a number of respondents with limited mobility had incorporated some of the rituals of social intercourse into their use of the telephone. In one case, a female respondent who was eighty-three years old and virtually housebound, had daily 'drinks on the phone at 5 o'clock' with an elderly male friend, who was in a nursing home on the other side of Melbourne. In another case, a respondent recorded in her diary that when her cousin, George, rang from England he suggested that next time they talked on the phone they make a cup of tea beforehand and drink it together (Williamson 1995, p. 233). The question which arises from this finding is: what telecommunications equipment will enhance the lives of people in this kind of isolated position? It could be a video phone, for example. This is an example of basic research having practical applications.

In the same research, respondents indicated that they faced barriers in the use of new technology, especially computers. Because of the likely disadvantages for older people in the age of the information super highway, this finding has led to further, more 'applied', study aimed at breaking down those barriers.

The major elements of a research project or proposal

As will be discussed in Chapter 2, the elements of research projects may differ according to whether the study is positivist or interpretivist, although there are steps which are common to both types of research. Very often researchers need to develop research proposals and these mostly have elements closely related to the research steps. Most of the steps or elements, listed below, are discussed in greater depth in later chapters. It is quite difficult to find information on the writing of research proposals in general social sciences texts or research methods texts. Sometimes university research offices provide instructions for their students and there are chapters in the information management literature. For example, Powell (1997) and Busha (1980) both provide chapters on this aspect. An old reference which still has relevance is Turney and Robb (1971). Sometimes books on research methods include sections on the writing of research reports. See, for example, Borg, Gall and Gall (1993); Bouma (1996); Busha (1980); and Powell (1997).

Research project elements

The main elements of research projects are:

- research questions or objectives. Hypotheses, if appropriate (see Chapter 3);

- literature search/literature review/theoretical framework (see Chapter 3);

- research design:

  - description of sample (see Chapter 13) – note that not all research designs include a sample;

  - method and techniques to be used for the research (see below for the methods and techniques covered in the book);

- analysis of findings (see Chapter 17); and

- interpretation and reporting of findings, and the writing of conclusions. (This element is not part of a research proposal, but rather of the research report. It is mentioned briefly in Chapter 18, in relation to critiquing published research.)

Book's coverage of methodology, methods, and techniques

Chapter 2 gives extensive coverage of research methodology, in terms of the major philosophies of research. The broad issues of positivist and interpretivist research, and their relationship to quantitative and qualitative methods, are discussed in this chapter.

The book includes the following research methods: survey (Chapter 5), case study (Chapter 6), experimental design (Chapter 7), system development in information systems research (Chapter 8), action research (Chapter 9), ethnography (Chapter 10), historical research (Chapter 11), and the Delphi method (Chapter 12). Coverage of techniques used for data collection are: questionnaire design (Chapter 14), interviewing (Chapter 14), focus groups (Chapter 15), ethnographic techniques, including observation (Chapter 16).

In the book, it was decided that a distinction should be made between 'research methods' and 'research techniques'. This is because a research technique, such as the questionnaire, is used in a number of different methods. It therefore makes sense not to treat it just as part of survey design, as typically occurs in books on research methods.

To describe what distinguishes a 'research method' from a 'research technique' is not always an easy task. In this book, a research method provides a design for undertaking research, which is underpinned by theoretical explanation of its value and use. Techniques for data gathering (such as questionnaires and surveys) and sample selection are usually included as part of this design. Given that sampling is not, on its own, a research method, it is grouped with techniques in the book, despite the important theoretical component involved.

The role which research can and should play in professional practice

Introduction

This section begins with some general reasons why research is important to professional practice in a range of fields. It then provides discussion of the key professional areas covered by this chapter: librarianship/information management; archives and records, which comes within the scope of information management; and information systems. Although these are treated separately, it should be remembered that there is an overlap of some of the issues.

Why undertake research in professional practice?

There are several reasons why research should play a part in professional practice. These vary somewhat according to the professional categories involved, but the answers include:

- to assist in understanding the problems and issues which arise in the workplace;

- to add to knowledge in the field and/or provide solutions to problems;

- to maintain dynamic and appropriate services;

- to meet requirements of accountability – research is important in the age of accountability as it can assist in policy formulation and provide data to justify present funding or increased funding;

- to maintain and improve professional status – it is generally believed that high quality research assists in improving the status of a profession; and

- to provide a body of research findings and theory to inform practitioners – professionals therefore need to be intelligent, critical consumers of research.

Research in librarianship/information management

Research can play a valuable part in the practice of information professionals. The profession will flourish where information workers develop inquiring frames of mind, underpinned by an understanding of research. It means that they can use these skills to service their clients better, to evaluate their products and policies, and to write grant proposals. Lowe (1999) makes a very strong statement about research in relation to information professionals:

> Research enables professionals to add value to their work and work practices ... [Its use] distinguishes between professionals who maintain the status quo without question and those who strive to develop their work practices through continual evaluation and investigation (Lowe 1999, p. 1).

Hernon (1991) postulates that research can play an important role wherever work is primarily intellectual and draws more on thinking processes than manual processes and routines. Librarianship, he argues, is well suited to benefit from research because it involves planning, management, decision making and other intellectual activities aimed at the resolution of specific information needs and, ideally, providing the best service possible (Hernon 1991, p. 9).

In taking up the issues outlined in the section above it is clear that there is much to be gained in information settings by using research to understand problems and issues which arise in the workplace. Research can add to knowledge and, in many cases, provide solutions. One example is research to develop performance indicators needed by all types of libraries. (See, for example, Broadbent and Lofgren (1991) and D'Avigdor (1997).) Another is the Digital Library Initiative in the USA which encompasses a number of research projects concerned with technological solutions for libraries. The projects are looking at ways in which libraries can expand their service delivery models to use technological developments. The National Science Foundation (NSF), National Aeronautics and Space Administration (NASA) and Defence Advanced Research Projects Agency (DARPA) are the major funding bodies. For a list and outline of projects, see: http://dlt.gsfc.nasa.gov/Projects/Abstracts/projectRDL.shtml.

Research also has an important role to play where a major goal is the development or maintenance of services, as is the case with all types of libraries. If information services are to remain viable and relevant to their clientele, information specialists must continue to assess needs and evaluate their services, and to explore new approaches and methods for doing so. This also involves professionals keeping on the 'cutting edge', so that new and future user needs and demands can be predicted. As part of providing service to clients, it is also important to understand their information-seeking behaviour, for example, their preferences for sources of information and formats. Williamson (1997) and Kirk (1997) provide examples of this kind of study.

With respect to meeting the requirements of accountability, information professionals will undoubtedly attest to the fact that increasingly financial accountability and other types of accountability are permeating every facet of their lives at work. The methods and techniques of research are valuable for justifying library services, as well as supporting all major decisions and policies. In the case of many libraries, there is constant pressure to justify services and prove that they are vital to the continued development of the communities they serve. Research can also assist in policy formulation and provide data to justify present funding or increased funding.

The issue of status of the library and information profession in relation to research is raised by Lowe (1999) who points out that:

> The application of research to daily work practices can improve professional status because it enables librarians to add value, or a perception of value, to their users. In this way they raise user expectations, and make their services more desirable and vital within their particular user community (Lowe 1999, p. 1).

Hernon (1991) takes this issue further, suggesting that library and information studies should aim for the status of a discipline, as well as of a profession, and emphasising the role of research in the process.

> Recognition as a discipline should provide LIS [library and information science] with increased recognition and nurturing by other disciplines and professions. More importantly, a discipline only grows and thrives if its body of basic and applied research increases. Such research may sustain a discipline, provide a basis for the development of new fields of inquiry, and suggest approaches for studying problems (Hernon 1991, p. 9).

The last point in the section above, concerns the need for professionals to be intelligent consumers of research. On this point, Hernon (1991, pp. 11-12) concludes that professionals need to be trained to understand and apply research findings. The ability to read research reports with discernment is a very important first step in making use of the findings, if appropriate, in their own work. Professionals also need to be able to articulate research findings, and their importance, to library decision makers and to colleagues inside and outside their own organisations.

Grounding research in professional practice

To this point, the emphasis has been on the need for research in professional practice. Conversely, there is also a strong argument for library and information studies academic research (including that undertaken by students) to be grounded in professional practice. For example, Van House (1991) says:

> Theory provides the underlying concepts and methods for diagnosing and solving problems; practice supplies the problems and tests the utility of results. Innovation consists of bringing these two areas together: Looking to the profession for new questions to be answered using the methods and concepts of the social sciences; or starting with social scientific knowledge and looking at new applications in the professions (Van House 1991, p. 88).

This is similar to Biggs' (1991) view that researchers should form partnerships with practitioners: 'The practitioners communicating concrete problems of practice, the researchers devising ways to study and solve them, and the practitioners then testing and applying solutions' (p. 82). The Editor of *Library Trends* (1998) puts this slightly differently in saying that academics and practitioners share the responsibility for research in the complementary roles that they play in professional practice.

McClure (1989) explores these issues in relation to increasing the usefulness of research for library managers. He lists a set of propositions, which include:

- Research NOT initiated or at least agreed upon by those libraries or librarians most affected is unlikely to have much impact …

- The greater the interaction between the researcher and the primary stakeholders during the research project, the better the impact of the research for decision making ...
- Research results which do not include carefully designed, practical, step-by-step guidelines, for implementing results in a specific context are likely to have less impact ...
- When researchers serve as consultants, they greatly increase the likelihood that research findings will have an impact on library decision making (McClure 1989, pp. 285-287).

With regard to the last proposition, McClure (1989, p. 287) says that 'the model of interaction between a researcher and a client offers a powerful approach for increasing the usefulness of research'.

Others who discuss this issue include Hoadley (1991) who believes that librarians, themselves, should be involved in research. She outlines a number of constraints to practitioner involvement in research, as well as strategies to overcome these barriers. The latter include research interaction among practising librarians and academics from library and information studies and other faculties; continuing education related to the use of different research methodologies; more involvement in research opportunities; the incorporation of research committees or units into libraries; and making research an integral part of librarianship.

The role of conferences which involve practitioners and academic researchers is crucial in the development of research partnerships and the fostering of research related to professional practice. In Australia there are many conferences which are appropriate, including the Biennial Australian Library and Information Association (ALIA) Conference and conferences for various interest groups.

Other issues for library and information studies research

An examination of the library and information studies literature indicates that there is very little cross-sectoral research in the field. Academics and practitioners tend to confine their research to one library sector, particularly the academic sector. Related to this is a broader issue raised by Biggs (1991), Van House (1991) and Grover and Greer (1991), namely the need for a cross-disciplinary approach to library and information studies research, so that it is placed in a larger context, especially of social science theory. As Van House says, by borrowing approaches from other fields, library and information studies researchers will be encouraged to take a fresh look at problems and generate new solutions (Van House 1991, p. 85). Grover and Greer (1991) mention the following fields, within the family of social and behavioural science, as useful for library and information studies researchers to draw upon: history, anthropology, psychology, sociology, economics, communication, political theory, ethnography and linguistics. For the study of information systems, they list: theory from management, engineering, physics, systems theory, organisational theory, and other applied areas of inquiry (Grover and Greer 1991, p. 106). All of these writers also discuss the importance of the generation of applicable theory. An Australian writer (Maguire 1989, p. 1) regrets the lack of fruitful argument about theory amongst Australian researchers. A contrasting view of interdisciplinary research is presented by Gatten (1989) who sees 'paradigm restrictions', or problems arsing from different disciplinary approaches.

Another issue, raised by Lynch (1991), is that of qualitative versus quantitative research in the field. Grover and Greer (1991, p. 107) take up this point, seeing library and information studies research as often having been focused on the technologies of the profession rather than on the clientele. They see a paradigm shift, suited to contemporary society, which recognises a greater complexity of relationships among phenomena and which has provoked a concern for people. These views reflect a landmark paper, focusing on information needs and uses (Dervin and Nilan 1986), which called for an alternative to the all-pervasive quantitative approach to the study of information behaviour. This paradigm shift has resulted in a more frequent focus on 'the user'. Qualitative research methods are seen as being favoured in this new paradigm. (These issues are discussed in detail in Chapter 2.)

Finally, in the librarianship/information management field, there has been considerable discussion of the topics needing research and in some cases research agendas have been developed. Examples of topics and research agendas are Lynch (1991); Research notes (1988); and Whitlach (1992). Maguire (1989) discusses topics of particular interest to Australian researchers.

A number of the references noted above come from a book by McClure and Hernon (1991) entitled *Library and information science research: Perspectives and strategies for improvement* which includes a range of chapters discussing the issues of research in relation to professional practice. There are also chapters which are specific to research in public libraries (Durrance 1991); school libraries (Fitzgibbons and Callison 1991); special libraries (Matarazzo 1991); and academic libraries (Townley 1991). Another excellent reference with regard to research in academic libraries is Lynch (1990).

Archives and records [1]

Although the field of archives and records comes within the scope of information management, it is treated as a separate area in this chapter. As a field of study, recordkeeping is also closely associated with the disciplines of social science, history and

---

[1] The contribution of Professor Ross Harvey of Charles Sturt University to this section of Chapter 1 is acknowledged with thanks.

law. Indeed archival science itself is a very old discipline with close links to the study of law, diplomatics and paleography.

In more recent times, research in records and archives has experienced a rebirth as professional challenges relating to electronic recordkeeping have led to a questioning of the applicability of traditional theories and practice to managing records in cyberspace. As is the case with both information management and information systems, records and archives research and educational programs have been very closely related to practice. Much recordkeeping research in recent years has involved collaborative projects with academic and industry partners. The recordkeeping community in Australia and internationally has been vitally concerned with the quality of public and corporate recordkeeping in electronic environments, recordkeeping-related issues concerning the reliability, accessibility and accountability of online activities and services, and the persistence and accessibility of records of continuing value to society. Major problems in electronic recordkeeping have been linked to the lack of controls, frameworks and standards in this rapidly evolving area. The response to these concerns has been a proactive, innovative, collaborative approach to the research and development role.

In recent times, recordkeeping research has continued to draw extensively on the theories, models and methods of the disciplines of history and law, but increasingly it has also looked to sociology and information studies. Like their counterparts in information management and information systems, recordkeeping researchers have been involved extensively in the 'reinvention' of practice, generating theories and models about recordkeeping that are being applied and tested by practitioners in rapidly emerging and changing information environments.

Another emerging characteristic of recordkeeping research is involvement in multi-disciplinary research relating to the information ecology, information and knowledge management in enterprises in networked environments, and global initiatives relating to metadata management regimes. An Australian example is the inclusion of recordkeeping research in the work of the new Enterprise Distributed Systems Technology Collaborative Research Centre (http://www.dstc.edu.au/EDST/).

Research in information systems

Most of the issues discussed above, both in the general context and in relation to library and information studies, are also applicable to the information systems field. As a field of study information systems is also very closely related to practice and researchers and practitioners are constantly engaged in the reflective loop. Information systems researchers draw problems for investigation from practice and the results of their studies usually generate theories, which need to be applied and tested by practitioners in the context of the real world information systems. Information systems researchers are very conscious about the usefulness of their research results to industry as well as the rigour of their approaches and their contribution to the core knowledge of the information systems field. Information systems is a relatively young discipline which is still in the process of building its core theory. When talking about the future challenges of information systems research Keen (1991) argued that the relevance of information systems research to its audience (information systems practitioners and academics) is still the major concern of the field. He asserted that: 'Until the relevance is established, rigor is irrelevant. When the relevance is clear, rigor enhances it' (Keen 1991, p. 47).

The field of information systems is commonly recognised as a multi-disciplinary, applied discipline. This results in a large number of research studies, which are conducted applying the methods borrowed from related disciplines, such as organisational theory, behavioural psychology, and management science. Such a 'secondary' methodological approach is sometimes criticised in the research literature and questions are asked about the 'purity' of information systems as an independent academic discipline (Weber 1997). Information systems researchers are still actively engaged in defining the core of the information systems discipline, with the aim of formulating some general theories to be tested in empirical studies (Alter 1999; Watson et al. 1999).

Information systems practitioners are actively engaged in research processes through participation in surveys, case studies and action research initiated by researchers. On the other hand, professional societies, such as the National Australian Computer Society, International Association for Information Systems and the Association of Computing Machinery, are actively involved in the process of dissemination of research results in a wider professional community through annual conferences and journal publications. Electronic discussion groups and mailing lists (for example, ISWORLD) and World Wide Web resources (such as ISWorld Net http://isworld.dis.unimelb.edu.au/isworld.html) serve as useful media for sharing current topics of interests between researchers and professionals.

Conclusion

This chapter has covered a range of introductory issues concerned with research in the field of information management and systems. Definitions are important for anyone beginning the research journey. The chapter attempts to include a taste of the definitional diversity in its purview.

A major focus of the chapter is the role of research in professional practice. Here there is much common territory for information management, including archives and recordkeeping, and information systems. There is also an individual flavour for each of these key professional areas and this emerges in the separate sections which conclude the chapter.

Discussion questions

- Why is research important to professional practice?

- How can high quality research, relevant to the workplace, be achieved?

- How can information professionals be encouraged to monitor the research literature and learn from it for their professional practice?

- What could be key questions or issues which might warrant research in the type of professional practice which is relevant to you?

Further readings

Galliers, R.D. (ed.). (1992). *Information systems research: Issues, methods and practical guidelines.* Blackwell Scientific Publications: Oxford.

Lynch, Beverly. (1991). Research, theory, and the practice of LIS. In *Library and information science research: Perspectives and strategies for improvement*, eds. Charles R. McClure and Peter Hernon. Ablex Publishing: Norwood, NJ, pp. 360-366.

References for Chapter 1

Agnew, Neil McK. and Pyke, Sandra. (1994). *The science game: An introduction to research in the social sciences.* 6th edn. (Previously published by Prentice Hall: Englewood, NJ.)

Alter, Stephen. (1999). A general, yet useful theory of information systems. *The Communications of Association for Information Systems*, 1 (13). (online). http://cais.isworld.org/contents.asp

Biggs, Mary. (1991). Research in the development of a profession or a discipline. In *Library and information science research: Perspectives and strategies for improvement*, eds. Charles R. McClure and Peter Hernon. Ablex Publishing: Norwood, NJ, pp. 72-84.

Bouma, Gary D. (1996). *The research process.* 3rd edn. Oxford University Press: Melbourne.

Borg, Walter R., Gall, Joyce P. and Gall, Meredith D. (1993). *Applying educational research: A practical guide.* 3rd edn. Longman: White Plains, NY.

Broadbent, M. and Lofgren, H. (1991). *Priorities, performance and benefits: An exploratory study of library and information units.* CIRCIT and ACLIS: Melbourne.

Burns, Robert B. (1990). *Introduction to research methods in education.* Longman Cheshire: Melbourne.

Busha, Charles H. and Harter, Stephen P. (1980). *Research methods in librarianship: Techniques and interpretations.* Academic Press: Orlando, NY.

D'Avigdor, Richard. (1997). Indispensable or indifferent. The reality of information service performance measurement at UNSW library. *Australian Academic and Research Libraries,* **28** (4), pp. 264-280.

Dervin, Brenda and Nilan, Michael. (1986). Information needs and uses. In *Annual Review of Information Science and Technology,* **21**, ed. Martha E. Williams. Knowledge Industry Publications: n.p., pp. 3-33.

Durrance, Joan C. (1991). Research needs in public librarianship. In *Library and information science research: Perspectives and strategies for improvement,* eds. Charles R. McClure and Peter Hernon. Ablex Publishing: Norwood, NJ, pp. 279-289.

Fitzgibbons, Shirley and Callison, Daniel. (1991). Research needs and issues in public librarianship. In *Library and information science research: Perspectives and strategies for improvement,* eds. Charles R. McClure and Peter Hernon. Ablex Publishing: Norwood, NJ, pp. 296-312.

Farhoomand Ali and Drury, Don H. (1999). A historiographical examination of information systems. *The Communications of Association for Information Systems,* **1** (19). (online). http://cais.isworld.org/contents.asp

Gatten, Jeffrey N. (1989). Paradigm restrictions on interdisciplinary research into librarianship. *College and Research Libraries,* **Nov.**, pp. 575-584.

Goldhor, Herbert. (1972). *An introduction to scientific research in librarianship.* University of Illinois Graduate School of Library Science: Urbana-Champaign, Il.

Gorman, G.E. and Clayton, Peter. (1997). *Qualitative research for the information professional: A practical handbook.* Library Association Publishing: London.

Grover, Robert and Greer, Roger C. (1991). The cross-disciplinary imperative of LIS research. In *Library and information science research: Perspectives and strategies for improvement,* eds. Charles R. McClure and Peter Hernon. Ablex Publishing: Norwood, NJ, pp. 101-113.

Hernon, Peter. (1991). The elusive nature of research in LIS. In *Library and information science research: Perspectives and strategies for improvement*, eds. Charles R. McClure and Peter Hernon. Ablex Publishing: Norwood, NJ, pp. 3-14.

Hoadley, Irene B. (1991). The role of practicing LIS professionals. In *Library and information science research: Perspectives and strategies for improvement*, eds. Charles R. McClure and Peter Hernon. Ablex Publishing: Norwood, NJ, pp. 179-186.

Keen, Peter G.W. (1991). Relevance and rigor in information systems research: Improving quality, confidence, cohesion and impact. In *Information systems research: Contemporary approaches and emergent traditions*, eds. H.E. Nissen, R. Klein and R. Hirschheim. Elsevier Science Publishers B.V.: North-Holland, pp. 27-49.

Kirk, Joyce. (1997). Managers' use of information: a grounded approach. In *Information seeking in context*: *Proceedings of an international conference on research in information needs, seeking and use in different contexts,* Tampere, Finland, 14-16 August 1996, eds. Pertti Vakkari, Reijo Savolainen and Brenda Dervin. Taylor Graham: London, pp. 257-267.

Library Trends. (1998). [Editorial], **Spring**. (online). http://edfu.lis.uiuc.edu/puboff/catalog/trends/toc.html

Lowe, D. (1999). Introduction to research in relation to professional practice. Unpublished paper. School of Information Management and Systems, Monash University, Caulfield, Vic., p. 1.

Lynch, Beverly. (1991). Research, theory, and the practice of LIS. In *Library and information science research: Perspectives and strategies for improvement*, eds. Charles R. McClure and Peter Hernon. Ablex Publishing: Norwood, NJ, pp. 360-366.

Lynch, Mary Jo. (ed.). (1990). *Academic libraries research perspectives*. ALA: Chicago, Il.

McClure, Charles R. (1989). Increasing the usefulness of research for library managers: Propositions, issues and strategies. *Library Trends,* **38** (2), pp. 280-294.

McClure, Charles R. and Hernon, Peter. (eds.). (1991). *Library and information science research: Perspectives and strategies for improvement*. Ablex Publishing: Norwood.

Maguire, Carmel. (1989). Researching library and information science in Australia: Obstacles and opportunities. *International Journal of Library and Information Research*, **1** (1), pp. 1-11.

Marshall, Catherine and Rossman, Gretchen B. (1995). *Designing qualitative research.* 2nd edn. Sage: Thousand Oaks, Ca.

Matarazzo, James M. (1991). Research needs and issues in special librarianship. In *Library and information science research: Perspectives and strategies for improvement,* eds. Charles R. McClure and Peter Hernon. Ablex Publishing: Norwood, NJ, pp. 316-322.

Paranagama, P. C. and Burstein, F. (1996). Preliminary study of the relationship between decision makers' personality and models of their preferences. In *Proceedings of the International Conference on Implementing Systems for Supporting Management Decisions, IFIP Working Group 8.3,* London School of Economics, 22-24 July 1996, pp. 1-20.

Research notes: research questions of interest to ARL. (1988). *College and Research Libraries,* **49**, Sept., pp. 467-470.

Sekeran, Uma. (1992). *Research methods for business.* 2nd edn. Wiley: New York.

Townley, Charles T. (1991). Opportunities and challenges for LIS research in academic libraries: elements of strategy. In *Library and information science research: Perspectives and strategies for improvement,* eds. Charles R. McClure and Peter Hernon. Ablex Publishing: Norwood, NJ, pp. 267-277.

Turney, Billy and Robb, George. (1971). The research proposal. In *Research in education: An introduction.* Dryden: Hinsdale, Il.

Van House, Nancy A. (1991). Assessing the quantity, quality, and impact of LIS research. In *Library and information science research: Perspectives and strategies for improvement,* eds. Charles R. McClure and Peter Hernon. Ablex Publishing: Norwood, NJ, pp. 85-100.

Watson, Hugh J., Taylor, Kenneth P., Higgins, Guy, Kadlec, Chris and Meeks, Michael. (1999). Leaders assess the current state of the academic IS discipline. *The Communications of Association for Information Systems,* **2** (2). (online). http://cais.isworld.org/contents.asp

Weber, Ron. (1997). *Ontological foundations of information systems.* Coopers and Lybrand: Australia.

Whitlach, Jo Bell. (1992). Research topics from the program – unanswered questions: Gaps in reference effectiveness. *RQ*, **31**, Spring, pp. 333-337.

Williamson, Kirsty. (1995). Older adults: Information, communication and tele-communications. PhD Thesis. RMIT: Melbourne, Vic.

Williamson, Kirsty. (1997). The information needs and information-seeking behaviour of older adults: an Australian study. In *Information seeking in context: Proceedings of an international conference on research in information needs, seeking and use in different contexts,* Tampere, Finland, 14-16 August 1996, eds. Pertti Vakkari, Reijo Savolainen and Brenda Dervin. Taylor Graham: London, pp. 337-350.

Zikmund, William. (1994). *Business research methods.* 4th edn. Dryden: Chicago, Il.

CHAPTER 2
The two major traditions of research
Kirsty Williamson with Frada Burstein and Sue McKemmish

Objectives

At the end of this chapter you will be able to:

- understand the major philosophical debates in the research field at an introductory level;

- understand the differences between deductive and inductive reasoning;

- describe positivist approaches to research and the ways in which they have been used traditionally;

- describe interpretivist research approaches and the ways in which they are applied;

- perceive ways in which quantitative and qualitative methods can be usefully combined to investigate problems in professional practice; and

- understand how the different research methods have been used in professional practice.

Introduction: The two major traditions of research

In this chapter we examine the two major traditions of research in the social sciences. The first is termed *positivist*, where researchers attempt to apply research methods used in the natural sciences to the social sciences; the second *interpretivist* (sometimes written as *interpretive*), where researchers emphasise the meanings made by people as they interpret their world. These philosophies are sometimes referred to as ontologies, meaning they are approaches to social inquiry which are based on particular assumptions. An understanding of these philosophies is necessary, along with key terms, if professionals are to integrate research effectively into professional practice. Remember that a glossary of these labels, and other major terms used to describe various aspects of research, is included at the end of this book. The chapter begins with reasoning styles which are important to understand in relation to these schools of thought and concludes with particular examples of the ways in which research has been used in professional practice.

The positivist and interpretivist traditions of research have, by and large, been considered to be very different; in fact, dichotomous. The debate about these approaches has been taking place since at least the mid-nineteenth century (Hammersley 1992, p. 39). It is fundamentally *epistemological*, which means that it is concerned with questions such as: 'what constitutes knowledge?' and 'how is knowledge formed?'

As part of this debate, qualitative approaches to research are mainly, but not exclusively, linked with interpretivism and quantitative approaches are linked with positivism. Any attempt to understand the debate is confused by the different labels which are sometimes used to describe the same or very similar research approaches. This reflects the complexity of the differences between the many philosophical schools of thought associated with research methods in the social sciences. Those differences may sometimes be very subtle. For those who wish to go beyond a basic understanding, Blaikie (1993) and Denzin and Lincoln (1994) offer profound and stimulating discussions.

Reasoning styles

Before discussing positivism and interpretivism, it is necessary to examine two styles of reasoning, with which the approaches are associated: 'deductive' and 'inductive' reasoning styles. Deductive reasoning is mainly associated with the scientific (or positivist) approach to research. Interpretivist approaches are associated with inductive reasoning. These differences will be described further below in relation to the discussions of the two schools.

Deductive reasoning

Deductive reasoning is linked with the hypothesis testing approach to research. With deductive reasoning, the argument moves from general principles to particular instances, for example:

1. People who are aged sixty or over are unlikely to be users of the Internet.
2. Tom Carter is aged seventy-five.
3. Therefore Tom Carter is unlikely to be a user of the Internet.

In this example, the first two statements are the premises, and include a general and a specific statement. The third statement, or conclusion, is specific. The truth of the premises guarantees the truth of the conclusion.

Inductive reasoning

Inductive reasoning begins with particular instances and concludes with general statements or principles. An example is: *Tom Carter, Jim Brown and Pam Eliot, who are all aged sixty or over, are not users of the Internet.* If there were many other instances which were identical and only a few that were not, it could be concluded: *People aged sixty or over are unlikely to be users of the Internet.*

Inductive reasoning is associated with the hypothesis generating approach to research. Field work and observations occur initially and hypotheses are generated from the analysis of the data collected. Thus if data were collected which showed that a large majority of people aged sixty or over were not using the Internet (in comparison with those aged under sixty), it could be hypothesised that: *Older people (aged sixty or over) are less likely than younger people (aged under sixty) to be users of the Internet.*

Positivism and post-positivism

Although the *positivist* paradigm has been mainly associated with *quantitative* methods of research, *qualitative* methods are also used, particularly by *post-positivists* (Myers 1999; Denzin and Lincoln 1994). *Paradigm* in this context means 'a set of interrelated assumptions about the social world which provides a philosophical and conceptual framework for the systematic study of that world' (Kuhn 1970, p. 10). The term positivist was first used by the philosopher Comte, one of the founding fathers of sociology, in 1830. Later, in the 1920s, a brand of positivism, known as 'logical positivism', was developed by a group of scholars known as the Vienna Circle, members of which moved to the USA in the 1930s.

The central themes of positivism are:

- the claim that the natural sciences and the social sciences should be investigated in the same way. Like scientific research, positivist research seeks to link cause and effect. The goal is the ultimate unification of all sciences (Dick 1991, p. 232); and

- the proposition that all scientific knowledge is based on experience (empirically observable impressions). Positivists consider that knowledge can only be based on what can be objectively observed and experienced (empiricism).

Positivists see the world as a collection of observable events and facts which can be measured. Hence the emphasis on quantitative data in this paradigm. Common research designs most likely to be linked to the positivist paradigm are 'experimental design' and 'survey', provided the latter is carried out with rigour. For example, the sample must be scientifically selected and principles of *validity* and *reliability* must be adhered to. Validity and reliability are complex terms. The former is concerned with accuracy. Validity in measurement refers to the extent to which a research instrument measures what it is designed to measure. Reliability is concerned with obtaining consistent, stable research results with replication, that is, when a study is repeated. For a deeper understanding, see Powell (1997, pp. 37-42).

Positivist research designs

Positivist research is based mainly on deductive styles of reasoning, as used in the natural sciences. Firstly, the deductive or hypothesis testing style begins with theories and models. It defines *variables* for study (for example, age of library users and their frequency of library use), predicts their relationships through the framing of *hypotheses* and tests those hypotheses. The sample is randomly selected and mostly quantitative data are collected, although qualitative data may also be included. Generalisations are eventually made. This search for general laws, central to the positivist approach is termed *nomothetic* which means, literally, 'pertaining to the search for general laws'.

The deductive process is seen as clear-cut and linear, as illustrated in Figure 2.1 (although remember the island of research in Figure 1.1).

The aim of deductivists is to refute their hypotheses, or to falsify them. Karl Popper is the best known exponent of this approach. According to Popper, deduction involves the '... putting forward of a tentative idea, a conjecture, a hypothesis or set of hypotheses that form a theory' (Blaikie 1993, p. 145). The hypotheses are then tested by the collection of observations or the undertaking of experiments. If the data are not consistent with the hypotheses, the latter must be rejected, and the theory regarded as false. Very importantly, if the data are consistent with the hypotheses, '... the theory is temporarily supported, it is *corroborated*, not proved to be true' (Popper 1959, pp. 32-5, cited in Blaikie 1993, p. 145). This must be emphasised: both hypotheses and theories are **supported** by the data, **not** proved. Powell (1997, pp. 12-44) provides a detailed and complex discussion of the processes involved in the deductive approach. Busha and Harter's (1980) account of the scientific method of research is easier reading.

Post-positivism

Although post-positivists, like positivists, assume that reality exists, the former believe it is not easy to discover '... because of basically flawed human intellectual mechanisms and the fundamentally intractable nature of phenomena' (Denzin and Lincoln 1994, p. 110). Post-positivists therefore believe that reality must be subjected to the widest possible critical examination. Research methods involve the use of more natural settings and the soliciting of *emic* (or insider) views, as opposed to a reliance on outsider (or *etic* perspective). Qualitative methods are therefore important. This approach has some similarities with interpretivist perspectives (discussed below).

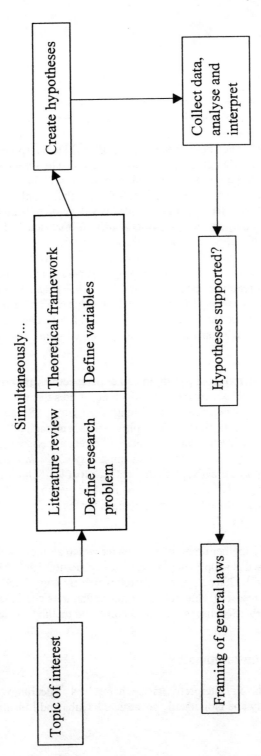

Figure 2.1: Positivist research design

Interpretivism

This is an umbrella term which is mainly associated with qualitative methods of research, but quantitative techniques can also be used. Researchers who are interpretivists favour *naturalistic inquiry* (where field work usually takes place in the 'natural setting') and are concerned with 'meaning'. They believe that the social world is interpreted or constructed by people and is therefore different from the world of nature. The school had its origins in *hermeneutics*, an intellectual tradition concerned, originally, with the interpretation of texts, but later of social life. The central tenet of interpretivism is that people are constantly involved in interpreting their ever-changing world. They develop meanings for their activities together, that is, they socially construct reality, as analysed in the famous book, *The social construction of reality: A treatise in the sociology of knowledge* (Berger and Luckmann 1967). They also make sense of their world on an individual basis, that is, they develop their **own** meanings, which often differ from one person to another. In other words, they personally construct reality, as postulated by Kelly (1955). This latter process is encapsulated in Dervin's 'sense making' theory, which has had a major impact in the information management field. (See, for example, Dervin (1992); Dervin and Nilan (1986).) According to Dervin, people are constantly involved in making sense of, or interpreting, their world.

Constructivism is a key interpretivist paradigm. Other perspectives are *critical theory* (discussed in Chapter 10) and *phenomenology* which penetrates the essences of human experiences by focusing on phenomena or the 'things themselves' (Sutton 1993, p. 414). It involves description and classification of those phenomena, embracing '... the host of personal meanings that are derived from the context of direct experiencing' (Burns 1990, p. 9). The sociological theory which is most in keeping is *symbolic interactionism* which emphasises the individual as a creative, thinking entity, capable of choosing behaviour rather than simply reacting to large-scale forces, as implied by functionalist theories. *Ethnography*, which was developed by anthropologists for the study of culture, is a key method used by interpretivists.

To add to the complexity, another umbrella term under which all these various conceptual approaches can be gathered is simply *qualitative* research (Patton 1990; Mellon 1990; Gorman and Clayton 1997). Other types of research which are considered 'qualitative' are case study and historical research, although the former often uses combined quantitative and qualitative approaches. (See discussion about combined methods, below.)

The perspectives of interpretivists

Regardless of particular labels, interpretivists see themselves as dealing with multiple realities which are socially and individually constructed. Guba and Lincoln (1981) refer to these multiple realities as the layers of an onion, nesting within or complementing each other. 'Each layer provides a different perspective of reality, and none can be considered more "true" than any other' (Guba and Lincoln 1981, p. 57).

Interpretivist researchers regard their research task as coming to understand how the various participants in a social setting construct the world around them (Glesne and Peshkin 1992, p. 6). Their concern is with the beliefs, feelings and interpretations of participants, who are also often referred to as actors, and with recording these perspectives as accurately as possible. They therefore often provide some opportunity for participants to comment on what has been recorded about them. Good interpretivist researchers are aware there can be difficulties in understanding fully the perspectives of others very different from themselves. Glesne and Peshkin discuss this problem at length, examining also the impact of postmodernism.

> The researcher becomes the main research instrument as he or she observes, asks questions and interacts with research participants. The concern with researcher objectivity is replaced by a focus on the impact of subjectivity on the research process ... [Postmodernists look] ... carefully for ways in which the historical and cultural context shapes the researcher's preconceptions. Postmodernists are particularly concerned with issues of 'intersubjectivity', that is, how researcher and researched affect each other (Glesne and Peshkin 1992, pp. 6 and 10).

Sutton (1993, p. 423) believes that 'the incorporation of the researcher into the field of research is inconsistent with the paradigm of the researcher as neutral observer' and points out that '... one can understand something observed only through the tinted lens of one's own experience'. He sees the fact that the researcher inevitably has a point of view as a strength, as a source of insight and understanding, as long as there is an awareness of it (Sutton 1993, p. 425).

Interpretivist research designs

Research designs are mainly based on inductive reasoning. Researchers attempt to make sense of the situation, without imposing pre-existing expectations (Patton 1990, p. 44). Data are collected, analysed, and then '... researchers develop concepts, insights and understanding from patterns in the data ...' (Reneker 1993, p. 499). This is similar to the use of induction in *grounded theory* (Glaser and Strauss 1967) which is theory literally built from the ground upwards, that is, from data observed and collected in the field.

Interpretivist researchers plan their studies, but are much less 'linear' in their approach than positivist researchers. They undertake a literature search to gain an understanding of their topic, they develop theory and research questions and they plan how they will collect their data. On the other hand, they 'seek to be totally open to the setting and subjects of their study' (Gorman and Clayton 1997, p. 38). For example, it might be that the initial stage of data collection reveals unexpected perspectives on research questions. The researcher may then adjust the research questions and data collection plan to take these new perspectives into account. The research design therefore tends to be non-linear and *iterative* (meaning that various elements in the research are interwoven, with the development of one influencing decisions about the others). For example, data analysis is undertaken throughout the project not just in the concluding stage. Figure 2.2 illustrates this iterative process, emphasising the interconnectedness of the stages.

Notice that the word 'hypothesis' is not mentioned in the Figure 2.2. Interpretivists do not usually test hypotheses, although they may develop working 'propositions' which are grounded in the perspectives of the participants. Nor is 'generalisation' mentioned on the diagram. Within the qualitative paradigm, generalisation is not essential: in fact generalisations usually cannot be made. It is wholly acceptable that a qualitative study should be *idiographic* which means 'the intensive study of an individual case', as is undertaken in a case study. In contrast to positivism, there are also not the same demands about the capacity to replicate research. There is a recognition that certain phenomena are confined in time and place, and that the particular styles of observation and explanation which may be relevant in one case may not be capable of repetition. Samples tend to be quite small and the need for random sampling is not emphasised as in the positivist paradigm. The form of sampling which is popular in qualitative research is *purposive or theoretical sampling* where a sample, appropriate to the investigation of a particular problem or which is representative of a special population, is selected (Grover and Greer 1991, p. 106).

Nevertheless, qualitative research needs to be rigorous. Glazier (1992, p. 211) says that, because a satisfactory means of evaluating qualitative research methods has not been found, *validity* and *reliability* are left as the primary means of ensuring integrity. He suggests that validity can be checked, for example, by undertaking a number of observations of similar people engaged in similar activities in similar situations and then comparing the results to see if the methods of observation are accomplishing what they are expected to accomplish. With reliability, which is a check on consistency, he suggests that findings can be compared with those in the literature, or triangulation can be used. The latter involves several different methods of collecting roughly the same data and comparing the results. (See further discussion of 'triangulation' below.) Lincoln and Guba (1985, cited in Kirk 1997, pp. 261-264) talk about 'trustworthiness' of findings, rather than validity and reliability, but their recommended checks are similar. Once again, triangulation is seen as vital.

Sutton's (1993) view is slightly different. He postulates that the priorities of positivists are different from those of interpretivists: the problem of error absorbs positivists, because they accept the notion of facts and objectivity as unproblematic, whereas:

> ... in the participatory research mode, where shared understanding is more salient than the
> objectively observed fact, the problem of error has a lower priority than the problem of
> finding appropriate modes of comprehending what is observed and placing it into its own
> explanatory context (Sutton 1993, p. 424).

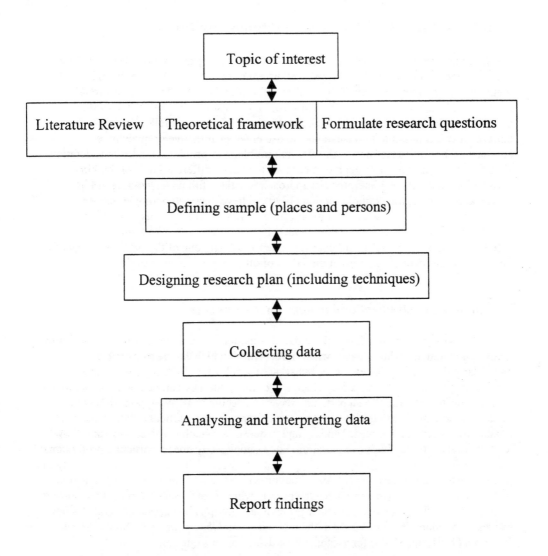

Figure 2.2: Qualitative research design

Combining quantitative and qualitative methods

While some writers (for example, Sutton (1993) and Bradley and Sutton (1993)) believe that positivism and interpretivism represent different ways of viewing reality and that the methods favoured by each cannot be easily combined, others would disagree strongly. Denzin and Lincoln (1994) include 'positivism' and 'post-positivism' as two of their alternative inquiry paradigms under the 'qualitative research' umbrella. Ford (1987), believes that it is possible for researchers to use either quantitative or qualitative approaches, or both, according to the research problem, or problems, under consideration. He argues a strong case for integration because the use of different kinds of thinking involved in positivist and interpretivist approaches make a full understanding of topics more likely. Others, for example Mellon (1990), believe that methodologies can be profitably combined, but warns that great care needs to be taken because they '... are separate and distinct from one another, with different purposes, methods and outcomes' (Mellon 1990, p. 5). Another reference (Brannen 1992) and one of the further readings for this chapter (Bryman 1992) present the views of other writers, on this subject.

Matching research questions to appropriate designs

There exists certain straight-forward factual information (for example, 'what', 'who' 'how many', 'how much', 'where', and 'when' information) which can be measured at a particular point in time. For example, 'what' are the rules for eligibility for the aged pension in Australia? The rules may change over time, but they can be reliably ascertained (barring misinterpretation) on a particular day of a specific year. What proportion of a random sample of Victorians bought *The Age* newspaper on a particular date? This can be reliably measured. On the other hand, complex questions which involve 'why' and 'how' lend themselves to qualitative exploration. For example, why does a particular professional group have a certain set of attitudes or approaches to work? Why do people read *The Age* in preference to another newspaper? Any situation which requires understanding in depth is well suited to a qualitative approach. One reason, which should not determine the choice of a qualitative method, is that a particular professional group is bad at maths! This has been suggested by more than one writer in the literature. See *Library and Information Science Research* (1991, pp. 85-88) for a vituperative debate on this question.

It must be noted that some 'why' and 'how' questions in more technical fields may require the high level of control afforded by experiments. For example, Shanks, Rouse and Arnott (1993) believe this to be the case in 'information systems' research. In this field, they would see qualitative methods to be particularly appropriate for exploratory research:

> **Exploratory research** (sometimes termed formulative research) is aimed at formulating more precise questions that future research can answer. It is used in the theory-building stage of research. Exploratory researchers frequently use qualitative

research methods such as case studies and phenomenological studies (Shanks, Rouse and Arnott 1993, p. 7).

This notion of an exploratory, qualitative study providing the basis for quantitative research is useful in other fields as well. (See Box 2.1 for an example of a research group which favours qualitative research, but uses a quantitative approach if this is required by the research questions and the audience for the research.)

Box 2.1: Example of one research group's approach to research

The focus of Information and Telecommunications Needs Research (ITNR), originally at RMIT as the Telecommunications Needs Research Group and now a joint venture of Monash University and Charles Sturt University, has been social and cultural research in the field of telecommunications. The research group is particularly interested in the investigation of the needs of telecommunications users and the ways new technologies can enhance their lives. A central belief is that most research in the field has been driven by the technological possibilities, rather than the needs of users. The research approach is ethnographic: there is a focus on contexts and how telecommunications are integrated into the lives of users. Thus qualitative research is favoured.

Nevertheless, the research sometimes uses quantitative methods in order to obtain a broader view with a much larger sample than can be used in a qualitative study. In one case, a detailed (qualitative) study of eleven very different telecommunications users was undertaken, to identify the important social and cultural features of people's telecommunications behaviour. Using the rich detail from this study, a survey was developed, so that some of these social factors could be defined and their links with telecommunications uses described and measured.

The researchers were conscious that, by using a quantitative approach, the contexts of telecommunications use were being limited and the dynamic of everyday use over-simplified. However, at the time, there existed very little hard data about Australians' familiarity with information technologies, or the distribution of that data on key demographic lines, such as age and gender. These kinds of data are well suited to quantitative collection. Furthermore, because the research group is publicly funded, it believes that it should also contribute quantitative data to current debates. It is a fact of life that not everyone is convinced by small samples and rich, qualitative data. Thus it is not only the type of question which should determine the choice of method, but also the audience for the research.

There is often scope within a research project to use both quantitative and qualitative methods. They can be complementary and, in combination, give both the broader, larger-scale picture, as well as a more detailed understanding of a specific situation. (For an example of combined qualitative and quantitative approaches see Box 2.2.)

Box 2.2: Example of combined qualitative and quantitative approaches

At the University of Melbourne, the Division of Library and Information Studies undertook a study of the use of resources in the Victorian Certificate of Education (VCE) subject, Australian Studies. The researchers began by considering a survey (a quantitative approach), but the exploratory interviews indicated that this was a very complex task, requiring detailed understanding of both the way the subject was being taught and how resource use was integrated.

It was therefore decided to undertake case studies in ten secondary schools. Using a qualitative approach, most common in case studies, interviews were conducted with coordinators and teachers. Documents were examined, both from the Victorian Curriculum and Assessment Board (VCAB) and the schools themselves. A few student assignments were also examined and the students who wrote them were interviewed.

Another strand of the research was quantitative. Students undertaking Australian Studies in each of the ten schools were surveyed. This gave broad, quantifiable data on the types of resources students were using, as well as the resources which teachers were introducing to students in class. It complemented, and provided confirmation of, the more detailed picture obtained from coordinators, teachers and the few student assignments which were examined. This kind of approach is called triangulation. (See Williamson (1995).)

Triangulation

There are two major types of *triangulation*: methods and sources. *Methods triangulation* is the checking of the consistency of findings by using different data-collection methods. The methods may be all qualitative, for example unstructured interviews and observation, or all quantitative, for example questionnaires and structured interviews, or a mixture of the two. *Sources triangulation*, on the other hand is the cross-checking for consistency of the information derived at different times and from different people, for example managers and para-professionals in a library situation.

The advantage of triangulation is that conclusions are likely to be more reliable if data are collected by more than one method and from the perspective of more than one source. If different methods are used, the researcher can take advantage of the strengths and offset the weaknesses of each. Both the broad and narrowly focused (or macro- and micro-level perspectives) can be combined in a single project (Gorman and Clayton 1997, p. 32).

Summary of research approaches

Before proceeding to examples in professional practice, the following provides a summary of the major research approaches covered by this chapter.

The two major approaches are broadly labelled 'positivist' and 'interpretivist'. The former attempts to apply scientific methods to the social sciences, and is most usually associated with deductive reasoning and quantitative data collection. Because of their use of natural settings and greater emphasis on qualitative data collection, post-positivists have some characteristics in common with interpretivists, although they still believe that there is a reality which can be measured. Interpretivists, on the other hand, are concerned with meanings constructed by individuals and groups, use principally inductive reasoning and collect qualitative data. Labels which fit under the interpretivist umbrella include naturalistic inquiry, constructivism, and phenomenology.

To many researchers combined perspectives and approaches are acceptable, and even desirable. There is a strong case to argue that research designs should be matched to the questions to be investigated. Triangulation is a popular approach which enables the checking of findings by using different data collection methods. These may be both quantitative and qualitative and therefore involve combined approaches.

An important note

It must be emphasised that the field of research includes many labels and approaches and that this chapter presents only some major ways of conceptualisation. Research is a dynamic, ever-changing field and this also makes it difficult to categorise in clearly defined ways. Moreover, researchers do not always make explicit that their research fits into, or has similarities with, a particular philosophical paradigm. This does not necessarily lessen the value of the research, provided that it has been undertaken with rigour and does not contravene basic tenets such as the limitations on generalisations from non-random samples or incomplete samples (discussed in Chapter 13).

It is also important to emphasise that, because a study is mainly 'quantitative' in its research approach, it does not necessarily meet all of the 'positivist' criteria. This may be particularly the case with many surveys where mainly quantitative data are collected but samples are not randomly selected. To add to the complications, some of the researchers involved may be committed to positivist philosophy, but have to make compromises at times where, for example, it is impossible to select a random sample. Conversely, purists amongst 'interpretivist' researchers may object to this label being applied to research which does not appear to be sufficiently open to the setting and the subjects and where strong elements of the deductive approach are evident. Interpretivists also may need to make compromises for practical reasons.

Another problem is that researchers apply different labels to very similar research styles. For example, a study which one researcher labels as an interpretivist case study, can appear to be very similar to a study labelled as an ethnography (using participant observation). 'Action research' can be considered to provide a set of strategies for 'systems development' (Baskerville and Wood-Harper 1998) . It is important to recognise this as a fact of life in the research field and to try to learn to accept, and deal with, the fluidity and rich diversity of terminology.

Examples of quantitative and qualitative research in professional practice

Both quantitative and qualitative methods have been used in all three (overlapping) areas of professional practice which are the focus of this book. There are many examples which could be chosen from each. Those below have been singled out from a vast field. Some of the examples are Australian.

Librarianship/information management

A key research area in librarianship has been 'user studies'. This is an umbrella term which covers all kinds of studies of users of library and information services, as well as of non-users. Principal questions have concerned: who uses services and why, and who does not use services and why not. There are also many other issues, often concerned with specific areas of service, which have been investigated. Both quantitative and qualitative methods have been employed for user studies, but the emphasis has been on quantitative approaches. Examples of quantitative user studies are: Power (1996); Wells (1995); Flowers (1995); Ng and Williamson (1992); Grosser and Bagnell (1989); and Williamson (1986). Examples of qualitative user studies are Burns and Tredinnick (1994) and Mellon (1990). When the topic is broadened to include studies of information-seeking behaviour more qualitative studies can be found, for example Kirk (1997) and Reneker (1993). Kirk (1997), in particular, presents a cogent justification for the location of the study within what she labels the naturalistic paradigm.

A study of user needs is often included as part of an evaluation of an information service. Conversely, a study of users is often encompassed within an evaluative study. Childers (1989, p. 251) says: 'To be evaluative research, an investigation must focus on a program (a service or product) and on a consumer (client or customer, actual or potential)'. A widely used form of evaluation in librarianship/information management is referred to as *performance measurement* where output measures are used to determine what has been accomplished by specific programs, services or resource availability. This is a quantitative approach. A well known Australian example is Broadbent and Lofgren (1991) and Lofgren

(1992). Two references deal specifically with evaluation from a qualitative perspective – Patton (1990); and Mellon (1990). The latter contains examples relevant to librarianship/information management.

An example of the use of a combined qualitative/quantitative approach to user studies can be found in Williamson (1995), referred to in Box 2.2.

Archives and records [1]

As mentioned in Chapter 1, archival science is an old discipline with a tradition of research in *diplomatics* and *historiography*. Both diplomatics and historiography have continued to be applied to research in the field of records and archives. For example the InterPARES project, a collaborative international research endeavour that is addressing issues relating to the long-term preservation of electronic records, is using diplomatics to develop a taxonomy of record types in electronic systems, and to help to identify the functional requirements for preserving authentic records in electronic systems. (See http://www.interpares.org/ for detailed information on the InterPARES project.) Historiographical studies of archival institutions, the evolution of archival law and the development of archival practice and systems also continue to feature in research programs.

More recently, research in records and archives has employed a range of other research methods drawn for the most part from social science disciplines, including surveys, structured interviews, case studies, action research, ethnography, grounded theory development, analysis of literary warrant and best practice, and narrative analysis.

The University of Pittsburgh study of the functional requirements, for evidence in records, used analyses of literary warrant and of current and historical best practice to establish recordkeeping requirements and develop a metadata specification for business acceptable communications (see http://www.sis.pitt.edu/~nhprc). In Australia, Pederson (1999) has undertaken a survey to establish the character traits of practising archivists and archival educators, using questionnaires developed by psychologists to type/stereotype personalities. Iacovino's (1997) surveyed the development of recordkeeping education and the place of legal studies in the curricula, using historiographical methods and analyses of literary warrant and best practices. She also conducted an extensive case study of the place of legal studies in the Monash recordkeeping programs and the teaching of law in the Monash Law Faculty. Her work has also drawn on theories relating to legal and juridical systems. Upward (1996; 1997) has been involved in grounded theory development through his exploration of records continuum theory and his development of the records continuum model. His research has drawn in particular on the theories of sociologists, especially the

---

[1] The assistance of Professor Ross Harvey of Charles Sturt University with this section is acknowledged with thanks.

structuration theory of Anthony Giddens (1984), and he has used *narrative analysis* to trace the evolution of a recordkeeping professional discourse.

Upward's (1996; 1997) records continuum thinking has provided the frame of reference for much of the applied research and development in Australia relating to the role of recordkeeping in society, the recordkeeping-accountability nexus, and the development of electronic recordkeeping regimes. It has also underpinned the development of recordkeeping standards and best practice, for example the Australian Standard on Records Management (AS 4390, currently under redevelopment as an international standard), the National Records and Archives Competency Standards, and the standards-based regimes being established for the Commonwealth and NSW public sectors by the National Archives of Australia (http://www.naa.gov.au) and the State Records Authority of NSW (http://www.records.nsw.gov.au/).

Much of the research undertaken has been collaborative, involving academic and industry partners. Increasingly, as is also evident in the international arena, collaborative research is becoming multi-disciplinary in nature.

The 1998-1999 Australian Research Council and industry funded SPIRT Recordkeeping Metadata Project (see http://www.sims.monash.edu.au/rcrg/; McKemmish and Acland (1999); and McKemmish, Cunningham and Parer (1999)), has developed a standardised set of recordkeeping metadata. It has involved collaboration between Monash University, University of New South Wales, the National Archives of Australia, the State Records Authority of New South Wales, the Queensland State Archives, the Records Management Association of Australia, the Australian Council of Archives and research scientists from the Distributed Systems Technology Centre (DSTC). This project used analysis of current and historical literary warrants and best practice to identify and map recordkeeping metadata requirements. It also contributed to the development of grounded theory in the field by the development of conceptual models of recordkeeping and its business context, and high level logical models of the Recordkeeping Metadata scheme itself.

The Victorian Electronic Records Strategy (VERS) project, which has developed a prototype of an electronic records system that captures records and their contextual metadata into a long-term format, has involved extensive collaboration between the Public Record Office of Victoria, its client agencies, Ernst and Young consultants, and CSIRO research scientists (Public Record Office of Victoria 1998).

Information systems

In the field of information systems both quantitative and qualitative approaches are widely used to explore various aspects of roles, functions and use of information systems in organisations and society.

Quantitative methods are mostly used for surveys, analysis of organisational data and some types of case studies. Historically they were more accepted as a valid approach to the investigation of information systems phenomena. However, there has been a significant shift in the level of use and interest in descriptive/qualitative studies in the field. This is well justified given the state of information systems theory which still needs a lot of exploratory work done to reveal the major concepts and influences associated with information systems development and use from the socio-human perspective (Myers 1999).

A wide range of examples of the quantitative studies performed internationally can be found published in the leading information systems research journals, such as *MIS Quarterly, Information Systems Journal, International Journal of Information Systems Applications*. An excellent resource for guidelines for survey design and some tested instruments in information systems area are available from the *ISWorld Net* (see Newsted, Huff and Munro (1999)).

Some examples of quantitative studies conducted in Australia can be found at the School of Information Systems, Curtin University of Technology. One study attempts to answer the question of how chief executives in organisations conduct their work, what information they utilise and how information systems can support them. A survey was conducted to investigate what are the key issues in uses of Executive Information Systems (EIS) across the top 200 Australian companies. In this study it was particularly interesting to see the comparison of the results obtained in the Australian context with similar studies performed earlier in the USA. (See Pervan (1992) for details.) A similar study was carried out in the Department of Information Systems, Monash University, by Arnott, Gilbert and O'Donnell (1994). Its focus was on the use of computers by senior executives in Australia.

Another example of a survey-based quantitative study is by Ching, Holsapple and Winston (1996). It is an empirical study, which investigated the use of information technology to support managers in coordinating network (virtual) organisations. The study identified the major areas of concern (the authors called them *dimensions*) that require information technology support to coordinate operation of a network organisation and how it is currently implemented. The results are presented as a model that has been further validated empirically.

An example of a quantitative study, which did not involve direct data collection through a survey, but relied on statistical analysis of a wide collection of secondary data from various sources is presented by Tam (1998). It is a study of the relationship between information technology investment and firm performance with a particular focus on newly industrialised economies in Asia, such as Hong Kong, Singapore, Malaysia and Taiwan. The main purpose was to document empirical findings of the relationship, and lay some groundwork for future comparative study of the results with similar studies performed in different cultural contexts.

A major collection of resources and references for qualitative research in information systems is provided by Michael Myers (1999) in his 'Qualitative Research in Information Systems' Website. An example from the School of Information Management and Systems, at Monash University, is Darke and Shanks (1997). These researchers conducted a study to investigate variations of requirements of users and the approaches to reflect those differences in data modelling for information systems development. Darke and Shanks have undertaken three case studies that have been thoroughly analysed using qualitative approaches.

Discussion questions

- What are the major differences between the positivist and interpretivist approaches to research as you understand them?

- Can you think of a research question, or a set of related research questions, appropriate to a particular work place, which would suit: (a) a quantitative research approach? (b) a qualitative research approach? or (c) a combination of quantitative and qualitative approaches? Explain the reasons for your choices.

- What role can triangulation play in research?

Further readings

Bryman, Alan. (1992). Quantitative and qualitative research: Further reflections on their integration. In *Mixing methods: Qualitative and quantitative research*, ed Julia Brannen. Avebury: Aldershot, Hants.

Galliers, R. (ed.). (1992). *Information systems research: Issues, methods, and practical guidelines*. Blackwell Scientific Publications: Oxford.

Gorman, G.E. and Clayton, Peter. (1997). *Qualitative research for the information professional: A practical handbook*. Library Association Publishing: London, pp. 29-31.

Wildemuth, Barbara M. (1993). Post-positivist research: Two examples of methodological pluralism. *Library Quarterly*, **63** (4), pp. 450-468.

References for Chapter 2

Arnott, D., Gilbert, A. and O'Donnell, P. (1994). *Preliminary results of a survey of senior executives computing use in Australia.* (Technical Report 1/94.) Department of Information Systems, Monash University: Clayton, Vic.

Baskerville, R. and Wood-Harper, A.T. (1998). Diversity in information systems action research methods. *European Journal of Information Systems*, **7**, pp. 90-107.

Berger, Peter L. and Luckmann, Thomas. (1967). *The social construction of reality: A treatise in the sociology of knowledge.* Anchor Press: New York.

Blaikie, Norman. (1993). *Approaches to social enquiry.* Polity Press: Cambridge.

Bradley, Jana and Sutton, Brett. (1993). Reframing the paradigm debate. *The Library Quarterly*, **63** (4), pp. 405-410.

Brannen, Julia (ed.). (1992). *Mixing methods: Qualitative and quantitative research.* Avebury: Aldershot, Hants.

Broadbent, M. and Lofgren, H. (1991). *Priorities, performance and benefits: An exploratory study of library and information units.* CIRCIT and ACLIS: Melbourne.

Burns, Jenny and Tredinnick, Mark. (1994). Knowledge is power: The case for consumer research in book publishing. *The Australian Library Journal*, **43** (2), pp. 81-103.

Burns, Robert B. (1990). *Introduction to research methods in education.* Longman Cheshire: Melbourne.

Busha, Charles H. and Harter, Stephen P. (1980). Research and the scientific method. In *Research methods in librarianship: Techniques and interpretation.* Academic Press: Orlando, NY.

Childers, Thomas. (1989). Evaluative research in the library and information field. *Library Trends*, **38** (2), pp. 250-267.

Ching, Chee, Holsapple, Clyde W. and Winston, Andrew B. (1996). Toward IT support for coordination in network organisation. *Information and Management: The International Journal of Information Systems Applications*, **30**, pp. 179-199.

Darke, P. and Shanks, G. (1997). User viewpoint modelling: Understanding and representing user viewpoints during requirements definition. *Information Systems Journal*, **7**, pp. 213-239.

Denzin, Norman K. and Lincoln, Yvonne S. (eds.). (1994). *Handbook of qualitative research.* Sage: Thousand Oaks, Ca.

Dervin, Brenda. (1992). From the mind's eye of the user: the sense-making qualitative-quantitative methodology. In *Qualitative research in information management*, eds. Jack D. Glazier and Ronald R. Powell. Libraries Unlimited: Englewood, Co, pp. 61-84.

Dervin, Brenda and Nilan, Michael. (1986). Information needs and uses. In *Annual Review of Information Science and Technology*, **21**, ed. Martha E. Williams. Knowledge Industry Publications: n.p., pp. 3-33.

Dick, A. L. (1991). Influence of positivism on the design of scientific techniques: Implications for library and information science techniques. *South African Journal of Library and Information Science*, **59** (4), pp. 231-239.

Flowers, Louise. (1995). Non-users of the upper Goulburn Library Service. *The Australian Library Journal*, **44** (2), pp. 67-85.

Ford, Nigel. (1987). Research and practice in librarianship: A cognitive view. In *Current Trends in Information Research and Theory,* eds. Bill Katz and Robin Kinder. Haworth: New York, pp. 21-47.

Giddens, Anthony. (1984). *The constitution of society.* Polity Press: Cambridge.

Glaser, Barney G. and Strauss, Anselm L. (1967). *The discovery of grounded theory: Strategies of qualitative research.* Aldine de Gruyter: New York.

Glazier, Jack D. (1992). Qualitative and nonqualitative research methodologies: Thesis, antithesis, or synthesis? In *Qualitative research in information management*, eds. Jack D. Glazier and Ronald R. Powell. Libraries Unlimited: Englewood, Co, pp. 187-200.

Glesne, Corrine and Peshkin, Alan. (1992). *Becoming qualitative researchers: An introduction.* Longman: White Plains, NY.

Gorman, G.E. and Clayton, Peter. (1997). *Qualitative research for the information professional: A practical handbook.* Library Association Publishing: London.

Grosser, Kerry and Bagnell, Gaye. (1989). External students and public libraries: Student perspectives. *The Australian Library Journal*, **38** (4), pp. 303-317.

Grover, Robert and Greer, Roger C. (1991). The cross-disciplinary imperative of LIS research. In *Library and information science research: Perspectives and strategies for improvement*, eds. Charles R. McClure and Peter Hernon. Ablex Publishing: Norwood, NJ, pp. 101-113.

Guba, Egon G. and Lincoln, Yvonne S. (1981). *Effective evaluation*. Jossey-Bass: San Francisco.

Hammersley, Martyn. (1992). Deconstructing the qualitative-quantitative divide. In *Mixing methods: Qualitative and quantitative research*, ed. Julia Brannen. Avebury: Aldershot, Hants, pp. 39-55.

Iacovino, Livia. (1997). Teaching law in recordkeeping courses: The Monash experience. *Archives and Manuscripts*, **25** (2), pp. 266-287.

Kelly, George. (1955). *The psychology of personal constructs*. Vols 1 and 2. Norton: New York.

Kirk, Joyce. (1997). Managers' use of information: A grounded approach. In *Information seeking in context: Proceedings of an international conference on research in information needs, seeking and use in different contexts*, Tampere, Finland, 14-16 August 1996, eds. Pertti Vakkari, Reijo Savolainen and Brenda Dervin. Taylor Graham: London, pp. 257-267.

Kuhn, T.S. (1970). *The structure of scientific revolutions*. 2nd edn. University of Chicago Press: Chicago.

Library and Information Science Research. (1991). **13**, pp. 85-88.

Lincoln, Y.S. and Guba, E.G. (1985). *Naturalistic inquiry*. Sage: Newbury Park, CA, cited in Kirk, Joyce. (1997). Managers' use of information: a grounded approach. In *Information seeking in context: Proceedings of an international conference on research in information needs, seeking and use in different contexts*, Tampere, Finland, 14-16 August 1996, eds. Pertti Vakkari, Reijo Savolainen and Brenda Dervin. Taylor Graham: London, pp. 257-267.

Lofgren, Hans. (1992). Priority and performance evaluation: A tool for libraries. *The Australian Library Journal*, **41** (1), pp. 14-30.

McKemmish, Sue and Acland, Glenda. (1999). Accessing essential evidence on the Web: Towards an Australian recordkeeping metadata standard. In *Proceedings of AusWeb99,*

The Fifth Australian World Wide Web Conference, Ballina, NSW, 18-20 April 1999. Southern Cross University Press: Lismore, pp. 263-277. (online). http://ausweb.scu.edu.au/aw99/papers/mckemmish

McKemmish, Sue, Cunningham, Adrian and Parer, Damian. (1999). Metadata mania: Use of metadata for electronic recordkeeping and online resource discovery. In *Place, interface and cyberspace: Archives at the edge. Proceedings of the 1998 Conference of the Australian Society of Archivists,* Fremantle, WA, 6-8 August 1998. Australian Society of Archivists: Canberra, pp. 129-144. (online). http://www.sims.monash.edu.au/research/rcrg/publications/recordkeepingmetadata/sm0 1.html

Mellon, Constance. (1990). *Naturalistic inquiry for library science: Methods and applications for research, evaluation and teaching.* Greenwood Press: New York.

Myers, M. D. (1999). Qualitative Research in Information Systems, *MIS Quarterly,* **21** (2), June 1997, pp. 241-242. (online).
MISQ Discovery, archival version, June 1997, http://www.misq.org/misqd961/isworld/
MISQ Discovery, updated version, Feb. 1999, http://www.auckland.ac.nz/msis/isworld/

Newsted, Peter, Huff, Sid and Munro, Malcolm. (1999). *MIS survey research.* (online). http://www.acs.ucalgary.ca/~newsted/surveys.html

Ng, Yim Mooi and Williamson, Kirsty (1992). Weekend use of the State Library of Victoria by VCE students. *The Australian Public Libraries and Information Services,* **5** (1), pp. 32-40.

Patton, Michael Quinn. (1990). *Qualitative evaluation and research methods.* 2nd edn. Sage: Newbury Park, Ca.

Pederson, Ann. (1999). Understanding ourselves & others: Australian archivists & temperament. Proceedings of the Conference of the Australian Society of Archivists, Brisbane, 30-31 July 1999. (online). http://www.archivists.org.au/events/conf99/pederson.html.

Pervan, G. P. (1992). Issues in EIS: an Australian perspective. *Journal of Computer Information Systems,* **32** (4), pp. 6-10.

Popper, K. R. (1959). *The logic of scientific discovery.* Hutchinson: London, cited in Blaikie, Norman. (1993). *Approaches to social enquiry.* Polity Press: Cambridge, p. 145.

Powell, Ronald. (1997). *Basic research methods for librarians.* 3rd edn. Ablex Publishing: Norwood, NJ.

Power, Christine. (1996). Consolidating information for IT managers. *The Australian Library Journal,* **45** (4), pp. 290-299.

Public Record Office of Victoria. (1998). *Victorian electronic records strategy: Final report.* Public Record Office of Victoria: Melbourne.

Reneker, Maxine H. (1993). A qualitative study of information seeking among members of an academic community: Methodological issues and problems. *Library Quarterly,* **63** (4), pp. 487-507.

Shanks, Graeme, Rouse, Anne and Arnott, David. (1993). *A review of approaches to research and scholarship in information systems.* (Working Papers Series). Department of Information Systems, Monash University: Caulfield, Vic.

Sutton, Brett. (1993). The rationale for qualitative research: A review of principles and theoretical foundations. *Library Quarterly,* **63** (4), pp. 411-429.

Tam, Kar Yan. (1998). The impact of information technology investment on firm performance and evaluation: Evidence from newly industrialized economies. *Information Systems Research,* **9** (1), pp. 85-98.

Upward, Frank. (1996). Structuring the records continuum: Part 1, Post-custodial principles and properties. *Archives and Manuscripts,* **24** (2), pp. 268-87.

Upward, Frank. (1997). Structuring the records continuum: Part 2, Structuration theory and recordkeeping. *Archives and Manuscripts,* **25** (1), pp. 10-35.

Wells, Jennifer. (1995). The influence of library usage on undergraduate academic success. *Australian Academic and Research Libraries,* **26** (2), pp. 121-128.

Williamson, Kirsty. (1986). Information seeking by users of a Citizens Advice Bureau. *The Australian Library Journal,* **35** (4), pp. 197-195.

Williamson, Kirsty. (1995). Independent learning and the use of resources: VCE Australian studies. *Australian Journal of Education,* **39** (1), pp. 77-94.

CHAPTER 3
The beginning stages of research
Kirsty Williamson

Objectives

At the end of this chapter you will be able to:

- understand the ways in which research problems are identified;

- formulate clear research questions;

- formulate concise and testable hypotheses;

- understand the role of theory in research and how theory is generated;

- describe the role of the literature review in a research project; and

- understand the elements of a good literature review.

Research problems and research questions

Introduction

Before undertaking a research project of any kind, you need to have a research problem and a set of clear, well-focused research questions. As mentioned in Chapter 1, the purpose of this book is not necessarily to create fully-fledged researchers. Nevertheless, the early stages of research need to be mastered so that you can write research proposals, a consultant's brief, or a pertinent literature review. If you are to be intelligent consumers of research, you also need to be able to gauge whether other researchers have begun with clear research questions. Einstein and Infield are quoted by Powell (1997, p. 19) as saying that 'the formulation of a problem is often more essential than its solution'.

One of the most common reasons for identifying a research problem arises from students having to find a topic for a research project. Some achieve this by reading the literature: by finding out what has already been done and where the gaps might lie. Others, who are already working in a professional field, have the opportunity to observe their work setting and identify problems and issues which seem to require investigation. If they are conscientious professionals, they will probably try to keep up with the research being reported in their field.

One of the principal purposes of this subject is to encourage the use of research in the workplace where, as discussed at length in Chapter 1, it has much to contribute to the understanding of needs, and the development of services, systems and programs. Observation in the workplace is important, as is the sharing of ideas with colleagues. It is also still important to check the literature to ascertain what has already been done. As Powell (1997, p. 21) says:

> ... a problem does not have to be entirely new and unresearched in order to be worthy of investigation. Some of the most important research builds on and improves or refines previous research. The degree of uniqueness desired will in part depend upon the purpose of the research.

Problems which emerge from a workplace situation can still involve conceptual thinking. We need at least some of the research in our field to be concerned with ideas and theoretical concepts, in order to bring innovative approaches to problems and their solution and ensure the dissemination of those ideas to other professionals in the field.

Statement of the problem and major questions

The first step is to write a clear statement of the problem, or major questions. This should be done in full grammatical sentences, not just as phrases. Powell (1997, p. 22) gives a very clear description of the process. Box 3.1 contains an example of major questions and Box 3.2 presents an example of a statement of a research problem. Boxes 3.3 and 3.4 refine these into sub-questions or specific research questions. Note that there is some flexibility in the way all these elements can be expressed. In each case the first examples are from a minor thesis, based on quantitative research using a questionnaire and a quasi-experiment, by a Masters student (Ellul 1996). This student was interested in whether many primary school libraries (in 1995) were providing their students with access to Online Public Access Catalogues (OPACs) and CD-ROMs and whether the use of OPACs and CD-ROMs meant an improvement in search outcomes (compared with traditional methods). In her second attempt at expressing her problem, the wording became: The extent to which OPACs and CD-ROMs are being used at primary school level and the extent to which students are able to retrieve information successfully and efficiently using this new technology. She further refined this into two major questions, as shown in Box 3.1. Notice that these questions are more specific again than the second attempt at the problem statement. As Powell (1997, p. 22) says, the manageability of the study which will investigate the problem needs to be considered.

Box 3.1: Examples of major research questions for a quantitative study

1. What is the extent of OPAC and CD-ROM use at primary school level in Victoria?

2. How successfully and efficiently are senior primary school students able to retrieve information using OPACs and CD-ROMs (as compared with traditional methods of information retrieval)? (Ellul 1996, p. 9).

With a qualitative study, the researcher tries to phrase a problem statement to indicate the kind of understanding that the project seeks to achieve, rather than to state relationships between variables as happens in quantitative research (Gorman and Clayton 1997, p. 72). Box 3.2 contains a research problem developed for a qualitative study which was undertaken with an ethnographic approach using participant observation. (Ethnography and participant observation are described in Chapters 10 and 16.)

Box 3.2: Example of a research problem for a qualitative study

'The primary goal of this study was to enhance the understanding of the networked learning community that emerged in an Internet-based, graduate-level course' (Rice-Lively 1994, p. 20, cited in Gorman and Clayton 1997, p. 72).

Sub-questions or specific research questions

Virtually every problem or major question can be broken down into a number of component parts. By framing sub-questions or specific questions, all of which fall within the scope of the larger problem or major question, the researcher makes manageable or easily researchable chunks. Powell (1997, pp. 22-23) warns that, when combined, the sub-questions or specific research questions should equal the whole of the main problem or question, but not exceed the whole. This means that the sub-questions should provide complete coverage of the research problem, but not introduce issues which are beyond its scope. If you find that that some of the specific questions do not fit within the scope of the main question, you need to make adjustments until the necessary fit is achieved. As illustrated in Box 3.3, usually a researcher will formulate five to eight sub-questions, or specific questions. These questions relate to the major questions (for a quantitative study) in Box 3.1.

Box 3.3: Examples of specific research questions for a quantitative study

- How widespread is the use of OPACs and CD-ROMs at the primary school level?

- Are OPACs and CD-ROMs available at all primary schools in Victoria?

- How successful are students at retrieving required information using both of the technologies, mentioned above?

- Are students' success rates using OPACs and CD-ROMs the same as when they use card catalogues and print encyclopedias?

- What are the processes used by students to locate information using these technologies?

- Do students follow the same processes they used when using card catalogues and print encyclopedias?

- What form of teacher instruction has been provided in conjunction with the introduction of these two forms of Information Technology? (Ellul 1996, p. 9).

It might be argued that some of these specific questions are not directly matched to the major questions, for example the processes of use or teacher instruction. A counter argument would be that the processes used are likely to affect success and efficiency, as will the form of teacher instruction provided. The specific research questions, related to the research problem (for a qualitative study) in Box 3.2, are set out in Box 3.4.

Box 3.4: Examples of specific questions for a qualitative study

- Will a class conducted in a mostly electronic environment form a unique culture, complete with rules for communication and behaviour?

- Do the traditional educational roles of the students and the instructor change in the virtual classroom? If so, how are these new roles different?

- To what extent can ethnographic research techniques, using the traditional data-gathering methodologies of observation, interviews, and recording of field notes, be applied in an electronic community? (Rice-Lively 1994, p. 2, cited in Gorman and Clayton 1997, p. 72).

You will undoubtedly note that each of this last set of questions is much broader than those for the quantitative study. Remember that Rice-Lively's study was qualitative, and thus aiming to uncover the unexpected and to explore new avenues (Marshall and Rossman 1995, p. 26). Questions therefore require more flexibility than those used in the quantitative research style. Marshall and Rossman (p. 26) suggest that in a qualitative study, 'the research questions should be general enough to permit exploration but focused enough to delimit the study. Not an easy task'.

The exploration of the literature needs to be undertaken in conjunction with the development of research questions. It is very important to understand the way in which other researchers have viewed the topic (if at all) and to take into account other research. Maybe there has been quite a lot of research undertaken on your topic of interest, but maybe approaches have been mainly quantitative and, in your opinion, there has not been a deep understanding of the issues involved. Conversely, you may believe that the broader perspective of a quantitative approach is missing. Theory formulation also plays a part in this initial stage of research (with question development and reviewing of the literature).

Gorman and Clayton (1997, p. 73) emphasise the interactive, iterative nature of the process of research question development, theory formulation and reviewing the literature. They see this interaction as a triangle, with each of these components at one point of the points. If hypotheses are developed they, too, should be part of this iterative process. The formulation of hypotheses is dealt with in the next section.

Suggestions for setting questions

The following steps may assist you to formulate your questions:

STEP 1. Write down your broad area of interest.

STEP 2. Write down a specific sub-area of this broad area in which you have a particular interest. Try to formulate a question based on this.

STEP 3. List five to eight unanswered questions you have in respect to the specific sub-area.

You need to scrutinise your questions carefully to make sure they are communicating exactly what you mean. Note that questions may relate to your sample. For example, if the main focus of your study is the factors influencing library use, sub-questions might concern the differences between males and females, or the differences between certain age groups in your sample.

Hypotheses: Their role in research and their formulation

Introduction

Hypothesis testing is central to the positivist or quantitative approach to research, as described in Chapter 2. The following long paragraph from Busha and Harter (1980) provides a definition of the term, 'hypothesis', together with an explanation of the role of hypotheses in research and how they are derived:

> In scientific inquiry, the *hypothesis* is a tentative, declarative statement about the relation between two or more variables which can be observed empirically. As a vitally important intellectual instrument of research, the hypothesis is a scientific guess about the relationship among variables related to a practical or theoretical problem. Hypotheses can be derived from intuition or theories, and from relevant facts produced during the course of previous observation, research, or experience. Hypotheses offer explanations for certain phenomena and serve as guides to the collection and analysis of research data. Implicit in the process of hypothesis formulation is the notion that statements of the relationship between or among variables must be tested. The essential function of the hypothesis in scientific inquiry is to guide the collection of research data and the subsequent discovery of new knowledge (Busha and Harter 1980, p. 10).

As Busha and Harter suggest, convenient and logical sources of hypotheses are theory and the findings of other studies reported in the literature (discussed further below). Each hypothesis should be closely related to at least one of the research sub-questions. In other words, there should be a close link between research questions and hypotheses.

Types of hypotheses

Burns (1990, p. 78) talks about a hierarchy of hypotheses – each becoming tighter and more testable. The first level is the *problem* or *general hypothesis*, from which the more specific *research hypothesis* is developed. When this is re-expressed in operational terms, it becomes an *operational hypothesis*. He provides the following example:

> Problem or General Hypothesis: You expect some children to read better than others because they come from homes in which there are positive values and attitudes to education.

> Research Hypothesis: Reading ability in nine-year-old children is related to parental attitudes towards education.

> Operational Hypothesis: There is a significant relationship between reading ability for nine-year-old children living in major cities in NSW as measured by standardised

reading test X and parental attitudes to education as measured by attitude test Y (Burns 1990, p. 79).

It is this last hypothesis – the operational one – which is sufficiently specific to be testable.

Powell (1997) lists several different types of hypotheses. One of the most important of these is the *directional hypothesis* which Powell defines as:

> ... a hypothesis that indicates the nature of the relationship between or among variables. For example, it could be hypothesized that the assignment of term papers results in more library use by certain students (Powell 1997, pp. 28-29).

Burns' operational hypothesis, above, is a directional hypothesis. Borg (1981) in the further reading list at the end of the chapter, gives several examples of directional hypotheses. Boxes 3.5 and 3.6 provide further examples of directional hypotheses. Those in Box 3.5 are two of the four hypotheses developed for a study which focused on users of a Citizens Advice Bureau (CAB), the kinds of problems they brought to the Bureau and the degree of their dependence or independence in their information seeking.

Box 3.5: Examples of directional hypotheses: Information seeking in a CAB

- Higher and lower socio-economic groups will present different categories of problem.

- The preferred responses of people in lower socio-economic groups indicate they are more dependent in their information seeking than those in higher socio-economic groups (Williamson 1984, p. 35).

Notice that each of these hypotheses involves a comparison of variables. In the first case, it involves higher and lower socio-economic groups and the different categories of problem which they brought to the CAB; in the second case, higher and lower socio-economic groups and different levels of dependency in information seeking.

Ellul (1996), whose research questions are outlined in Box 3.3, also framed directional hypotheses. If you look at her hypotheses (in Box 3.6) alongside her research questions you will notice the close relationship between three of the research questions and the four hypotheses.

Box 3.6: Examples of directional hypotheses: OPAC/CD-ROM study

- That students using OPACs to locate information follow steps similar to those they use with card catalogues.

- That students using CD-ROMs to locate information follow steps similar to those they use with print encyclopedias.

- That success rates for OPACs will be better than those for card catalogues for the same students.

- That success rates for CD-ROMs will be better than those for print encyclopedias for the same students (Ellul 1996, pp. 9-10).

The converse of the directional hypothesis is the *null hypothesis* which Powell (1997, p. 29) defines as:

> ... a hypothesis that asserts that there is no real relationship between or among the variables in question. It involves the supposition that chance rather than an identifiable cause has produced some observed result. It is used primarily for purposes of statistical testing.

Box 3.7 shows how the hypotheses developed for the CAB study would have appeared had null, rather than directional, hypotheses been chosen.

Box 3.7: Example of null hypotheses: Information seeking in a CAB

- There will be no difference in the categories of problem presented by higher and lower socio-economic groups.

- There will be no differences between the higher and lower socio-economic group in the responses they prefer from the CAB.

When hypotheses should be used

If you have a quantitative approach in mind (and provided your sample, as discussed in Chapter 13, is appropriate), you should develop operational hypotheses, along with your research questions. Hypotheses often help to clarify what it is you are trying to find out. Mostly used in positivist research, they are usually regarded as inappropriate for qualitative research which uses small samples, does not submit its data to statistical tests, and which aims to uncover the unexpected and explore new avenues of related inquiry as they open up. However, for some interpretivist studies, researchers develop propositions which are similar to research hypotheses (described above). They do not require such precise wording, nor the rigorous testing associated with operational hypotheses. They, nevertheless, can help to provide a similar kind of clarification as hypotheses give to a quantitative study. Historians also sometimes use hypotheses of the 'research' kind.

Criteria for good hypotheses

Good hypotheses should:

- be stated in correct terminology;

- be as brief and clear as possible;

- state an expected relationship or difference between two or more variables;

- be testable; and

- be grounded in past knowledge, gained from the literature review or from theory.

A hypothesis should *never* be double barrelled. Box 3.8 gives an example of an *unacceptable* hypothesis.

Box 3.8: Example of an unacceptable hypothesis

The older age group is much more likely than the younger group to do press ups and eat porridge first thing in the morning.

This hypothesis is problematic because there could be different results for the separate variables concerning press ups and porridge. The two issues need separate hypotheses.

Theory: Its role in research and its development

What is theory?

Very simply, a *theory* is a viewpoint or perspective which is explanatory. According to Babbie (1989, p. 46), social science theory is 'a systematic explanation for the observed facts and laws that relate to a specific aspect of life'.

There is a sense in which we develop theories all the time in our everyday lives, for example, to account for someone's behaviour or explain certain problems which we face. Professionals, such as information service providers, also construct viewpoints or theories. For example, suppose staff from a particular public library observe that the children's collection of the library is used less than would be expected (or they believe that is the case). Their theory of why this is so could include the fact that there are very good school libraries in the area; and that the area is basically working class with the result that parents do not encourage their children to use the library as much as middle-class parents do. They might develop other theories about what can be done to change this situation.

Likewise researchers act on the basis of theory, but differ in the extent to which they are aware of it, make it explicit and develop it. There are also differences between quantitative and qualitative researchers with regard to the stage of the research at which they focus on theory development. With regard to positivist approaches, Powell (1997, p. 24) says '… theory or theory construction is the first major component of the scientific method of inquiry'. On the other hand interpretivists, or qualitative researchers, use theory at various stages of the research process. In particular, those who are users of 'grounded theory' (Glaser and Strauss 1967) will be seeking to generate theory based on data collected from the field work stages of their research. These differences were discussed at greater length in Chapter 2.

A number of the definitions of 'theory' mention the relationships between variables. In addition to the definition of social science theory, above, Babbie also defines theory as 'a complex set of relationships amongst several variables' (Babbie 1989). Sekaran says that:

> The theoretical framework is the foundation on which the entire research project is based. It is a logically developed, described and elaborated network of associations among variables that have been identified through such processes as interviews, observations, and the literature survey (Sekaran 1992, p. 73).

One metaphor which might help is to think of a project's theoretical framework (sometimes described as the 'conceptual framework') as an architect's plan of a house. Just as a house plan describes the rooms of the house and how they are connected, the theoretical framework describes the key ideas underpinning the research and how they are related.

The role of theory in research

Theory is very important in research. It 'informs' the research process and helps to direct it. When an investigator is aware of the theoretical implications of a study, more pertinent and potentially significant research questions are likely to be posed. When researchers set out to develop theory, they will usually search for other theories and research to inform the process. They, themselves, will then contribute theories and research on which others can build. In this way, theory helps to encourage a cumulative, rather than a fragmented approach. From the theoretical framework, hypotheses are usually easily formulated.

Powell (1997, pp. 24-25) provides a very good discussion of the role of theory in research. Schauder (1989) eloquently expounds the role of theory in research in professional practice. The latter's axiom is: 'Don't be afraid to theorise: the rest is implementation' (Schauder 1989, p. 318). He begins with definitions of 'theory' and 'model' then discusses how the use of 'theory' is implicit in library work, as in other fields. He makes a sound case for the benefits of using metaphor to aid the understanding of theory, for developing the capacity to theorise, and to enable the creation of alternative perspectives. His major theme is the power that imaginative, alternative theories can bring both to research and professional practice.

How theory is developed

How theory is developed depends, to some extent, on whether a researcher is from the quantitative or qualitative tradition. Nevertheless, most researchers generate some theory initially, using observation and discussions, as well as a review of the literature. A period of deep thought and gestation is usually very beneficial. An interesting article, providing a conceptual framework for theory building in library and information science, is provided by Grover and Glazier (1986). At least in quantitative research and, to some extent in a qualitative study, the theoretical framework for a study should emerge from the literature review. Box 3.9 provides an example of the development of part of a theoretical framework.

Box 3.9: Part of a theoretical framework: How it was developed

For research concerning the information, communication, and telecommunication needs of older adults (Williamson 1995), one of the key components of the theoretical framework was concerned with how information is acquired. The central question became: is information always purposefully sought or is it sometimes incidentally acquired? The idea for this came from Wilson's (1977) theory of informing behaviour. Wilson talked about the habits or routines which people use to keep their internal model of the world up-to-date. He postulated that this involves monitoring the environment by personal observations, discussions with friends, relatives and colleagues and use of the mass media. Such routines, he considered, may or may not have the gathering of information as their goal. In the latter case, information is incidentally acquired.

In the theoretical framework for the Williamson study, this concept of purposeful/incidental information acquisition was related to a range of different sources of information for everyday living, for example, family, friends and the mass media. Another related key concept was everyday life activities and the effect these might have on information needs and the sources used to satisfy them. All these concepts were defined and explained in relation to the relevant literature and to each other.

At the conclusion of the research described in Box 3.9, a diagrammatic model of the theory was developed based on the findings of the study. (See Figure 3.1.) It incorporated the initial theoretical ideas, which had been supported empirically in the study, and illustrated the relationships between the concepts as they emerged from the research. For example, as illustrated in the model, purposeful information seeking and incidental information acquisition occurred with all sources of information, except institutional sources, from which information was almost always purposefully sought. In information systems research, particularly, but also in information management, researchers will often begin with diagrammatic models which represent their theoretical framework.

The literature review plays an important part in the formulation of the theoretical framework. Innovative theoretical frameworks will draw on a range of literature, not necessarily restricted to the field of the proposed study. For example psychology, sociology, education, anthropology and computer science, may all have interesting ideas to contribute to a study in the field of information management.

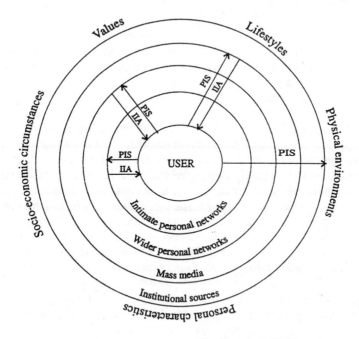

PIS - Purposeful information
      seeking
IIA - Incidental information
      acquisition

(Williamson 1998, p. 36.)

Figure 3.1: Everyday life information: An ecological model of use

The literature review

The role of the literature review

The literature search and review involve identifying, locating, synthesising, and analysing
the conceptual literature, as well as completed research reports, articles, conference papers,
books, theses, and other materials about the specific problem or problems of a research
topic. It is important that a literature review should include evaluative and critical
judgments about the literature, and that it should present a comparison of ideas and research
findings, tying them together. As mentioned above, at least in the quantitative paradigm, the
theoretical framework for the proposed research study should emerge from the literature
review.

The literature review has a crucial role in research. According to Marshall and Rossman (1995, p. 28) 'a thoughtful and insightful discussion of the literature builds a logical framework for the research that sets it within a tradition of inquiry and a context of related studies'. In other words, it provides a background and context for a study. It also assists the researcher in understanding the problem and its context.

As pointed out above, the literature review plays an important role in the generation of theory and in the formulation and refinement of research questions and hypotheses. In addition, a thorough search of the literature enables the researcher to identify the gaps in previous research and thus to justify a proposed study in relation to a demonstrated need. Gorman and Clayton (1997, p. 74) state that '... a chosen topic should aim to fill the gap, or at least put a new complexion on existing research'. In other words, the absence of coverage in the literature is a good indication that an investigation of a topic will break new ground. It is still possible to write a literature review which covers related areas, especially if you look for inspiration beyond the specific field of study, as discussed above. Pointing out the gaps in the literature, through the literature review, is very important.

Very importantly, the literature can help in the choice of a research method for the study. Not only are the findings of research reported in the literature, but the methods used will usually be discussed. This may enable a researcher to say that the chosen method is well accepted by other researchers. Alternatively it may be that a particular problem has been investigated only by quantitative methods and that a researcher can see that a qualitative approach will provide a greater depth of understanding. For example, if the use of public libraries has mainly been examined through a survey approach, a deeper understanding of what motivates use by some groups, in comparison with others, may be lacking.

A further role is the documentation of the research results already available for the topic. Researchers can then use these results for comparison with the findings of their own studies. In this way, results are placed in the context of the findings of past research.

Undertaking a literature search

Because of the discipline areas to which this book relates, many readers will be trained in retrieval of information. Given the vast range of possible sources of literature, it is not feasible to include more than a brief mention of the literature search. As discussed in Chapter 1, it is important not to limit your thinking to your own disciplinary field. There is much to gain from thinking laterally to other fields (depending on your topic).

The World Wide Web is now an important source of material, but should be used in conjunction with other sources. Sometimes you can be lucky enough to find a review article which gives a detailed coverage of the literature of your topic. If you are initially lucky enough to locate one or more recent key articles, the bibliographies of these will very often lead you to other relevant items. If you are writing a literature review, you should try to include a range of literature – not all books, journal articles, or Internet sites, for example. Remember to look for theses, conference papers and government or industry reports, if relevant.

Basic steps for writing a literature review

Below is a list of basic steps for writing a literature review. The relevant further readings and references will provide more information.

1. Categorise your literature into subject/topic areas. **Categories should be clearly related to your research questions**.

2. Begin with an introduction to the topic, including its significance and importance.

3. End the introduction with an overview of the contents of the review.

4. Organise the body of the review under headings **which relate to your research questions**.

5. Critically analyse the relevant literature – conceptual, anecdotal and research – under those headings.

6. Write a conclusion which draws the threads together, indicating the gaps in the literature and other reasons why research, or further research, is needed. The key concepts for the proposed research should be highlighted.

7. End with the research questions which the proposed research will investigate.

8. Finally, check that you have written a **critical** and **evaluative** literature review. For example, did you examine the quality of the research which you discussed? Or did you simply assume that the findings are useful and valid? Did you simply report the views of other authors, rather than questioning and evaluating those views?

(Note that an alternative is to place the research questions towards the end of the introduction. If you are writing a literature review which is not part of a research project, it is still a good idea to write some questions which the review is intended to answer. In this case, the questions would be placed towards the end of the introduction.)

References for a literature review

There must be a high standard of referencing for a literature review. The best approach is to use *Style manual for authors, editors and printers* (1996). Whichever style you choose, it is important to use it consistently. The Harvard System is recommended.

Conclusion

All the components of the beginning stages of research, discussed above, are inextricably linked. The development of research questions needs to be undertaken in conjunction with an exploration of the relevant literature and the development of the theoretical framework. If hypotheses are appropriate to the research, they should be developed in association with the research questions. When the research is written up, the links between these elements should be clear. The researcher's research questions, hypotheses and key concepts should be clearly related to each other, and to the literature review. For example, all the issues encompassed in the research questions should be covered in the literature review. Conversely the literature review should reflect the issues of the research questions. Conscientious attention to the beginning stages of research lays the foundation of a good research project.

Discussion questions

- How can problems which warrant research be identified in the work place?

- What do you think are the elements of good research questions?

- When is hypothesis testing appropriate in research and what should you consider when formulating hypotheses?

- How can theory be generated so that a study can be informed and enriched?

- What are the elements of an effective literature review?

Further readings

Powell, Ronald. (1997). *Basic research methods for librarians.* 3rd edn. Ablex Publishing: Norwood NJ, pp. 19-28 (for setting questions and theory).

Borg, Walter R. (1981). *Applying educational research: A practical guide for teachers.* Longman: New York, pp. 69-72 (for hypotheses).

Schauder, Don. (1989). Research in librarianship and information services: the scope for innovation and inquiry in Australia. *Australian Library Journal*, **38** (4), pp. 318-324 (for theory).

Cooper, H.M. (1989). *Integrating research: A guide for literature reviews.* 2nd edn. Sage: Newbury Park, Ca.

References for Chapter 3

Babbie, Earl. (1989). *The practice of social research.* 5th edn. Wadsworth: Belmont, Ca.

Borg, Walter R. (1981). *Applying educational research: A practical guide for teachers.* Longman: New York.

Burns, Robert B. (1990). *Introduction to research methods in education.* Longman: Melbourne.

Busha, Charles H. and Harter, Stephen P. (1980). *Research methods in librarianship: Techniques and interpretations.* Academic Press: Orlando, NY.

Ellul, Rita T. (1996). An evaluation of the impact of OPACs and CD-ROMs on the information retrieval skills of upper primary school students. Master of Business (Information Technology) thesis. RMIT, Department of Information Management and Library Studies, Faculty of Business: Melbourne.

Glaser, Barney G. and Strauss, Anselm L. (1967). *The discovery of grounded theory: Strategies of qualitative research.* Aldine de Gruyter: New York.

Gorman, G.E. and Clayton, Peter. (1997). *Qualitative research for the information professional: A practical handbook.* Library Association Publishing: London.

Grover, Robert and Glazier, Jack. (1986). A conceptual framework for theory building in library and information science. *Library and Information Science Research*, **8**, pp. 227-242.

Marshall, Catherine and Rossman, Gretchen B. (1995). *Designing qualitative research.* 2nd edn. Sage: Thousand Oaks, Ca.

Powell, Ronald. (1997). *Basic research methods for librarians.* 3rd edn. Ablex Publishing: Norwood, NJ.

Rice-Lively, Mary Lynn. (1994). Wired warp and woof: An ethnographic study of a networking class. *Internet Research,* **4** (4), cited in Gorman, G.E. and Clayton, Peter. (1997). *Qualitative research for the information professional: A practical handbook.* Library Association Publishing: London.

Schauder, Don. (1989). Research in librarianship and information services: the scope for innovation and inquiry in Australia. *Australian Library Journal,* **38** (4), pp. 318-324.

Sekaran, Uma. (1992). *Research methods for business.* 2nd edn. Wiley: New York.

Style manual for authors, editors and printers. (1996). 5th edn. Australian Government Publishing Service: Canberra.

Williamson, Kirsty. (1984). Information seeking by users of a citizens advice bureau. Master of Librarianship thesis. Monash University: Clayton, Vic.

Williamson, Kirsty. (1995). Older adults: information, communication and tele-communications. PhD Thesis. RMIT: Melbourne, Vic.

Williamson, Kirsty. (1998). Discovered by chance: The role of incidental information acquisition in an ecological model of information use. *Library and Information Science Research,* **20** (1), pp. 23-40.

Wilson, Patrick. (1977). *Public knowledge, private ignorance.* Greenwood Press: Westport, Ct.

CHAPTER 4
Ethics in research
Graeme Johanson

Objectives

At the end of this chapter you will be able to:

- understand the relevance of ethics to research;

- describe the main features of ethical thinking, and why most researchers want to think ethically;

- observe that ethical principles in research pervade many other spheres of influence on our daily lives;

- appreciate why ethics have been built into good research techniques; and

- practise drawing conclusions about the ways that researchers make decisions, by trying out the ethical validity of your own views on a set of research problems posed towards the end of this chapter.

The practice of ethics in research

It is impossible for any research to avoid ethics. They are inextricably entwined. Ethics are demonstrated in intentional conduct or the values that lie behind actions (MacIntyre 1998, p. 85). The act of research itself inevitably disturbs the status quo. Every decision in research affects other decisions somehow; no decision can be taken in isolation. Any personal value needs to be related to all mutually-supporting values. Buckminster Fuller, the visionary sailor, accountant, engineer, architect, and inventor, wrote of the interconnections in this way:

> One of the modern tools of high intellectual advantage is the development of what is called general systems theory. Employing it we begin to think of the largest and most comprehensive systems, and try to do it scientifically. But if we don't really know how big 'big' is, we may not start big enough, and are thus likely to leave unknown, but critical variables outside the system, which will continue to plague us. If we are to be effective, we are going to have to think in both the biggest and most minutely-

incisive ways permitted by intellect and by the information thus far won through
experience (Fuller 1963).

If you put yourself in the shoes of a person being researched, you will appreciate that ethical
questions arise inevitably. Ask yourself, how would you want a researcher to handle you,
evaluate you, examine you, or report on you. (Bouma 2000B, pp. 190-202). Think of the
dilemmas posed by the following simple questions, by way of further illustration. Is stored
information about you, or any technology that you use, value-free in all contexts? What
about images of you, used by others after being gathered by secret electronic surveillance?
What if your image is matched with someone else's mistakenly, and covertly stored? Is a
virtual world more likely to encourage amoral behaviour than are face-to-face interactions?
Is there any role for concepts like personal integrity or individual rights in that world? How
can confidentiality about individuals be secured on any computer network? Who owns or
should own public information? How do you draw the boundaries between private and
public information? When new systems directly lead to unemployment, or to obsolescence
of respected skill sets, who is to be held responsible? Who will preserve alternative
knowledge and culture for the future? Who should fund organisations to recycle potentially
valuable data which may be worth little in today's marketplace? Should the lifespan of
politically-damaging knowledge be restricted? For how long should controversial
information be curated if it severely affects the reputation of people or groups? Should
information from the past be protected with the purpose of constraining future behaviours or
progress? Answers to these sorts of questions have exercised the minds of all researchers in
the fields of information management and information systems, not to mention the minds of
other people more generally (Christians 2000).

Ethical research involves and uses humans respectfully and equitably without trying to
change them or their surroundings. Ideally it collects data that is kept confidential to the
researcher, it destroys private data after use within a reasonable time, and it allows the
researcher (without excessive extraneous pressures) to choose the subject of research, the
manner of conduct of the research, and the method of dissemination of the results of the
research. Peers will review its ethical basis frequently. It permits the subjects of the research
to opt out at any time. On the whole, research is motivated by honourable intentions
(MacIntyre 1998, p. 85). Ethical research is practised within accepted moral systems based
on broadly-understood human duties, maybe with a strong dose of plain common sense.
Ethics are applied to help to find fair, responsible solutions to practical problems.

What if things go wrong? Saunders (1994), a Salem librarian, has thought this through. She
sets out what an organisation should do when an ethical crisis occurs. She might just as well
be referring to ethical problems created by bad research. She recommends standard
problem-saving techniques as a set response. These are: specify the facts of the problem
situation; define the moral dilemma posed; identify the concerned constituencies and their
interests; clarify and prioritise the values and principles at stake; formulate options for
action by the researcher (and managing supervisor); and identify the potential consequences
of acting on the problem, or failing to act.

Social ideals and research

Ethical dilemmas posed by research are age-old. The combined power of knowledge and human enquiry have long been viewed as very beneficial and potentially dangerous at the same time – two sides of the same coin.

The major benefits of research are threefold. First is the benefit to society as a whole. In modern Western culture the pursuit of knowledge per se is universally valued. Tax-funded universities and research organisations are given the responsibility to initiate, undertake and guide objective, public research (Smith and Hasnas 1999, p. 112). Extending knowledge generally is in the community interest. Inventive researchers are rewarded for elevating the quality of human lives and experience, by awards, and research funds.

Also, we believe that knowledge ennobles and dignifies humans as individuals. It increases self-awareness, promotes personal growth, and self-fulfilment, and ultimately creates a better person, a well-rounded, humane citizen able to develop fully by means of informed self-determination.

Thirdly, knowledge derived from research is said to encourage useful activities, and the adoption of worthy research outcomes. It supports progress in health, educationally, culturally, politically, and economically. We constantly measure (albeit crudely) the value of our plans. Individuals, politicians, and managers speak daily of good decisions, and in retrospect they analyse the impact of their thoughts and actions on their constituencies, be they peers, friends, family, nations, organisations, budgets, social acceptability, or predetermined bottom lines. This reflective process is a regular form of primary research in practice. It can expand into a greater scale. Yet our aspiration for success must be tempered at times with ethical limitations, and certainly success alone does not amount to an ethical code in its own right. In a similar way, research which seeks to quantify only success that might be derived from adopting ethical codes is delusory.

The detrimental side of research is to be found in the abuses of it, or unintended bad side-effects of it. Examples can be found in the ambivalence with which we regard scientific research, although we could also look elsewhere for other examples.

The end of the nineteenth century experienced 'scientism' at its peak, a blind faith in the virtues of the neutrality of science. The word 'science' itself is from *scientia,* the Latin word for knowledge. In our culture it is only three hundred years since distinctions began to be drawn between experience and experiment, practice and theory or formula, subjective and objective knowledge, the chaos of nature and the rational mind, and between art and science. The scene was set then for tensions that still prevail in many ethical and disciplinary discussions, especially between interpretivist and positivist schools of thought, explained elsewhere in this book.

Scientific beliefs, and the ethics that informed them, spilled over into the world of politics, although the originators did not intend the transfer. Thus in various forms they lay behind the philosophies of the American Declaration of Independence (1776), the ideals of the French Revolution (1789) and the Bolshevik Revolution (1917). In the American Declaration, Thomas Jefferson wrote about obvious, universal truths:

> We hold these *truths* to be *self-evident*, that all men are created *equal*, that they are endowed by their creator with certain inalienable rights, and among these rights are life, liberty, and the pursuit of happiness.

In the French Declaration of the Rights of Man, the pursuit of enlightened public knowledge was seen as a major benefit. The Bolsheviks used a prescription for revolution which aimed to bring about world peace and prosperity; they wanted to apply all labour and resources for the benefit of a united, classless community. Marxism seemed almost a mechanistic scheme, many believing it to be 'scientific', applicable to any society anywhere. An equally authoritarian belief is that computers are superior thinking machines to human minds, guardians of absolute truth, reliable replacements for human error, capable only of perpetually consistent behaviours (Langford 1995).

We know well today that science combats ignorance and provides many important benefits. Yet it can have drawbacks. Overdependence on science was challenged dramatically by the horrible destruction it facilitated in two European wars (1914-1918, and 1939-1945), by the technological threats of the ensuing Cold War, by financial crises around the world (especially in 1929) which showed the fallibility of economic science, and more recently by the demise of the centralist Soviet experiment (USSR) once known as 'scientific socialism' (1989). We have nominated only a few examples here of misleading applications of research; there are many more.

Principles and ethical codes

In looking for alternatives to scientific absolutism, we check beneath the surface of research decisions for the ethical origins behind them (Blaikie 1993, p. 212). It is possible to identify two main schools of thought. The first school, titled the deontological, emphasises ideals about the pre-existing duty of any researcher, principles based on universal rules which should guide research actions and duties. The second focus, titled the teleological, is primarily about the ends, purposes, goals of research activities, and the consequences of those acts.

Many groups, such as professional associations and universities, choose the first approach (prescribed duty) and try to codify behavioural guidelines, in order to provide broad ethical rules, for staff and students. Such guidelines were invented by Isaac Asimov for the fictional context of his Three Laws of Robotics. Those laws were that a robot may not injure a human being, or, through inaction, allow a human being to come to harm, that a robot must obey the orders given it by human beings except where such orders would conflict with the First Law, and that a robot must protect its own existence as long as such protection does not conflict with the First or Second Law (Asimov 1950). The laws are simple, but realistic.

The old Hippocratic oath is another example of general guidelines, still sworn by new doctors today:

> I swear by Apollo the Physician and by Asclepius and by Health and Panacea and by all the gods as well as goddesses ... to bring the following oath and written covenant to fulfillment, in accordance with my power and my judgment. And I will use regimens for the benefit of the ill in accordance with my ability. Into as many houses as I may enter, I will go for the benefit of the ill. And about whatever I may see or hear in treatment, or even without treatment, in the life of human beings – things that should not ever be blurted out outside – I will remain silent, holding such things to be unutterable. If I render this oath fulfilled ... may it be [granted] to me to enjoy the benefits both of life ... being held in good repute among all human beings for time eternal (Von Staden 1996).

The complex ethics involved in the separation of private life from public space is highlighted later in this book in relation to ethnographic research. (See the section 'Gaining permission to enter the field', in Chapter 16.)

Most universities set out rights and responsibilities of research students in various policies, handbooks and Websites. Commonly ethics committees within organisations vet research projects at the time they are proposed, and compliance with the committee requirements is strict and compulsory. Organisations can be subject to litigation for side effects of bad research. Research proposals which do not take ethics into account are rejected outright. The ethics policy on research into humans of the National Health and Medical Research Council (1999) outlined below is endorsed by the Australian Vice Chancellors' Committee, the Australian Research Council, the Australian Academy of the Humanities, the Australian Academy of Science, the Academy of the Social Sciences in Australia and the Academy of Technological Services and Engineering.

An urgent need to standardise rules surrounding medical research in Australia led to the evolution of the general 'National statement on ethical conduct in research involving humans,' which is widely adopted (National Health and Medical Research Council 1999). The statement is useful for most researchers in that it espouses five fundamental principles:

- researchers must treat with dignity and respect the persons, groups and organisations which participate in their research;

- research must be based on the work of others in the researched area and be conducted and/or supervised by persons qualified to do the work who have the necessary facilities to ensure the safety of the participants;

- the potential benefits of the research project must substantially outweigh any potential harm to participants, or users of the research output;

- participants in the research must be able to make a voluntary, informed decision to participate; and

- research is a public activity, conducted openly and accountably to both the researcher's community and to participants in the research (Bouma 2000B, pp. 194-199).

The Australian Library and Information Association also has broad ethics policies, as do the Australian Computer Society and the Records Management Association of Australia, and in the United States the American Association for Information Science, the Association of Computing Machinery (ACM) and the Computer Ethics Institute, to mention a few.

Ethics committees

To see what sorts of issues are at stake, an example of an ethics application form from Monash University can be found at http://www.monash.edu.au/resgrant/human_ethics/forms-reports/index.html. The form is extremely relevant to all research: it applies to *any* researcher who is gathering information (even archived data) about human beings and organisations. In writing a research application, the committee urges the applicant to understand the viewpoint of participants in research:

> How would you feel if you were asked these questions, asked to undergo these procedures, or were asked to give approval for your child to take part in this research? What would you like to know about it? What would you need to know to give informed consent for yourself or for a dependent? (Bouma 2000A).

There are many complexities in an ethics approval process. Applicants for ethics clearance have to submit an outline of the purposes of their research. They need to provide the ethics committee with copies of their interview schedules, and if there are no precise, pre-determined questions, then the applicants need to provide a thorough description of the key topics being examined. A consent form can be downloaded by the applicants, from the World Wide Web, and presented to the ethics committee, for later use by the researcher, to present to the interviewee or other subject of the research. The consent form will be signed by the participant in the research as permanent evidence, kept by the researcher, of willingness to be subjected to it.

Power and influence

The second way of thinking about underlying ethics (emphasising consequences of actions) is observable in techniques for undertaking research or failure to carry out basic responsibilities. Many of the consequences of unethical research behaviour relate to abuse of a researcher's power and influence, to complacency and carelessness, to failure to carry through the original research commitments, to subjecting participants in research to duress, to failing to protect confidentiality, to falsifying data, or not disseminating findings properly as promised. Despite admirable efforts, it is proving hard to standardise research practice globally. It is hoped that honourable motives guide research acts: honesty, integrity, respect and a sense of communal duty.

Motivations of researchers vary according to the contexts of the projects. Some are more public or international than others. Some will emphasise disciplinary or professional norms, which may be very specialised. Others will focus on research resourced by employers, maybe primarily with commercial outcomes such as patents in mind (Foray 1998, pp. 170-171). Other researchers will not be seeking the entire truth, but will concentrate on selective evidence for purposes of persuasion and manipulation – in the realms of business analysis, public relations, marketing, politics, and promotional media, for example. The contexts of the management and supervision of research will vary too, as well as the extent, form and style in which the research is publicised (Connolly 1994). Some groups will deliberately aim to manage research to stifle any work outside their immediate hegemony, as does IBM (Kitson and Campbell 1996, p. 165).

Monitoring and supervision involves obvious actions as well as subtle consequences. The supervisor can be in a temporary position of great influence over research projects (Elphinstone 1994, p. 5), while sometimes there may be little obvious effect. Typically the role of the research investigator or supervisor is to guide and inspire a research project, and to monitor ethical implementation.

Publishing research

Normally research results are published. This is one obvious consequence of completing research. Indeed, some researchers believe it unethical not to publish. The process of giving credit for original work raises the need for a fresh set of ethical decisions. Who has been involved in publication and the research? If a number of authors contribute to a single research project, they will often individually declare their contribution when it is published. In differing research contexts they might declare that: they have participated in the conception, execution or interpretation of at least that part of the publication in their field of expertise; they take public responsibility for their part of the publication; the responsible author accepts overall responsibility for the publication; the original data are stored at known locations and will be curated for several years, for re-examination if required; and potential conflicts of interest have been disclosed to editors or publishers, where necessary.

'Several authors' are alluded to above. If these include graduate students, colleagues, paid research assistants, other students, technicians, mentors, then the relative contribution of each of them should be publicly acknowledged, maybe if only in a foreword or footnote. In some disciplines, the order in which authors to a publication are cited indicates status and the quantity of each author's contribution. At this point some research supervisors seek to promote their contributions unfairly by asserting their primacy in the attribution of authorship.

Unethical publishing practices do occur. The originality of the contribution of the researcher's work is a significant arbiter of quality at the stage of public release of the results. Most of us know of examples of bad practices, because we have encountered them in relation to our decisions about plagiarism or collusion when writing assignments for academic assessment. It becomes easier and easier to steal the work of others, or use others' work illegitimately; nevertheless, *how* to steal has never been the main issue of contention. The real problem lies in the ultimate destructive effects of plagiarism or collusion for fraud. The consequences of freely purloining without checking authenticity and veracity create enormous ethical problems. Theft destroys utterly the entire principled research infrastructure.

Recently several cases of assisting to secretly 'borrow' other researchers' output have been publicised. Here is one recent example which also includes deliberate bias. A large drug company in the United States paid ten experts to write articles which all presented its drugs in a very favourable light. The company then asked university professors to put their names on the ghosted articles as authors. Some did. The plot was uncovered by the American Medical Association only after two of the articles had been published, one in the prestigious *New England Journal of Medicine* (Ornste 1999; Bor 2000; Klein 2000, p. 111).

Hypothetical dilemmas: links between practice, ethics and research

The malpractice in that case was premeditated, but many ethical problems are not so clear-cut, especially not at the start of research activities. In this section key characteristics of modern information creation, design, dissemination, evaluation and use are identified, and ten hypothetical problems for researchers in information management and information systems are presented (in italics) for discussion after each example. The given examples, which are all based on real events, pose many ethical dilemmas. Try the discussion questions in each case.

Ease of dissemination of information; globalisation of economies

Discussion example

A university researcher explores the connections between good information management, efficient information systems, and productivity in the olive growing industry in Australia. She discovers that some companies are much better at all three than others, and that there is a significant causal connection between them. She realises that a number of multinational companies are willing to pay large sums for information on good olive investments in Australia. She tries to keep her findings secret, but drinks a few glasses of burgundy too many and accidentally leaves a zip disk full of industry analysis on a chair at an Israeli conference on managing information in the olive industry. It is lost to her, but found by an unscrupulous entrepreneur from Calabria, Italy.

- *What should she do?*

- *Can the companies which form her case studies do anything?*

Data integration, interoperability of systems; built-in obsolescence

Discussion example

A research team is commissioned by a newly-elected government to design a new dispatch system for emergency vehicles in a capital city. The team decides to begin from scratch, and to just pay lip-service to the interaction of its new system with the old existing one. In this way it aims to complete the contract faster. The pressure of a deadline to produce 'a new answer' to the research problem, crucially within the finite life of a new government as client, increases the expectation of quick solutions. The old data in the pre-existing system is more or less moth-balled, and never fully analysed for transfer to the new, in the interests of completing the new project quicker.

- *In practice should researchers ever design systems which they know have in-built limitations?*

- *Should they be subject to everyday time constraints, political pressure, and restricted funds?*

- *Should full testing of this new life-critical system be an integral part of the project?*

- *If you were one of the researchers would you 'blow the whistle' on the conduct of the research?*

Intellectual property is very hard to protect

Discussion example

A secondary school teacher of information technology works in country Queensland. From her school, in addition to classroom teaching, she services a wide geographical area by assisting distant students with on-line instruction delivered via a government network. She designs the computer interface in an original way, and her students find the appealing structure and content of her presentations (multimedia learning packages) very helpful. She disseminates the packages via a local area network. The teacher also integrates text-reading features for some of her visually-impaired rural students. The design and function of the navigation icon buttons on the computer displays are apparently different from any others that have been used before.

A Gympie company which sells agricultural produce (seed, fertiliser, agrichemicals) adopts the same icon buttons as the school site on its own Internet Website, and uses them to receive orders, sales, and payments from all over rural Australia. The company grows into a massive e-business, making millions from its interactive commerce. Because of its success, it is taken over by a Canadian company. Realising the potential for features of its site, the Gympie company lodges a patent application and claims ownership of the design and function of it, to prevent any other enterprises from using it.

- *Did the teacher as researcher 'invent' something? Who knew about it at the time?*

- *In the eyes of the law, would the teacher have any standing to protect her invention?*

- *If the original inventor worked for a private company, would her standing be any different from her role as teacher?*

- *On what basis might the users of the research output, for example the students or customers of the company, claim any legal protection?*

- *Are there remedies which might be cheaper than costly litigation?*

- *Are there any non-commercial solutions to these problems of ownership of research output?*

Capacity to monitor private opinions, to covertly manipulate public opinion

Discussion example (See Klein (2000, p. 316).)

A public relations researcher is hired by the Ironic Oil Company to monitor the World Wide Web and accessible discussion groups to identify the image of the Company whenever it is mentioned. The researcher discovers that most of the references are negative, and that the Company ranks very low in public opinion. A research associate is paid to develop an intelligent program which will automatically cut in to any live discussion about the Company, and 'listen in' in real time. When the program identifies instances of negative portrayals, it automatically cuts off the negative contributor totally, in their place it inserts positive references to the Company, in natural language, imitative of the style of the pre-existing discussion, in such a way that the inserts appear realistic and integrated without drawing attention to any change. Although the software development costs millions of dollars, the Company believes that its image is worth far more.

- *Would you join a research team that develops such software?*

- *Should the program remain proprietary? If not, who should control it?*

Discussion example (See the sections 'Gaining permission to enter the field' and 'Entering the field' in Chapter 16; and Jesdanun (2000).)

In order to follow a potential research topic, viz., virtual information communities created for health self-support, a research student joins a number of chat groups on the World Wide Web. Initially she just observes, not participating in on-line discussions. Then she becomes fascinated with one – a support group for sufferers of leukaemia. She adopts a pseudonym and posts comments simply to observe the reaction from participants. She lurks, with no intent to get consent before monitoring. She notices that she can shift the content and tone of discussion, and by suggestions she can prompt participants to say things which they otherwise would not.

- *Where do you draw the line between simple curiosity and serious research?*

- *Should the researcher record and publish the on-line discussions anonymously?*

- *If she wanted to, how could she obtain genuine consent on-line, or prove her bona fides, when the discussion group is scattered across the globe?*

Determination of rights of authorship and ownership of ephemeral, reformatted publications

Discussion example (See Banham (2001).)

A researcher is seeking to identify sound recordings of early live Australian radio shows from the 1940s, but can find none which survive. Only some scripts of a few early shows are in the personal archive of a 'personality' who worked for a Sydney broadcasting company, and who migrated with them to Germany in the 1950s. The researcher has a passionate concern about the preservation of national culture. She also discovers that in the 1980s the bulk of video-taped Australian television series were wiped, unless re-sales were sustained. She lobbies an international beverage company to fund the digitisation of all extant Australian radio and TV series, to be preserved in perpetuity in the National Radio and Image Centre in Canberra. The private corporation gains naming rights to the Centre. It will promote Web-accessibility from its own corporate site to the collection.

- *Who 'owns' what?*

- *What guarantees should she offer owners when she solicits publications for digitised preservation?*

- *Is the World Wide Web a secure place for national heritage?*

Information and data are insecure

Discussion example (See Gammack and Goulding (1999, p. 74); and Kitson and Campbell (1996, p. 201).)

An investigation is under way into the nature of the content of e-mail messages used to communicate internally within a company. The ultimate aim is to collect summarily the substance of day-by-day contacts to help with the design of a decision support system to assist in archiving the organisation's 'corporate memory'.

None of the employees are aware of the research. The company's systems operator is told by the Managing Director not to interfere with the consultant-researcher in any way. The researcher has access to all internal communications at all times. The researcher discovers many libellous comments made by employees about the incompetence of the manager and the poor management of the company.

Half way through the project, the researcher obtains an additional well-paid consultancy which involves advising on construction of an internal communications system of a major competitor company.

- *How might this researcher balance the potential conflicts of interest?*

- *Who should control the systems and data?*

Discussion example

The loans records of individual library users are a rich resource for research. A researcher for an educational software company wants to correlate academic library borrowing habits, Internet search patterns, and levels of academic success. The university librarian refuses her access to the necessary student loans data, on the ground that it is confidential.

The researcher is annoyed because a criminologist, who was undertaking a longitudinal study of the reading habits of criminals in gaols, and its therapeutic potential, tells her that he has been able to buy copies of loans records and information on Internet use from the company which owns all of the libraries and networks in the privatised prisons in Victoria.

- *Why is some data protected, and some not? Who should control it?*

- *Is information about a university student different from that about a prisoner? How?*

Suppression of controversial research information, and data encryption to limit access

Discussion example (See Linnell (2000).)

One in every two Australians owns a mobile phone. A researcher has worked for a major telecommunications company for twenty years. He is familiar with all the scientific literature on the effects on humans of electromagnetic radiation from mobile phones. Two years ago five of the company's employees, who had used mobile phones heavily, complained of continuous head and shoulder aches, and needed to retire. They have since died from brain tumours. The medical researcher aimed to follow up their case histories, to determine whether there might be a link between their mobile phone usage and their illnesses. He was sacked as soon as he made his intentions known.

- *How would you as researcher balance the public health interest against your company's fears about losing all mobile customers?*

- *Should this researcher try to continue the research in spite of his sacking?*

Discussion example (See Markoff and Schwartz (2001).)

A researcher creates encryption that allows a user to affix a personal signature to any document, or a specified segment within a document, using a private signature key. Only the user can then verify the authenticity of the signature. The document cannot be altered. The researcher sells the encoding system to a powerful national government, which proposes to use it exclusively in all its international transactions. The system will be under the direct control of the country's finance minister. No global digital signature standards exist. This system may become the standard.

- *Should this researcher have the power to behave in this way?*

- *In whose interests is he acting?*

- *What are the long-term consequences of his action?*

Conclusion

As time goes by, and on reflection you will probably want to vary your answers to the questions above. It is hoped that, with discussion, the above dilemmas will challenge your thinking, and maybe enable you to practise applying your own moral views to research situations. Drawing conclusions about the ways that researchers make ethical decisions is never easy, but you can gain some insights into what might be involved, from trying them out here for yourself.

This chapter has aimed to help you to understand the value of ethics to research, and to relate ethics to the examples of research given in other chapters of this book. The main features of ethical thinking, and why researchers try to think ethically, have been described.

Ethics in research pervades many other activities in our daily lives, even when we make mundane but well-informed decisions, or regularly use others' inventions and products. On a more intellectual level, many of the abstract notions behind ethics also affect our personal values about health, education, politics, culture, belief, social welfare and relationships (Blaikie 1993, p. 85). By accepting that ethics should bolster good thinking, acting and research analysis and techniques, we affirm the universal validity and usefulness of all research and its outputs.

I am grateful to my colleagues John Crossley, Livia Iacovino, Don Schauder, and Kirsty Williamson for their beneficial discussions with me of many aspects of this chapter.

Further readings

Baase, Sara. (1996). *A gift of fire: Social, legal and ethical issues in computing*. Prentice Hall: Upper Saddle River, NJ.

Davison, Robert, and Kock, Ned. (eds.). (2000). IS Worldnet. Professional ethics; information about professional ethics concerning the information systems profession. (online).
http://www.cityu.edu.hk/is/ethics/ethics.htm

Ethics and IT journal. A description of the contents of the first six issues of *Ethics and IT* (online).
http://www.kluweronline.com/

Johanson, Graeme. (1997). Information, knowledge and research. *Journal of Information Science*, **23** (2), pp. 103-109.

Karamjit, S.G. (1996). *Information society: New media, ethics, and postmodernism.* Springer: London.

Mason, Richard O., Mason, Florence M. and Culnam, Mary J. (1995). *Ethics of information management.* Sage: Thousand Oaks, Ca.

Parliament of Victoria. (2000). *Information Privacy Act 2000*, Act No. 98/2000, assented to 12 December. (online).
http://www.dms.dpc.vic.gov.au/sb/index.html

Postman, Neil. (1990). Informing ourselves to death. In *Computers, ethics and society*, eds. M. David Ermann, Mary B. Williams and Claude Gutierrez. Oxford University Press: New York, pp. 128-136.

Singer, Peter. (1993). *How are we to live? Ethics in an age of self-interest.* Text: Melbourne, Vic.

Spinello, Richard. (1997). *Case studies in information and computer ethics.* Prentice Hall: Upper Saddle River, NJ.

Williams, Mark. (2000). Ethics in information systems research? AICE2000: Second Australian Institute of Computer Ethics conference. (online).
http://www.cm.deakin.edu.au/aice/aice2000/wil.pdf

References for Chapter 4

Asimov, Isaac. (1950). Handbook of Robotics, 56th Edition, 2058 A.D. In *I, Robot*. Panther: St. Albans, Herts.

Banham, Cynthia. (2001). Cuts to staff in ABC library and archives. *Sydney Morning Herald,* 14 April. Reprinted in *Background Briefing*, **3** (2), p. 7.

Blaikie, Norman. (1993). *Approaches to social enquiry*. Polity Press in association with Blackwell: Cambridge, UK.

Bor, Jonathan. (2000). Medical journal admits, apologises for ethical lapses: doctors wrote reviews of drugs despite ties to the manufacturers. *The Baltimore Sun*, 24 February. (online).
http://www.blancmange.net/tmh/articles/ethicallapses.html

Bouma, Gary. (2000A). *A human ethics committee application survival kit*. (online).
http://www.monash.edu.au/resgrant/human-ethics/survival-kit.html/index.html (Revised 13 July, 2001).

Bouma, Gary. (2000B). *The research process*. Oxford University Press: Melbourne, Vic.

Christians, C.G. (2000). Ethics and politics in qualitative research. In *Handbook of qualitative research*, eds. Norman K. Denzin and Yvonna S. Lincoln. Sage: Thousand Oaks, Ca., pp. 133-155.

Connolly, Anne. (1994). Call for supervisor code. *The Australian* (Higher Education supplement), 25 May, p. 25.

Elphinstone, Leonie. (1994). *Surviving a research thesis; Issues and options*. Student Services, RMIT: Melbourne, Vic.

Foray, Dominique. (1998). The economics of knowledge openness: emergence, persistence and change of conventions in the knowledge systems. In *Trust and economic learning*, eds. Nathalie Lazaric and Edward Lorenz. Edward Elgar: Northampton, Ma., pp. 162-189.

Fuller, Buckminster. (1963). General systems theory. In *Operating manual for spaceship earth*. E.P. Dutton: New York, section 5. (Also online).
http://www.bfi.org/operating_manual.htm

Gammack, J.G., and Goulding, P.R. (1999). Ethical responsibility and the management of knowledge. *Australian Computer Journal*, **31** (3), August, pp. 72-77.

Hippocratic oath. (online).
http://www.rs.org/hippocraticoath.htm

Jesdanun, Anick. (2000). Chat group snoops slammed. *The Australian*, 17 October, p. 45.

Kitson, Alan, and Campbell, Robert. (1996). *The ethical organisation: Ethical theory and corporate behaviour*. Macmillan: London.

Klein, Naomi. (2000). *No logo*. Flamingo: London.

Langford, Duncan. (1995). *Practical computer ethics*. McGraw-Hill: London.

Linnell, Garry. (2000). Doctor's job cut after phone concerns raised. *The Age*, 16 December, p. 3.

MacIntyre, Alisdair. (1998). *A short history of ethics*. Routledge: London.

Markoff, John, and Schwartz, John. (2001). Microsoft system aid to vandals. *The Age* (Business section), 5 June, p. 5.

National Health and Medical Research Council. (1999). National statement on ethical conduct in research involving humans. (online). http://www.health.gov.au/nhmrc/publications/synopses/e35syn.htm

Ornste, Charles. (1999). Drug company's ghost research. *The Australian*, 26 May, p. 39.

Saunders, Laverna M. (1994). Ethics in Cyberspace. (online). http://www.cpsr.org/program/ethics/ethics.cyberspace.saunders

Smith, H. Jeff, and Hasnas, John. (1999). Ethics and information systems: the corporate domain. *MIS Quarterly*, **23** (1), pp. 109-127.

Section 2: Methods

Introduction

The second section, Chapters 5 to 12, examines research methods which are defined as designs for undertaking research, including the theoretical background to these designs. The research methods included are survey, case study, experimental design, systems development in information systems research, action research, ethnography, historical research and the Delphi method.

CHAPTER 5
Survey research
Kerry Tanner

Objectives

At the end of this chapter, you will be able to:

- differentiate descriptive and explanatory surveys, and the appropriate circumstances for their use;

- explain the links between the sampling method selected for a survey and conditions for valid generalisation in reporting survey findings;

- discuss the relative advantages and disadvantages of printed, telephone and electronic forms of survey;

- explain the main phases involved in planning and implementing a survey;

- identify the most suitable form of survey design, given a particular research topic and research constraints; and

- devise an effective survey research design for a particular project.

Introduction to survey research

Survey research involves the collection of primary data from all or part of a population, in order to determine the incidence, distribution, and interrelationships of certain variables within the population. It encompasses a variety of data collection techniques, for example, questionnaires (print or electronic), interviews (face-to-face or telephone), and observation techniques. Surveys have been a very widely used method in both information management and information systems research.

Sampling and the ability to generalise in survey research

A sound understanding of sampling concepts is essential for anyone undertaking survey research. The reader is referred to Chapter 13 for a fuller discussion of the concepts that are introduced briefly here.

Firstly, to define a few key terms:

- A *population* is the aggregate of all cases sharing at least one common characteristic, for example: Australians, information systems managers, IBM employees, Malaysian small businesses, New South Wales school libraries.

- Populations can be further subdivided into *strata* according to specified criteria, for example: for people – age or lifestyle categories, or for organisations – geographic or industry groupings.

- A *case* or *element* is a single unit or member of the population about which data are collected.

- A *sample* is a defined subset of a particular population.

- A *sampling frame* is a list of all elements within the population from which a sample is selected. Examples of sampling frames are employee databases, electoral rolls, telephone books, specialist directories.

One common misunderstanding of novices undertaking survey research is confusing the concepts of *population* and *sample*. Where a population is small, for example, a small business of fifty employees, it is feasible to survey all elements of that population. *Descriptive statistics* (that is statistics that describe population characteristics) are used in reporting the results of a survey of a population.

For larger populations, it is not practicable to survey all cases, so sampling techniques are used to identify a particular subset of the population to be surveyed.

Researchers using samples in survey research usually aim to generalise from the sample to the broader population from which the sample was selected. There are definite constraints on a researcher's ability to do this, and the ability to make valid generalisations varies greatly according to the sampling technique used. *Probability sampling* techniques are required for valid generalisations. With probability sampling, it is possible to specify the probability of an element being included in the sample. For instance, with *random samples* (one type of probability sample), each element has an equal probability of inclusion. For example, if there are 6000 cases in a population, in a random sample the probability of one element being included is 1:6000. With probability sampling techniques, samples can be accepted as reasonable approximations of proportions existing within the broader population. However, even then there is no guarantee that the sample is a completely accurate representation of the population. There is always a *margin of error*, which the researcher can quantify statistically. Researchers use descriptive statistics when they describe the characteristics of a sample, and *inferential statistics* when they generalise their findings from their sample results to the broader population.

Non-probability samples are generally used for reasons of convenience and economy. *Accidental sampling* is a type of non-probability sample where the researcher selects cases close at hand, such as his/her classmates or workmates. Another type is *purposive sampling,* where the researcher on the basis of personal knowledge hand-picks subjects with the required expertise or background for the study.

With non-probability sampling, there is no way of estimating the probability each element has of inclusion in the sample, nor of estimating bias (that is, by how much results from the sample are likely to deviate from 'true population' figures). While descriptive statistics can be used in reporting results of a survey based on a non-probability sample, inferential statistics cannot be used. Use of a non-probability sample is appropriate when the researcher does not need to generalise from the sample to the broader population, but merely wishes to gather ideas or gain some insights into a particular phenomenon, for example in a survey pilot test, or for exploratory research.

Where there is no available or suitable sampling frame, or where the size and composition of a population is indeterminate, the researcher may have no other choice than to opt for a non-probability sample.

The crucial point to watch in reporting survey results involving non-probability samples is that no untenable claims are made concerning characteristics of the broader population.

Descriptive (or status) surveys

Definitions and overview

As the term suggests, the main purpose of a *descriptive survey* is to describe a particular phenomenon: its current situation, its properties and conditions, that is, to answer 'who', 'what', 'when' or 'where' (rather than 'how' or 'why') questions about it. It is also known as a status survey, that is, a survey of the *status quo*.

Descriptive surveys are primarily concerned with fact gathering, with enumerating and describing, and most tend not to do anything very sophisticated with the data they collect. Although in discussion of results there may be some mention of likely explanations of a particular phenomenon, there is often no attempt at formal statistical hypothesis testing. When analysing data, descriptive surveys tend to use a significant amount of qualitative, verbal data, and with quantitative data to draw more on descriptive statistics than inferential statistics.

Questionnaires (print or electronic) and interviews (face-to-face or telephone) are the primary techniques used in descriptive surveys. (See Chapter 14 for an overview.)

Typical stages in planning and conducting a descriptive survey

Typical stages involved in planning and implementing a descriptive survey are outlined below (though the order may vary).

- A general idea of the area to be investigated is derived from a literature search and/or from other sources (for example, a request from a professional association).

- The broad area is narrowed down in focus to ensure the project is manageable. Precisely what information is required? Anything that is unnecessary or of doubtful value should be excluded. If a researcher attempts to cover too much ground, the questionnaire or interview will become too long or too complex, which will tend to reduce the response rate. Where questions are very imprecise and general, data generated are likely to be superficial and of little value.

- A specific set of research questions and hypotheses is devised – questions the survey is setting out to address.

- The target group for the survey is precisely defined, that is, who is to be surveyed.

- A decision is made about whether the entire population will be targeted, or whether a sample will be taken. If there is to be a sample, the type of sample must be decided, given the goals of the research. Subsequently, a sampling frame is obtained or compiled, and a sample drawn. (See Chapter 13.)

- The most appropriate type of survey technique (mail or email questionnaire, face-to-face interview, telephone interview) for the project is determined. Considerations such as the geographic extent and dispersion of the sample/population and depth of information sought and cost constraints will affect this decision.

- The survey instrument (questionnaire, interview schedule) is written, and pilot tested on a number of the intended target audience. After this, any necessary revisions are made (for example, questions or instructions which were unclear or ambiguous are clarified).

- An initial letter or email is sent explaining the nature and aims of the survey and enlisting participation. This step may be dispensed with for a questionnaire, or combined with the actual survey distribution.

- The survey is conducted (either questionnaires with an accompanying cover letter are mailed or emailed or interviews held with participants).

- With questionnaires, after the designated due date for return (indicated on the questionnaire cover letter) has passed, one or more follow-up letters or emails are sent to those who have not returned their questionnaires. This is necessary to increase response rate, and hence the validity of findings. However reassurances about confidentiality in relation to this will be necessary.

- The returned questionnaires, or completed interview schedules, are collected for data analysis. Respondents' answers to each question are systematically recorded for subsequent analysis. An email or Internet-based questionnaire can facilitate data analysis further through automatic downloading of data into a spreadsheet or statistical package.

- Results are recorded, analysed and interpreted, and conclusions drawn. (See Chapter 17 for coverage of data analysis.)

Advantages of descriptive surveys

Compared with some other research designs, descriptive surveys are relatively straightforward and easy for a novice researcher to implement.

Limitations of descriptive surveys

This section addresses some major research issues involved with descriptive surveys.

Non-cooperation

With an increasing number of academic programs requiring students to conduct formal research, many individuals and organisations are tiring of being continually surveyed. Some will routinely relegate all questionnaires to the wastepaper basket. Others will do likewise if the survey seems ill-conceived, poorly prepared, unnecessarily long or complex, or requiring data that are difficult to procure. A low response rate impacts negatively on the generalisability of results.

Rival explanations (threats to internal validity)

In natural settings (as opposed to controlled settings such as laboratories), it is difficult to control for rival explanations, or the possibility that some intervening variable rather than the variable under consideration may have produced the results observed. This is a major problem with descriptive surveys, and inevitably affects the conclusiveness of findings. Because of this, survey researchers must always be careful to qualify statements on their findings so that they are not claiming too much, or more than can be supported by their data.

Accuracy of self-report data

Generally surveys involve respondents answering questions about their own situation or behaviour. Some question the accuracy of such 'self-report data', given factors such as the natural human tendency to present oneself to others in the most positive light.

Generalisability of results (threats to external validity)

The generalisability or external validity of surveys is affected by the sampling technique employed. Another factor threatening the external validity of surveys is the response rate achieved. A high response rate is essential if survey results are to be generalised accurately from a sample to the broader population. Researchers taking this issue very seriously will take every possible step to maximise response rate, for example, by sending out three or four follow-up letters or emails to non-respondents. There is a definite trend that the more focused the target group, the higher the response rate; and, conversely, the more generalised the target group, for example, the 'general public', the lower the response rate. Other factors affecting response rate are noted under 'Non-cooperation'.

Box 5.1 illustrates the application of a descriptive survey approach.

Box 5.1: Example of a descriptive survey: Survey of information technology outsourcing in Australia

The issue under investigation

From the late 1980s, governments and business:

- were seriously questioning whether their huge information technology investments were delivering value;
- were looking to business process restructuring and drastic downsizing to maintain competitiveness in an adverse market climate; and
- saw information technology outsourcing as an attractive means of cost cutting, while still delivering services.

By 1993:

- information technology outsourcing was a pervasive management practice; and
- Federal, State and Local government agencies were required to market test their information technology with a view to outsourcing.

Box 5.1 (cont.): Example of a descriptive survey: Survey of information technology outsourcing in Australia

---

Research questions related to information technology outsourcing involved:

- motives/influencing factors;
- current Australian trends;
- public/private sector differences;
- functions and processes; and
- business, structural, technological and staff impacts.

The research design:

- a review of relevant (management, computing) literature and a descriptive survey using a mailed questionnaire;
- the literature review found little objective data on the Australian experience with information technology outsourcing;
- insights from the literature review formed the basis of the questionnaire; and
- there was an initial pilot validation of the questionnaire, and revisions made prior to the mail-out.

The sample:

- the target population comprised Australian public and private sector bodies with large information technology infrastructures;
- information technology managers seemed the most appropriate personnel to target within organisations (needed both information technology knowledge and a strategic perspective);
- a sample was needed, as there was no feasible way of surveying this entire population;
- the most suitable sampling frame identified at the time was MIS 2000 (1993). (This directory listed details of 1,800 Australian public sector (Federal, State, Local) and private sector organisations with a significant information technology infrastructure, and included names of information technology managers.)

Considering prevalent low response rates of, for example, 20%, and the need to have around 300-400 responses for meaningful analysis, it was decided to include all Australian organisations.

Box 5.1 (cont.): Example of a descriptive survey: Survey of information technology outsourcing in Australia

Questionnaire design:

- *The introductory section* was designed to profile the respondent organisation – for example, its sector, industry grouping, size, the size and maturity of its information technology department, degree of alignment of the information technology function with overall corporate strategy. These were important variables for subsequent cross-matching in the data analysis phase.
- *The main part* focused on significant information technology outsourcing issues for example, planning, management, costs, vendor relationships, and staff impacts.
- *The final section* attempted to assess the organisation's overall evaluation of its outsourcing experience.

The questionnaire:

- used primarily closed-ended questions – 'tick the box', rating scales (for example, grading of 'relative importance – minimal, moderate or significant – of various factors affecting the outsourcing decision') and rankings (for example, 'Rank the following information technology functions in the order of their importance to your organisation.');
- included some open-ended questions for deeper insights;
- sought both objective/factual data and personal evaluation/subjective data; and
- channelled respondents according to whether they had or had not already outsourced, were still planning, or had rejected outsourcing.

The response rate:

- November 1993 – 1,794 questionnaires distributed;
- 447 responses received from the initial mail-out;
- January 1994 – follow-up letter sent;
- follow-up yielded an additional 51 responses;
- 498 responses – a 27.8% response rate;
- further follow-ups were considered, but rejected – significant expense for minimal gain;
- the generalisability of findings with less than one-third response rate is problematic, as there is no guarantee that non-respondents would have answered in the same way, or would have exhibited the same characteristics as did respondents. Given the low response rate, care was taken in writing up the results not to claim more than was justified.

(Karpathiou and Tanner 1995.)

Explanatory (or analytical) surveys

Definitions and overview

While descriptive surveys primarily collect and arrange data, and identify trends, explanatory (or analytical) surveys attempt to probe further, to explain 'how' and 'why', to explore interrelationships of variables and likely causal links between them.

With explanatory surveys, data tend to be more numerically based, with greater emphasis on the application of statistical tests, and confirming or refuting statistical hypotheses (that is, the realm of inferential statistics). Explanatory surveys require probability sampling techniques.

In natural (as opposed to controlled) settings, it is very difficult to establish causation, as all possible alternative explanations (intervening variables) must be dismissed. Take the case of observed data apparently supporting the hypothesis 'Computer skills decrease with age'. Here a researcher would need to be able to discount rival explanations of 'computer access' and 'computer training' as factors.

Although a researcher must exercise caution in claiming definite links between variables, it is easy to err in the opposite direction: not claiming enough from the findings of an explanatory survey. For instance, if all major rival explanations are identified from the literature review, and are addressed in a formal way in the research using a technique such as elaboration analysis, and are dismissed, considerable confidence can be placed in the survey findings.

Particular designs used for explanatory surveys

Note that these designs involve some type of simulation of an experimental design. However, in contrast to a formal experiment, there are significant limitations in inferring causality due to the natural setting and associated lack of rigorous controls (for example, lack of random assignment to different 'conditions').

Static group comparison design

The basic design for static group comparisons is given in Figure 5.1. Note that:

> X = The characteristic under study (that is, the *independent* variable)
> O = An observation or measurement (that is the *dependent* variable)

GROUP 1	X	O_1
GROUP 2	Not-X	O_2

Figure 5.1: Basic design for static group comparisons

An example of this design is a study of the personality characteristics of executives who do and do not succumb to major illness (for example, heart disease) under sustained high stress conditions (Kobasa 1979, pp. 1-11). In the example in Figure 5.2 note that:

X = Illness under high stress conditions
O = Test for personality characteristics

GROUP 1	Executives with high stress and high illness rates	Personality test
GROUP 2	Executives with high stress and low illness rates	Personality test

Figure 5.2: Example of basic design for static group comparisons

The static group comparison is a *correlational* design rather than an experiment. There is a lack of random assignment to the two different 'conditions', which is characteristic of the formal experiment. Rather, subjects are divided into Groups 1 and 2 on the basis of whether or not they possess 'X'. For instance, in the example above, executives who had experienced high degrees of stress for an extended period were divided according to whether or not they had succumbed to serious stress-related illness such as coronary heart disease. Both groups were then given a personality test to identify distinguishing personality characteristics which may predispose one to the negative effects of stress (that is, stress-related illness). In this case, it is not legitimate to claim that there is a *causal link* between stress-related illness and personality, but rather that there is some *degree of relationship* between the two factors.

Claiming causation is really not possible with this type of design. To infer that 'X' (the independent variable) causes 'O' (the dependent variable), three criteria must be satisfied:

- X and O must co-vary;

- X must precede O in time; and

- there must be no alternative explanations of the group differences in O.

Clearly, these criteria are not satisfied by the example above as stress-related illness cannot be said to precede personality in time: in fact, the reverse is likely to be true. Indeed, in this type of design, even differentiating the 'independent' and 'dependent' variables can be difficult.

Longitudinal, or panel study

A longitudinal study is an investigation conducted over an extended period of time (often many years), which follows changes in certain variables amongst the sample.

There have been some very well known longitudinal studies. One British government study followed through a sample of babies born in one week in March 1946 at regular intervals to adulthood, and has collected a tremendous range of data about them since (Cherry 1978, p. 259). Other longitudinal health surveys have linked diet, smoking and related factors with particular diseases. Smaller scale longitudinal surveys are often used in market research, for example, Indra Kurzeme (1996) traced changes in characteristics of the clientele of VICNET (a Victorian community network) over an eight month period, during its developmental phase.

This type of study also does not fully satisfy the criteria for inferring causation given earlier. Although there may be a slight *hint* of causation, no definite causal links can be established due to potential rival explanations.

Cross-sectional, or pseudo-panel design

Cross-sectional designs attempt to achieve what a longitudinal design does, but in a single (horizontal) dimension, that is, at one point in time. With this design, the sample is divided into appropriate, and mutually exclusive, *strata*; then each *stratum* is compared with respect to the variable under consideration. This design is widely used in market research. For example, a sample may be divided by age group, and each group compared with respect to attitude towards a particular phenomenon (for example, heroin use; the Microsoft Company; or a political party). Differences in attitudes between the different age groups are assumed to trace changes that would occur over time.

Again, the nature of the design precludes any attribution of causation. Only an identification of possible correlations (relationships) of variables is feasible. These studies are often simply descriptive surveys, using stratified samples. (See Chapter 13 for a discussion of stratified sampling.)

Advantages of explanatory surveys

Explanatory surveys enable problems to be measured in their natural setting as opposed to the artificial setting of a laboratory. (It is impossible to investigate many natural phenomena in a laboratory situation.) They are appropriate when a researcher needs to:

- derive answers to 'how' and 'why' questions about a particular phenomenon; or

- explore interrelationships of variables and possible causal links between them (though they do not establish causal relationships as such).

Limitations of explanatory surveys

As just noted, explanatory surveys do not firmly establish causal relationships. Rather, they are correlational, identifying relationships of variables. These may be interpreted as giving a hint of causality, provided appropriate statistical techniques are applied to establish that correlations are not spurious relationships.

Telephone surveys

Definitions and overview

Telephone surveys are widely used in certain types of research, particularly market surveys. Professional market research companies utilise the latest technology in telephone surveying, for example, computer-based systems with automatic random digit dialling and forms for the easy and direct entry of response data.

Studies have shown that data collected in telephone interviewing are as valid as data collected by other survey methods (questionnaire, face-to-face interview). However, the researcher considering a telephone survey needs to be aware of certain limitations of this method of data collection. If the survey is planned accordingly, telephone surveys can be very successful.

The decision on whether a telephone survey is a suitable method for a particular survey will depend on factors such as: the topic under investigation; whether or not sensitive or complex issues are being explored; the depth of responses sought; and whether visual aids are necessary to explain the point.

Advantages of telephone surveys

Advantages of telephone surveys include:

- *Wide geographic extent* – with telephone surveys, a geographically dispersed population can be surveyed in a short period of time, saving interviewers' travel costs and time. Also, populations difficult to reach by other methods may be able to be accessed through a telephone interview.

- *Relatively low cost per interview* – telephone surveys are relatively inexpensive compared with face-to-face interviews, although generally a little more expensive than a mail survey. STD or IDD calls can become costly, but this problem can be overcome by employing a decentralised strategy, using telephone interviewers from different locations.

- *A quick way of obtaining information* – telephone surveys are an ideal means of collecting data when time is limited, and a quick response crucial, for example, weekly surveying during an election campaign of political preferences, voting intentions and preferred leader.

- *It is easy and convenient to derive a representative sample from the telephone book* (although this will contain some element of bias compared with the general population, as noted below). Either simple random sampling or systematic random sampling methods can be used.

- *Non-response rate is usually relatively low* – in comparison with a mail survey, the non-response rate of telephone surveys tends to be much lower: although some particular types of commercial telephone surveys may have a high non-response rate if they are considered to be invasive of personal privacy. Tyebjee (1979) in a 'state of the art' review of telephone surveys found response rates ranging from 45% to 95% in the studies identified.

With telephone surveys, there are two types of non-response needing to be addressed:

- *Refusal rate* – often a refusal is due to a respondent being temporarily occupied with something else. This type of refusal can be reduced if telephone interviewers ask if they can call back at a more convenient time, and make times for a subsequent phone interviews. Refusal rates also can be higher at certain times of the day/week. Response rates tend to increase if the respondent is addressed by name, and when the social value of the survey is stressed.

- *'Not at home' non-response* – to ensure a representative overall sample, it is important that repeated call-backs be made in an attempt to contact 'not at home' respondents.

Three or four call-backs may be necessary. Call-backs are relatively simple and economical to make.

Limitations of telephone surveys

Limitations of telephone surveys include:

- *The interview schedule must be short and to-the-point* – the interview must be quite brief (for example, five to ten minutes), requiring a limited number of questions, and questions which can be answered in relatively few words. It is difficult to probe in-depth in telephone surveys.

- *Some types of questions cannot be effectively asked over the telephone* – questions must be easily understood over the telephone, so complex lists of alternative options should be avoided. Telephone surveys are unsuited to questions requiring lengthy or involved responses. People are naturally reticent to disclose highly personal information, or information which may be interpreted as an invasion of privacy or risking their personal security, for example, questions pertaining to their income or possessions.

- *There are some problems with bias in a sample taken from the telephone book*, which omits non-telephone owners and people with unlisted numbers. About 97% of Australian households possess a telephone. Hence a sample taken from the telephone book no longer excludes a significant proportion of the general population. This was more of a problem years ago when telephone ownership correlated more with degree of affluence. A sample from the telephone book excludes unlisted numbers. However, commercial market research organisations using automatic random digit dialling facilities will access unlisted numbers as well as listed numbers.

- *The time of the day telephone surveys are conducted is another potential source of bias* – if conducted during the day, telephone surveys will yield an over-representation of certain community groups (the retired, parents caring for children, and the unemployed), and conversely an under-representation of others (especially the employed). A strict call-back policy where repeat calls are made in the evenings or on week-ends to numbers that did not answer during the day is essential to ensure a representative final sample.

- *It is difficult to target a particular group with telephone interviewing* – targeting a specific client group is difficult without access to a specialised listing or directory which contains the phone numbers of the desired target group.

Electronic surveys

Definitions and overview

Surveys can be conducted by a variety of electronic means, for example, fax, disks-by-mail, interactive kiosks, email, the Web and newsgroups. Data transmitted in electronic form are much more flexible and greatly facilitates the process of data collection, data capturing and data analysis, compared with print-based forms. Research processes involve developing the questionnaire; designing an online survey form; and creating a database for the electronic capturing of data.

Whilst electronic forms of survey are becoming more common, printed texts on the topic of methods for electronic survey research are still quite limited. Recent editions of established business research methods texts (for example, Zikmund 1997a; 1997b) devote a few pages to the topic. Some 'how-to' books on the Internet cover online surveys (for example, Emery (1997)) in relation to the design of forms for the Internet.

An Internet search on 'electronic surveys' tends to retrieve primarily home pages of software vendors, and management, market research or information technology consultancy firms engaged in the business of electronic survey design and administration—a burgeoning line of business. Some of these sites are worth exploring for examples of electronic survey design. However, some Websites focus on research issues associated with surveys, including electronic surveys. Those interested in information systems research are referred to resources on survey methodology and survey research instruments that can be accessed through the *ISWorld Net Research and Scholarship Section* site http://www.isworld.org/isworld, and the *MISQ Discovery* site http://misq.org/discovery The *MISQ Discovery* archive for December 1998 contains a useful online resource 'Survey instruments in IS [information systems]' by Newsted, Huff and Munro (1998). These authors claimed they would keep this resource updated through a 'living version', to be maintained by Newsted (1999).

Advantages and limitations of different types of electronic survey

Faxed surveys have the 'one-to-many' advantage of other electronic forms. They are quick to send and to receive. However, they lack some of the flexibility of other electronic forms.

Disk-in-mail surveys enable the recording and transfer of data through electronic means, but they have some of the attendant problems of surveys reliant on the post, and require more human intervention in the process of data transfer than do more direct electronic forms.

Email surveys have much appeal as a form of surveying, but the circumstances where they can be successfully used are limited, because a significant proportion of the population still lacks email access. The primary issue involved here is deriving a suitable sampling frame for a population under investigation. Email surveys are ideal for internal use within an organisation, such as for getting a fast employee response on a particular issue; or where email mailing lists are available, for example, customer or supplier lists. Companies with email lists of customers/prospective customers have a ready source of immediate market feedback, an ability to readily capture their customers' needs, feelings and views.

Emery (1997) recommends using personalised, casual and relatively informal approaches for success with email surveys (versus cold and impersonal bureaucratese), for example, signing with a person's name rather than an anonymous department name.

Advantages of email surveys can be summed up as:

- ease of surveying (due to the one-to-many feature of email systems);

- fast response time – as most people check and respond to their email each day;

- low cost – due both to reduced labour needed and to relatively low transmission costs compared with postal surveys;

- ease of design for survey instruments, and for collection and analysis of data, using available software packages;

- complete transcript of all responses is electronically captured;

- likelihood of more honest responses – as surveys are completed at one's leisure, they are more likely to elicit fuller, more considered responses (for example, compared with telephone surveys);

- ease and speed of questionnaire completion – especially when check boxes and radio buttons are used and responses are recorded by a simple 'click of the mouse';

- higher response rates than postal surveys (possibly partly due still to their novelty value); and

- particular appeal to certain target groups, for example, young males.

Some limitations of email surveys:

- email surveys should be relatively short, preferably only two or three screens in length. Response rates are greatly reduced with longer surveys. This has implications for the types of survey that work well in this format; and

- it can be very difficult to procure email lists of a particular population – other than one's own company records. Emery (1997, p. 599) advises against using another company's list, or 'renting' lists and sending surveys off unsolicited as they tend to arouse hostility and encourage bogus responses. He feels that email surveys work best where established relationships already exist (for example, a company with its clients or its employees), or where people already know of the survey and are expecting it.

Web-based surveys are relatively easy to set up and to administer, and will generally yield many responses if placed on busy Websites. However, there are difficulties where site traffic is low – when considerable effort will need to be devoted to promotion, and the establishment of links containing invitations to visit the survey site. As with email questionnaires, it is best if Web surveys are relatively short, for example, twenty questions, and with a majority of closed-ended questions.

Web surveys share many of the advantages, and the limitations, of email surveys, for example, fast response; low cost; targeting a wide and geographically dispersed audience; ability (with appropriate software) to process and disseminate results almost instantaneously.

Current software has made it relatively easy to design and create surveys for the Web, using HTML 'forms' conventions – for example, lists of options with radio buttons, drop-down lists, check boxes, fill-in-the-blanks, and filter questions which divide respondents into different channels according to the way they answer a particular question.

Web surveys are ideal for longitudinal research, for example, into changing customer patterns over a couple of years. The same instrument can be posted as often as needed, and trends compared. Kurzeme's (1996) study mentioned earlier is a good example of an online longitudinal survey.

Self-selection bias is a major issue with Web-based surveys. Who is most likely to complete the survey, and who is less likely? As there is no way of knowing whether or not those who responded to the survey are typical of site visitors, non-probability samples are inevitable with Web surveys. There are therefore constraints on the reporting of research results (in terms of generalisations).

Newsgroup-based surveys can also be a useful method. With their topical focus, newsgroups and discussion groups have the advantage of co-locating those who share a particular interest. These can be ideal potential targets for a survey on the particular topic. Targets can also be limited geographically with many newsgroups.

However, Emery's (1997, p. 601) advice is worth heeding in this context:

> Of all the ways to conduct surveys on the Internet, newsgroups are by far the most potentially explosive. Mistakes here can generate hate mail . . . – not to mention ruining your survey.

> The more closely your survey fits your audience, the less likely you are to receive bogus answers and angry replies.

Emery (1997) also stresses the importance of cautiously picking target newsgroups, as each one runs by different rules, and names can mislead. In order to become familiar with the content and style of the newsgroup, he recommends reading about a hundred messages from the newsgroup, as well as examining the FAQ (Frequently Asked Questions) list, which will cover rules for posting. Cross-posting of a survey in different newsgroups, he warns, is considered 'bad netiquette' and should be avoided.

One or two questions can easily be posted from an individual, placing a question mark at the end of the subject line of the message. This will generally elicit responses within a few days. This approach is ideal for finding answers to specific questions or reactions to certain ideas. However, more complex questionnaires pose problems in newsgroups. Even if they are completed, many respondents will ignore instructions and re-post their responses to the entire newsgroup, causing congestion and irritation to others. For more detailed questionnaires, posting an invitation to participate, and getting respondents to email a specific contact address is a better option.

Conclusion

Survey research designs remain pervasive in information management and information systems research. Surveys can appear deceptively simple and straightforward to implement. However valid results depend on the researcher having a clear understanding of the circumstances where surveys are appropriate and the constraints on inference in interpreting and generalising from survey findings. Initially, the researcher needs to determine whether survey research suits the nature and extent of the research problem being investigated, and the type of questions being addressed by the study. The sampling method chosen affects the researcher's ability to generalise from the survey sample to a wider population.

Newer electronic survey methods have much to offer, overcoming some of the difficulties of conventional survey administration. Nevertheless, achieving valid representative samples in electronic surveys can be problematic, and particular care needs to be taken in reporting findings to ensure that conclusions drawn from electronic survey data are justified.

In addition to the references cited throughout the chapter the reader is referred to Alreck and Settle (1995); Crockett (1989); Galliers (1992); Helleik (1984); Judd, Smith and Kidder (1991); Leedy et al. (1997); and Salant and Dillman (1995).

Discussion questions

• Have surveys outlived their usefulness?

• To what extent is the validity of the survey as a research method compromised through pervasive low response rates?

• Is survey research limited to the positivist paradigm? Or do surveys also have a place in interpretivist research?

• For what types of study would you consider using a survey?

• Will electronic surveys completely displace postal surveys and telephone surveys over the next decade or two?

Further readings

De Vaus, D. A. (1995). *Surveys in social research.* 4th edn. Allen and Unwin: North Sydney.

Fowler, Floyd J. (1993). *Survey research methods.* 2nd edn. Sage: Newbury Park, Ca.

Lavrakas, Paul J. (1993*.) Telephone survey methods: Sampling, selection and supervision.* 2nd edn. Sage: Newbury Park, Ca.

Newsted, Peter. (1999). [Surveys site, University of Calgary, Canada]. (online). http://www.acs.ucalgary.ca/~newsted/surveys.html

References for Chapter 5

Alreck, Pamela and Settle, Robert B. (1995). *The survey research handbook: Guidelines and strategies for conducting a survey.* 2nd edn. Irwin: New York.

Cherry, N. (1978). Stress, anxiety and work. *Journal of Occupational Psychology*, **51** (3), pp. 259-270.

Crockett, R.A. (1989). *An introduction to sample surveys: A user's guide.* Australian Bureau of Statistics: Melbourne.

Emery, Vince. (1997). *How to grow your business on the Internet.* 3rd edn. Coriolos Group Books: Albany, NY, pp. 596-605.

Galliers, Robert (ed.). (1992*). Information systems research: Issues, methods and practical guidelines.* Blackwell Scientific Publications: Oxford.

Hellevik, Ottar. (1984). *Introduction to causal analysis: Exploring survey data by crosstabulation.* Allen and Unwin: London.

Judd, Charles M., Smith, Eliot R. and Kidder, Louise H. (1991). *Research methods in social relations.* 6th edn. Holt, Rinehart & Winston: Fort Worth. TX.

Karpathiou, Vass and Tanner, Kerry. (1995). *Information technology outsourcing in Australia.* RMIT, Department of Business Computing: Melbourne.

Kobasa, Suzanne C. (1979). Stressful life events, personality and health. *Journal of Personality and Social Psychology,* **37** (1), pp. 1-11.

Kurzeme, Indra. (1996). VICNET's users: a longitudinal market survey of the users of Victoria's network, VICNET. MB(IT) Minor thesis. RMIT, Dept. of Information Management: Melbourne.

Leedy, Paul D. with contributions by Newby, Timothy J. and Ertmer, Peggy A. (1997). *Practical research: Planning and design.* 6th edn. Upper Merrill: Saddle River, NJ.

MIS 2000. (1993). Strategic Publishing Group: Sydney.

Newsted, Peter. (1999). [Surveys site, University of Calgary, Canada]. (online). http://www.acs.ucalgary.ca/~newsted/surveys.html

Newsted, Peter, Huff, Sid and Munro, Malcolm. (1998). Survey instruments in IS. *MISQ Discovery*, December. (online). http://misq.org/discovery/surveys98/surveys.html

Salant, Priscilla and Dillman, Don A. (1995). *How to conduct your own survey.* Wiley: New York.

Tyebjee, T.T. (1979). Telephone survey methods: The state of the art. *Journal of Marketing*, **43**, Summer, pp. 68-78.

Zikmund, William G. (1997a). *Business research methods.* 5th edn. Dryden Press: Fort Worth, TX.

Zikmund, William G. (1997b). *Exploring marketing research.* 6th edn. Dryden Press: Fort Worth, TX.

CHAPTER 6
Case study research
Peta Darke and Graeme Shanks

Objectives

At the end of this topic you will be able to:

- understand the nature of the case study as a research strategy and its strengths and weaknesses;

- appreciate the ways in which case study research can be used to achieve various research aims;

- understand the requirements of the effective design and conduct of case study research; and

- understand how to approach the data collection and data analysis activities of case study research.

The case study as a research approach

Definition of case study research

Case study research has been used extensively in the social sciences as a means of developing an understanding of social phenomena in their natural setting. A case study is:

> an empirical enquiry that investigates a contemporary phenomenon within its real-life context, especially when the boundaries between phenomenon and context are not clearly evident (Yin 1994, p. 13).

Multiple sources of evidence are used, and data collection techniques typically used include interviews, observation, questionnaires, and document and text analysis. Although both qualitative and quantitative data collection and analysis methods may be used, case study research is most often concerned primarily with qualitative data. Within the information systems research community it is the most widely-used qualitative research method (Orlikowski and Baroudi 1991).

Case study research shares characteristics with a number of related research strategies which also involve the collection and analysis of empirical evidence as a means of examining phenomena in their natural context.

Field studies differ from case studies in that the field study researcher generally has greater prior knowledge of constructs and variables (Cavaye 1996). The difference between the two research methods is often difficult to discern, however, and is really a matter of degree as case researchers may also have clear a priori definitions of variables to be studied and the ways in which they can be measured.

Ethnographic research differs from case study research in that the findings are not usually related to generalisable theory and are interpreted from the researcher's point of view (Cavaye 1996).

Action research differs from case research in that it involves the researcher entering the field as an active participant rather than as an independent observer. The researcher collaborates with participants at the site to help understand and solve their practical problems and concerns, and at the same time the problem solving process is also the subject of research (Benbasat, Goldstein and Mead 1987).

Case studies also need to be distinguished from *application descriptions*. These are accounts of events concerning a particular phenomenon which are intended to describe and inform readers of particular situations and experiences rather than to investigate specific research questions (Benbasat, Goldstein and Mead 1987).

Another use of case studies which is not concerned with research is as teaching devices, where the purpose is to illustrate particular situations and provide a framework for discussion amongst students (Yin 1994, p. 10).

Achieving various research objectives using the case study approach

Case study research can be used for description of phenomena, development of theory, and testing of theory (Cavaye 1996, pp. 234-236). It has been used to provide evidence for hypothesis generation and for exploration of areas where existing knowledge is limited. Approaches such as grounded theory, in which theoretical concepts and propositions emerge as the researcher gathers data and investigates phenomena, may be used to develop theory. Theory testing using case study research requires the specification of theoretical propositions derived from an existing theory or suggested by the results of prior research, for example, the outcomes of a survey. The case study findings resulting from analysis of the case data are compared with the expected outcomes predicted by the propositions. The theory is either validated or found to be inadequate in some way, and may then be further refined. Case study research can also be combined with other research methods. For example, it can be used to define constructs and develop theory which can subsequently be tested using survey research methods (Gable 1994, pp. 112-115).

Strengths and weaknesses of case study research

Case study research is particularly appropriate for situations in which the examination and understanding of context is important. Areas where there is little understanding of how and why processes or phenomena occur, where the experiences of individuals and the contexts of actions are critical, or where theory and research are at their early, formative stages can be usefully addressed using case study research. In particular, these include areas where a phenomenon is dynamic and not yet mature or settled, or where terminology and a common language and set of definitions are not yet clear or widely accepted. There are situations, however, where case study research may not be appropriate, such as areas where a phenomenon is well-understood and mature, where constructs exist already and are well-developed, where understanding of how and why the particular phenomenon occurs is not of interest, and where understanding of the contexts of action and the experiences of individuals in single settings is not relevant. Examples of research areas within information systems in which case study research has been useful and some for which it would not be appropriate can be found in Darke, Shanks and Broadbent (1998).

There are, however, disadvantages associated with the use of the case study research method. The data collection and data analysis processes in case study research are both subject to the influence of the researcher's characteristics and background, and rely heavily on the researcher's interpretation of events, documents and interview material. This may limit the validity of the research findings, although as Yin (1994, p. 10) notes, bias may enter into the design and conduct of other types of research. Case studies typically make use of qualitative data, often in combination with quantitative data. Data analysis can be difficult as qualitative data analysis methods are not as well-established as quantitative methods, and the volume and variety of data collected may make analysis time-consuming (Cavaye 1996).

Philosophical traditions and case study research

The case study research strategy has been used within both the positivist and the interpretivist philosophical traditions. Positivist case study research is designed and evaluated according to the criteria of the natural science model of research: controlled observations, controlled deductions, replicability, and generalisability (Lee 1989). Although manipulation of variables in the experimental sense is not possible, theoretical constructs can be defined and empirically evaluated and measured, and naturally occurring controls can be identified (Yin 1994, pp. 32-38). Interpretivist case study research focuses on the evolution of rich, complex descriptions of specific cases in order to understand social phenomena and their interaction with their context. Researchers acknowledge their own subjectivity as part of this process. The value of an explanation is judged in terms of the extent to which it allows others to understand the phenomena and makes sense to those being studied. The concept of generalisation refers to the value of explanations of phenomena and processes in understanding them in other settings and in providing rich insights rather than to their predictive ability (Walsham 1995). Discussion of recent information systems case study research within both the positivist and interpretivist traditions, including examples of published case studies drawn from each, can be found in Doolin (1996) and Darke, Shanks and Broadbent (1998).

Designing case study research

In order to design and scope a case study research project it is necessary to undertake a comprehensive literature analysis. This allows the researcher to understand the existing body of research within the area, to position the proposed research within the context of that literature, and to frame the research question(s) accordingly. The literature analysis provides a basis for careful design of the research project structure and scope so that an appropriate number of cases and unit of analysis can be determined. The design of case study research also requires selection of suitable data collection methods and data analysis strategies to ensure that the adequacy and validity of the evidence collected is established, that the process by which the research results are arrived at is made clear, and that the validity of the research findings can be demonstrated.

The research question

Research within applied disciplines generally should have an applied orientation directed at improving practice. The research questions to be addressed must be appropriate in terms of their interest, significance and value for both the research and practitioner communities and they must be able to be answered in a useful way. Definition of the research questions is a critical step in the design of a research study, and sufficient time and effort must be spent on ensuring that they are appropriate and feasible. The research questions must have both *substance*, which indicates what the study is about, and *form*, which indicates the nature of the questions in terms of whether they are 'who', 'where', 'how', 'what', or 'why' questions (Yin 1994, p. 7). It is essential to ensure that the research approach adopted is appropriate for the substance and the form of the research question or questions.

The unit of analysis

A complete collection of data for one study of the unit of analysis forms a single 'case'. The unit of analysis may be an individual, a group, an organisation, or it may be an event or some other phenomenon. It is related to the way the major research question is initially defined and is likely to be at the level being addressed by the question (Yin 1994, pp. 21-

24). The major research question informs the selection of the level and scope of the unit of analysis, and suggests 'where one goes to get answers, with whom one talks, what one observes' (Miles and Huberman 1984, p. 43). Consideration of the generalisations the researcher hopes to make at the conclusion of the research is also useful in determining the unit of analysis, that is, will the results be applicable to other individuals, groups, organisations or events? The unit of analysis must also provide for sufficient breadth and depth of data to be collected to allow the research question to be adequately answered.

Single-case and multiple-case designs

Either single-case or multiple-case designs may be used in case study research. Single-case designs are usually appropriate where the case represents a critical case (it meets all the necessary conditions for testing a theory), where it is an extreme or unique case, where it is a revelatory case, or where the research is exploratory (Yin 1994, pp. 38-40). Single cases allow researchers to investigate phenomena in-depth to provide rich description and understanding. A single case may also be used as a pilot study for a research project in which several cases are required, especially where the study is of an exploratory nature. The pilot case study can help to refine data collection and analysis procedures. Multiple-case designs allow cross-case analysis and comparison, and the investigation of a particular phenomenon in diverse settings. Multiple cases may also be selected to predict similar results (literal replication) or to produce contrasting results for predictable reasons (theoretical replication) (Yin 1994, pp. 46-51).

The focus of the research question should determine the number of cases to be studied. More replications generally give greater certainty, but in some situations, for example where rival theories that are very different are being tested, fewer replications may be necessary (Yin 1994, p. 50). Eisenhardt (1989) suggests that between four and ten cases are desirable for theory building. Both single- and multiple-case designs can be adopted for exploratory research. Where explanatory research is undertaken, a single case may provide the basis for developing explanations of why a phenomenon occurs, and these may then be further investigated by applying them to additional cases in other settings.

For the positivist case study researcher, a single case, like a single experiment, represents a single set of empirical circumstances. The findings of a single case are generalisable to other empirical settings when additional cases test and confirm those findings in other settings (Lee 1989). Multiple case studies can thus strengthen research findings in the way that multiple experiments strengthen experimental research findings (Benbasat, Goldstein and Mead 1987). Statistical generalisation to a population is not the goal of case study research as cases are not sampling units. Rather, theoretical or *analytical* generalisation is appropriate, where case study results are used to develop theory or to test previously developed theory (Cavaye 1996; Yin 1994, pp. 30-32). Within interpretive case study research, four types of generalisations can be identified: development of concepts; generation of theory; drawing of specific implications; and contribution of rich insight

(Walsham 1995). These allow explanations of particular phenomena derived from empirical research which may be valuable in other settings as interpretations of phenomena but which are not wholly predictive for future situations.

Selecting suitable case study sites

Selection of suitable sites for conducting case study research requires careful consideration of the nature of the research question, the number of cases required, and the unit of analysis. Where a single-case design is used, it is essential to ensure that the site selected will provide all the necessary characteristics of the unit of analysis and will allow all the necessary types of evidence to be collected. Miles and Huberman (1984, pp. 36-40) identify settings, actors, events and processes as parameters to consider when selecting sites for case studies. They discuss the need to ensure that each of these 'lines up' with the research question. Where a multiple-case design is used, the selection of sites also needs to take into account the rationale for investigating multiple sites. For example, literal replication requires selection of sites that would be able to produce similar results, while theoretical replication requires selection of sites that would be able to produce contrasting results. In discussing the use of case study research to develop theory, Eisenhardt (1989) suggests that as only a limited number of cases can usually be studied, the selection of cases involving extreme situations and polar types is useful where theory is emergent and the goal of the research is further refinement of theory.

Conducting case study research

Getting organisations to participate

If a research area is particularly relevant to an organisation and the specific research question is interesting and important to the organisation, then it is more likely that access to people and resources will be provided. The researcher needs to make clear what the research outcomes will be and how the organisation will benefit from involvement. The benefits may include an overview of the organisation's position in relation to the research question, or a rich description and understanding of the nature of the phenomenon within the organisation, or, within the limits of confidentiality requirements, insights gained from studies of other participating organisations. Before commencing field work at a case study site, it is essential to reach an agreement with the participating organisation concerning the confidentiality requirements relating to the case study data and findings, and any limitations on the disclosure of the identities of the case study participants and the organisation. Agreement also needs to be reached on publishing rights and restrictions on the publication of research in which the organisation has participated. Organisations also need to be assured that adequate preparation for the study at their site has been carried out. All potential case participants should be sent a brief covering letter describing the nature and context of the research project and its objectives. The letter should include attachments outlining the research timeframe, the proposed nature of the case participants' involvement in the project, and the expected research outcomes.

Collecting case study data

The collection of case study data from case participants can be difficult and time-consuming and requires careful planning and judicious use of both the case participants' and the researchers' time. Researchers should prepare themselves with sufficient background information about a case study site prior to commencing data collection. The names and positions of all potential case participants should be obtained before they are contacted for participation in interviews and other data collection activities, and interview time should be used only to obtain information that cannot be obtained in any other way. Factual and other straightforward information can be collected from other sources, for example annual reports, or by obtaining written answers to structured questions sent to case participants prior to interview sessions. Useful sources of information often overlooked are the internal magazines and other organisational bulletins which are circulated within larger organisations in particular. These can supplement information obtained from other sources and often reflect the culture within an organisation and the issues which are currently of interest or concern to both management and employees.

A case study database should be planned before data collection commences and maintained throughout the process (Yin 1994, pp. 94-98). A well-organised and categorised set of case data will facilitate the task of analysing the case study evidence and maintaining a chain of evidence to support the derivation of case study conclusions from the data collected. The case study database will include the case data, such as documents, video or audio tapes of interviews, survey or other quantitative data, and the field notes and other observations of the researcher during data collection activities. Methods of classifying case data and materials and mechanisms for accessing and retrieving them need to be considered to ensure ready access to the case data at any point during or after the study. Indexing and storage of case study materials can be assisted by the use of computerised tools. Myers (1998) is a source of information about these.

Adequate planning for dealing with the difficulties of gathering data in a real-life environment not controlled by the researcher is necessary to ensure efficient and effective data collection in the field. Sufficient resources, time and facilities should be provided for handling accumulated documents and other materials, for perusing and copying documents, and for making and reviewing field notes when necessary. Unanticipated changes to case participants' schedules and availability must be accommodated within the overall data collection schedule. Effective and timely communication with case participants is promoted by the use of fax, email and courier services rather than postal services.

Analysis of case study data

A general data analysis strategy is an important part of the case study design, as a major practical difficulty of analysis of case study evidence is dealing with the amount and variety of data collected (Yin 1994, pp. 102-125). The strategy will indicate what to analyse and why, and will help ensure that data collection activities are appropriate and support the ways in which the evidence is to be analysed. It will also help the researcher select from the various data analysis techniques that are available.

Some useful techniques for categorising, tabulating, and displaying qualitative data have been described by positivist researchers. Detailed case study descriptions and write-ups of the case data form the basis for data analysis which focuses on discovering regularities or patterns within the case study data. The inductive, grounded theory approach of Glaser and Strauss (1967) involves *coding*: the assignment of themes and concepts to a selected unit, combining these into related categories, identifying and verifying links between categories, and attempting to integrate the categories into a theory which accounts for the phenomenon being investigated. Miles and Huberman (1984, pp. 21-23) adopt a more deductive approach and describe three concurrent activities: *data reduction* to select, simplify, abstract, and transform the raw case data, *data display* to organise the assembled information to enable the drawing of conclusions, and *conclusion drawing/verification* to draw meaning from data and build a logical chain of evidence.

The goal of analysis in interpretive studies is to produce an understanding of the contexts of phenomena and the interactions between them and their contexts. The interpretive researcher is presenting their interpretation of the interpretations of others, and the strength of analysis derives from the strength of the explanation of the phenomena based on the interpretation of data. Myers (1998) discusses some *modes of analysis* associated with interpretive research including hermeneutics, narrative (a tale or recital of facts), and metaphor (a way of understanding or experiencing one thing in terms of another).

Possible biases in the researcher's collection and analysis of case data need to be considered. Two types of bias may be recognised: the effects of the researcher on events and the behaviour of participants at the case study site, and the researcher's own beliefs, values and prior assumptions which may prevent adequate investigation and consideration of possible contradictory data and unduly influence the analysis of the case study evidence. Biases arising from researcher effects at the site are in one sense unavoidable: the researcher is influencing what is happening just by the sharing of concepts and interpretations with personnel at the site. Biases of the researcher are accepted by the interpretive researchers who acknowledge the subjectivity of their analysis in that their predispositions, beliefs, values and interests shape their investigations. However, the effects of biases can be counteracted by using multiple sources of evidence (triangulation of data – as discussed in Chapter 2) to provide multiple instances from different sources. Case study findings are strengthened by the convergence of information from a variety of sources, providing multiple measures of the same phenomenon (Yin 1994, p. 92). Multiple sources of evidence also assist in corroborating information provided by different participants where there are conflicting accounts of events and actions.

Writing up case study research

In order to establish credibility to the reader, the researcher must describe in detail how the research results are arrived at, and to establish validity in the view of the reader, the researcher must present a coherent, persuasively-argued point of view (Walsham 1995). Sufficient evidence for the research results must be provided and alternative interpretations must be carefully considered and clear reasons given for their rejection. This will help enable the rigour and reliability of the research to be established. It is important to demonstrate the trail of evidence which the analysis has followed so that the derivation of the case study conclusions from the case data is made explicit.

Case study research can be difficult to write up due to the volume of data collected and the problems of analysis of evidence. When reporting case studies it is useful to follow a recognised case study reporting structure that has been used in published case study research literature within the field. Potential readers within the field can then more readily understand the research and its results. An exemplary case study paper may also be used as a template for presentation of case data and research results. Another means of helping to ensure the quality of the case study report is to have it reviewed by colleagues.

A case study should be presented as an interesting and convincing 'story'. Yin (1994, p. 151) notes that a case study report 'must be composed in an engaging manner' with not only a clear writing style but also 'one that constantly entices the reader to continue reading'. The case study report must be complete and must contain sufficient evidence to support the findings. Secondary data that is not essential for understanding and evaluating the case study analysis and conclusions should be omitted. Presentation of data in tabular form is useful for summarising and compressing data, and is effective when making comparisons either between cases or between features or aspects of a single case. The overall goals in writing up case studies are to present the critical evidence judiciously and effectively using a clear and lucid writing style.

Examples of case studies in information management and systems

Case studies have been used quite often in both information management and information systems. Box 6.1 provides an example of case study research from information systems, and Box 6.2 an example from information management.

Box 6.1: Examples of case study research (information systems)

This chapter's first author used case study research to undertake the empirical component of her PhD thesis (see Darke 1997). The theoretical component of the thesis included a conceptual framework for the development of stakeholder viewpoints during requirements definition. A model for the representation of stakeholder viewpoints was a part of the process. Requirements definition is the phase in the development of an information system in which the information and processing requirements of all potential stakeholders and users of the system are identified and documented. Different groups of stakeholders and users often have differing requirements or viewpoints. The case study research method was used to investigate the empirical validity of the concepts.

- Four extensive case studies of the requirements definition phase within systems development projects were undertaken in order to determine the empirical validity of the proposed concepts. The theoretical concepts being investigated were used to guide data collection. Qualitative data were collected, including transcripts of semi and unstructured interviews with both business and information technology project participants, annual reports, internally-circulated project bulletins, project planning and general system documentation, requirements definition documentation (both final and intermediate versions), informal notes, memorandums. Triangulation of data sources permitted cross-checking of data and convergence of data from multiple sources.

- Documents were examined to identify conceptual categories based on the concepts in the framework and the model, and interview transcripts provided a means of accessing the case participants' perceptions of the viewpoint development process and the relevance of the framework and model concepts. Case study analysis sought to interpret the data collected to determine whether and in what ways the concepts could be applied to the four cases. Cross-case analysis attempted to identify similarities and differences between the four cases and to relate these where possible to aspects of the cases revealed in within-case analyses.

- Case study analysis occurred in three interrelated phases. First, within-case analyses examined, analysed and interpreted field data to determine the applicability of the framework concepts in each case; the second phase involved similar analyses in terms of the concepts of the model (the concepts of the model are grounded in the framework concepts, so the applicability of the model concepts is interlinked with that of the framework); the third phase focused on comparison of results of the within-case analyses, and used the field data and the within-case analyses to provide a cross-case analysis of the four cases. Concepts were considered to be applicable to the cases where the analysis indicated that the case participants perceived the concepts to be both relevant and meaningful, or that conceptual categories based on the framework and the template components were present in the case data, or both. The concepts that were found to be applicable to the empirical data of the cases can be said to have empirical validity as they are grounded in empirical reality (see Darke 1997, Chapter 7). Not all concepts were applicable or applicable in the same way in all four cases. The cross-case analysis examined similarities and differences between viewpoint development in each of the four cases and identified how the applicability of the concepts of the framework and the model in each case can be related to the nature and features of the four cases.

Box 6.2: Example of case study research (information management)

At the University of Melbourne, the Division of Library and Information Studies undertook multi-site case studies of the use of resources in the Victorian Certificate of Education (VCE) subject, Australian Studies, in ten secondary schools (Williamson 1995). (This research was discussed in relation to triangulation in Chapter 2.) Multiple sources of evidence were used: interviews were conducted with co-ordinators and teachers; students undertaking Australian Studies in each of the ten schools were surveyed, using a self-administered questionnaire; and documents were examined, both from the Victorian Curriculum and Assessment Board (VCAB) and the schools themselves. A few student assignments were also examined and the students who wrote them were interviewed.

Data were both quantitative and qualitative. The data from the self-administered questionnaires were coded for computer analysis which was carried out using Statistical Package for the Social Sciences (SPSS). This analysis enabled comparisons to be made across cases. For the qualitative data, data reduction techniques as described by Miles and Huberman (1984) were used. The project team engaged in discussions to consider findings and impressions and to decide on the information to include under each selected heading in the individual case reports. A particular attempt was made to include a large number of comments from the teachers and teacher-librarians interviewed. After the individual case reports were completed, similarities and differences within each case, as well as across cases, were drawn out and issues and themes were identified for the final report (Williamson 1995, p. 82)

Conclusion

Case study research is a useful means of investigating phenomena in their natural setting which enables the capture and understanding of their context. It can be used to achieve a variety of research aims using diverse data collection and analysis methods. Weaknesses of case study research include difficulties in generalising research results and the subjectivity of the data collection and analysis processes. Case study research within applied disciplines requires the selection of research areas that are relevant to industry and practitioners.

Discussion questions

- What are the key characteristics of case study research?

- In what kinds of research situations is case study research most useful?

- What criteria can be used to judge the quality of case study research designs?

- In what ways can rigour be established in the collection and analysis of case study data?

Further readings

Benbasat, Izak, Goldstein, David K. and Mead, Melissa. (1987). The case research strategy in studies of information systems. *MIS Quarterly*, **11** (3), pp. 369-386.

Cavaye, Angele L.M. (1996). Case study research: A multi-faceted research approach for IS. *Information Systems Journal,* **6** (3), pp. 227-242.

Yin, Robert K. (1994). *Case study research: Design and methods.* 2nd edn. Sage: Thousand Oaks, Ca.

References for Chapter 6

Benbasat, Izak, Goldstein, David K. and Mead, Melissa. (1987). The case research strategy in studies of information systems. *MIS Quarterly*, **11** (3), pp. 369-386.

Cavaye, Angele L.M. (1996). Case study research: A multi-faceted research approach for IS. *Information Systems Journal,* **6** (3), pp. 227-242.

Darke, Peta. (1997). Viewpoint development in requirements definition. Unpublished PhD dissertation. Monash University: Melbourne.

Darke, Peta, Shanks, Graeme and Broadbent, Marianne. (1998). Successfully completing case study research: Combining rigour, relevance and pragmatism. *Information Systems Journal*, **8** (4), pp. 273-289.

Doolin, Bill. (1996). Alternative views of case research in information systems. *Australian Journal of Information Systems*, **3** (2), pp. 21-29.

Eisenhardt, Kathleen M. (1989). Building theories from case study research. *Academy of Management Review*, **14** (4), pp. 532-550.

Gable, Guy. (1994). Integrating case study and survey research methods: An example in information systems. *European Journal of Information Systems*, **3** (2), pp. 112-126.

Glaser, Barney G. and Strauss, Anselm L. (1967). *The discovery of grounded theory: Strategies of qualitative research.* Aldine de Gruyter: New York.

Lee, Allen S. (1989). A scientific methodology for MIS case studies. *MIS Quarterly*, **13** (1), pp. 33-50.

Miles, Matthew B. and Huberman, A. Michael. (1984). *Qualitative data analysis: A sourcebook of new methods*. Sage: Newbury Park, Ca.

Myers, Michael D. (ed.). (1998). Qualitative research in information systems. (online). http://www.auckland.ac.nz/msis/isworld/

Orlikowski, Wanda J. and Baroudi, Jack J. (1991). Studying information technology in organisations: Research approaches and assumptions. *Information Systems Research*, **2** (1), pp. 1-28.

Walsham, Geoffrey. (1995). Interpretive case studies in IS research: Nature and method. *European Journal of Information Systems*, **4**, pp. 74-81.

Williamson, Kirsty. (1995). Independent learning and the use of resources: VCE Australian studies. *Australian Journal of Education,* **39** (1), pp. 77-94.

Yin, Robert K. (1994). *Case study research: Design and methods.* 2nd edn. Sage: Thousand Oaks, Ca.

CHAPTER 7
Experimental research designs
Kerry Tanner

Objectives

At the end of this chapter, you will be able to:

- define and explain key concepts associated with experimental research;

- differentiate true experiments from pre-experimental and quasi-experimental research designs;

- describe and explain, with examples, typical experimental designs and research phases for true experiments, pre-experiments and quasi-experiments;

- explain the relative advantages and limitations of each type of experimental design, and the circumstances under which its use is appropriate;

- identify the most suitable form of experimental design, given a designated research question and research constraints;

- critically evaluate published reports of experimental research; and

- devise an effective experimental research design for a particular project.

Introduction

Experimental research is undertaken when a researcher wishes to trace cause-and-effect relationships between defined variables. However, there are major constraints on causal inference in experimental research, and the type of experimental design chosen has a significant influence on the inferences that can be validly drawn from experiment results.

This chapter begins by defining basic terms and explaining concepts which underpin experimental research. It then examines three broad types of experimental research designs: the true experiment (laboratory experiment); pre-experimental designs; and quasi-experimental designs; and looks at the relative strengths and weaknesses of each design in terms of the trade-off between establishing causation and enabling generalisability outside laboratory settings. Specific types of designs are outlined, along with relevant examples.

Important considerations in determining the most appropriate form of experimental design for a research project include: the type of research questions being addressed by the study; the degree of control the researcher has over conditions under investigation; and whether or not the phenomenon of interest can be studied outside its natural setting. These factors are explored in relation to each of the major types of experimental design examined in the chapter.

Key research concepts underpinning experimental research designs

Experimental research exemplifies classic positivist approach, or 'scientific method'. As discussed in Chapter 2, this research tradition is based on *hypothesis testing*, on a *deductive* process of logical inference, where reasoning proceeds from general principles to particular instances as shown in Figure 7.1.

Hypotheses and statistical probability testing

A hypothesis is a statement or proposition about a predicted relationship between two or more variables, which is empirically testable. Hypotheses are discussed at greater length, and in a more general way, in Chapter 3.

Taking an example which might be used for an experiment, a researcher may start with the hypothesis: '*Those with higher levels of computer literacy are the most successful in retrieving relevant documents in an Internet search.*' However, to empirically test this hypothesis, it is conventionally stated in its *null* form (expressed in shorthand form as H_0), for example, '*Computer literacy has no effect on success in retrieving relevant documents in an Internet search*'. Null hypotheses are designed for statistical probability testing purposes and are based on the assumption of 'no difference' between experimental and control groups. The researcher hopes that statistical tests will show that there is a statistically significant difference between experimental and control groups (that is, a difference not explained by chance), and thus establish a likely causal link between the variables under study. Research conventions are that an acceptable level of statistical probability is 0.05 (that is, $p <= 0.05$). Interpreted, this means that the researcher can be 95% confident that the 'true population mean' lies within the range recorded in the test results, with a 5% chance that it does not. At this level the null hypothesis can be rejected and an alternative research hypothesis (expressed in shorthand form as H_1, H_2, etc.) accepted. A statistical probability of 0.01 (that is, $p <= 0.01$) indicates a very strong result (a 99% confidence interval).

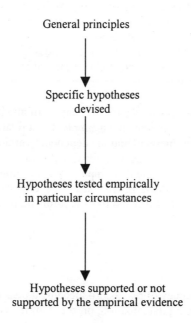

General principles

Specific hypotheses
devised

Hypotheses tested empirically
in particular circumstances

Hypotheses supported or not
supported by the empirical evidence

Figure 7.1: Deductive reasoning process

Variables

A *variable* is an element or factor which is under investigation in the experiment. The *independent* or *causal* variable is the factor manipulated by the researcher to see what impact it has on another variable(s). It is the presumed cause. For example, in an investigation into '*The impact of noise on task performance at work*', the independent variable is 'noise'. The researcher manipulates this factor (for example by varying levels of noise, or the nature and frequency of bursts of noise), and then observes its effects on subjects performing work tasks.

The *dependent* or *effect* variable is the factor which is measured to determine how it has responded to a particular treatment or cause. In the example just given, the dependent variable is 'task performance'. The researcher would need to devise a test or other means of measuring the task performance levels of subjects at work.

An *extraneous* or *confounding* or *intervening* variable is an unknown element, which is not the focus of the study, but which is assumed to account for some of the effects observed. In the example on task performance at work, it may not only be varying noise conditions which account for subjects' task performance. Other physical factors, for example poor lighting or unanticipated interruptions, or psychological factors such as severe emotional trauma, may act as confounding variables, having an impact on test results. That is, varying noise conditions may not be assumed to account for all variations in results observed. In a laboratory experiment, formal controls aim to limit the possibility of confounding variables impacting on results. However, in a natural (field) setting, it is much more difficult to eradicate such intervening variables.

A *moderating* variable in some way moderates the impact of another variable under study. For instance, it may be found that there is not a simple direct relationship between the independent variable 'computer literacy' and the dependent variable 'retrieval of relevant documents in an Internet search', but that attitudinal factors act to moderate the impact of 'computer literacy' (for example the highly computer literate subject who is overconfident and blasé may achieve poorer results in Internet searching than those with lower levels of computer literacy who are eager to learn and more careful and deliberate in their searching strategy).

Reliability

Reliability refers to the consistency of results produced by a measuring instrument when it is applied more than once in a similar situation; or, the stability, consistency and dependability of measures. Most experiments involve a series of tests, and it is important to ensure reliability in subsequent administrations of the experimental treatment.

Validity

Validity is the capacity of a measuring instrument to measure what it purports to measure, or to predict what it was designed to predict; or, the accuracy of observations.

Internal validity pertains to the conclusiveness of results, that is, the confidence that observed results are attributable to the impact of the independent variable, and not caused by other unknown factors.

External validity refers to the generalisability of research findings, that is, the extent to which they can be generalised to other populations, settings or treatments. Sampling measures have a significant impact on external validity.

Construct validity refers to the extent to which a measure actually measures the construct (abstract concept) it was designed to measure.

Validity in laboratory experiments and field experiments

Experiments conducted in laboratory settings are high in internal validity, as the researcher is in a position to control and manipulate the independent variable and accurately measure its effects on the dependent variable, and to ensure that confounding variables do not influence results. In field settings the researcher lacks such controls, and cannot be sure that the effects observed were attributable to the independent variable. Hence field experiments tend to rate low on internal validity, but high on external validity (generalisability to other settings). Laboratory experiments, based on artificial and contrived settings, have low external validity.

Experimental and control groups

Experimental research involves the differentiation of two basic conditions: exposure and non-exposure to the treatment condition of the independent variable. The *experimental group* is the group exposed to the treatment condition, while the *control group* is not subjected to treatment. There can be multiple experimental and control conditions in an experiment. Observations are recorded for each group, and the groups are then compared, with differences in the experimental group assumed to be attributable to the application of the treatment. As previously discussed in Chapter 5, 'X' is a shorthand form used in describing experimental designs to indicate the application of a treatment condition of the independent variable, and 'Not-X' the lack of such a treatment. 'O' is the abbreviation for an observation or measurement (the dependent variable). Multiple measurements are indicated as O_1, O_2, O_3, etc. These abbreviations are used when describing different experimental designs later in this chapter.

Randomisation (random assignment)

A necessary pre-condition for applying statistical testing procedures in experiments is that initially subjects must be *randomly assigned* to experimental and control groups. Randomisation ensures that experimental and control groups are equivalent in composition, and is an integral feature of a valid experimental design. The abbreviation 'R' is used in diagrams of experimental design to indicate 'randomisation' in assigning subjects to experimental or control conditions.

Inferring causation in experimental research

While it is difficult to establish cause-and-effect relationships conclusively with any research design, 'true experiments' offer the greatest potential of any design for inferring causal relationships. This is due to their careful control of experimental conditions, and to the practice of randomisation ensuring groups equivalent in composition.

To infer causation, a researcher needs to be able to eliminate alternative explanations (rival hypotheses), that the fact that observed changes in the experimental group may be due to factors other than the independent/treatment variable.

Some typical rival hypotheses include:

Selection effect – if subjects are permitted to select their own treatment condition (experimental or control), groups will not be equivalent. This alternative explanation can be overcome by the practice of randomisation.

Maturation – any naturally occurring process within persons which could account for the observed change.

History – any event to which subjects are exposed around the time of the experiment, which could account for observed differences between subjects.

Instrumentation – any change in measurement instrument or procedures from one application of a treatment to another.

Mortality – subjects dropping out from a study.

The true experiment

Definitions and overview

The true experiment is the classic example of 'scientific method' or the hypothetico-deductive research model referred to earlier. It is the most suitable of any method in testing hypotheses involving cause-and-effect relationships, due to rigorously controlled laboratory conditions, including the isolation of the independent and dependent variables from other intervening variables. Eliminating potential intervening variables is much easier in a laboratory situation than in a naturalistic setting (such as the subjects' own work environments).

The basic true experimental design model involves subjects (who have been randomly assigned to groups) experiencing some condition of the independent variable (experimental group), or lack of such a condition (control group), and then being measured on the dependent variable. Taking the example, *'The impact of noise on task performance at work'*, a researcher in a laboratory experiment manipulates 'noise' (the independent variable) by varying levels of noise or the nature and frequency of bursts of noise to which subjects are exposed while performing designated work tasks (dependent variable). Equivalent 'control' groups perform similar tasks but without the application of the noise treatment. Subjects' task performance is measured. Statistical tests are applied to results, and conclusions drawn on the effects of different noise conditions on subjects' task performance, compared with the group of subjects not exposed to the noise treatment.

Some particular true experimental research designs

The models illustrated in Figures 7.2 to 7.10 rely on the following abbreviations

R = Randomisation or random assignment
X = The application of a treatment; the independent or experimental variable; a
    cause
O = An observation or measurement; the dependent variable; an effect
$O_1, O_2, O_3, \ldots$ = The first, second, third, etc. measurement.

Simple experiment, or randomised two-group design

This is the simplest valid true experimental design. Figure 7.2 depicts the basic model.

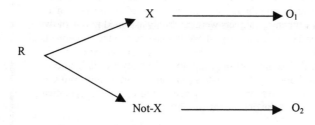

Example

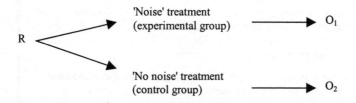

Figure 7.2: Randomised two-group design

Box 7.1 illustrates the application of this approach.

Box 7.1: Example of a simple (randomised two-group) experimental design

Tombros and Sanderson (1998) used a randomised two-group experimental design to investigate the usefulness of a new type of 'query biased summaries' to users making relevance judgements in lists of retrieved documents from an automated information retrieval system

Background explanation: The method used for generating query biased summaries involved the information retrieval system taking terms from a user's queries of the system, matching them against document text, and using sentence extraction methods to generate document summaries. Although not always fluent, these query biased document summaries are to some degree customised to the individual user. In contrast, typical document summaries from a traditional information retrieval system comprise title and the first few sentences of the retrieved document.

The central hypothesis was that 'the use of query biased summaries in a retrieved document list would have a positive effect on the process of relevance judgement by users' (Tombros and Sanderson 1998, p. 4).

There were two conditions of the independent variable in the experimental design: the use of query biased summaries, and the use of static pre-defined summaries, in a ranked list of retrieved documents. Subjects were randomly assigned to one of two task groups. One (the first experimental group) had to make relevance judgements of documents using query biased summaries, and the other (the second experimental group – that may be regarded as the control group) to make relevance judgements based on static, pre-defined document summaries (typical system output from a traditional information retrieval system). Performance on retrieval tasks, specifically accuracy and speed, constituted the dependent variable.

Each subject was given five separate queries, and a retrieved document list. Time to perform the relevance assessments was limited to five minutes per query. The experiment used queries and documents from the TREC test collection (see further explanation of the TREC experiments in Box 6.4). 'The only actions [subjects] ... could perform was to move through the list or to fetch the full text of the documents listed within it. Their task ... was to identify, in a limited amount of time, as many relevant documents as possible.' (Tombros and Sanderson 1998, p. 5). Subjects also completed a brief questionnaire based on their experience.

Criteria measured in the experiment included recall and precision, speed, the need to consult the full text of documents for clarification, and subjects' subjective assessments of the value of document summaries provided.

'The results from the evaluation indicate that the use of query biased summaries significantly improves both the accuracy and speed of user relevance judgments' (Tombros and Sanderson 1998, p. 2).

Variations on the basic model include two or more experimental conditions *and* a control group, or two or more alternative treatments *instead of* a control group. For example, the design in Figure 7.3 was used in a study into the stress-producing effects of an invasion of one's 'personal space' (Kanaga and Flynn 1981). One of the conditions involved an interview between experimenter and subject where a comfortable social distance was maintained (control); and the other two conditions involved two different levels of violation of spatial distance conventions (close, very close) through the interviewer moving to an inappropriate social distance at a designated point in the interview.

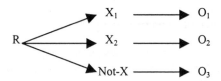

Figure 7.3: Variation on the basic two-group design

Pre-test/post-test control group design (also known as four cell experimental design, or before-and-after two-group design)

This is also one of the simplest, 'classic' types of experimental design. It involves experimental and control groups, selected through randomisation. Both groups are initially tested, and measured on the variable under consideration. Then the experimental group is subjected to the treatment, and subsequently re-tested. The control group is isolated from the experimental treatment, and is also re-tested. Results from the two groups are compared, the assumption being that any observed differences are attributable to the experimental treatment. The basic model for this design is shown in Figure 7.4.

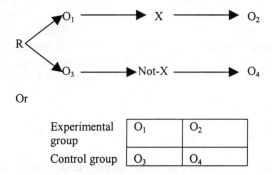

Or

Experimental group	O_1	O_2
Control group	O_3	O_4

Figure 7.4: Basic model for pre-test/post-test control group design

In the analysis of results, comparisons will be made between pre-test and post-test scores for each group (that is, O_1 and O_2; O_3 and O_4), and also the between-group scores (that is, O_1 and O_3; O_2 and O_4).

One potential problem with a pre-test preceding a post-test is that subjects may be sensitised to the purpose of the experiment, and hence bias their post-test scores (a *maturation* effect).

Variations on the basic design include:

- more than one experimental group and a control group; and

- two or more treatment groups in lieu of a control group.

A typical instance of a pre-test/post-test control group design is an experiment testing the efficacy of a training program in producing desired training outcomes or behaviours. Take the case of a state public library agency that has developed an Internet training program for older adults. The primary hypotheses are that the Internet training program yields significant improvements in Internet searching skills and improves the confidence of older adults in using the Internet. The Internet training is the independent variable, while Internet searching skills and confidence levels are the dependent variables.

Specific tests are developed to measure subjects' skills in Internet searching, and to rate their level of confidence in Internet use. Subjects from the relevant age range are randomly assigned to experimental (training) and to control (no-training) groups. An initial test of Internet searching skills and level of confidence is applied to subjects in both conditions. Certain basic demographic and other relevant personal data (such as previous exposure to computers and to the Internet) is also collected.

Those in the experimental group(s) then undertake the training program, while those in the control group(s) receive no training. All subjects (experimental and control) are tested again after the delivery of the training. It is hoped that the performance and confidence of those who have undertaken the training improves significantly more than that of subjects in the control group. As well as drawing conclusions on the efficacy of the training program in enhancing Internet searching skills and confidence, conclusions may also be drawn on the impact on results of moderating variables such as age, sex or subjects' prior exposure to computers and the Internet.

Factorial designs

A factorial design involves two or more independent variables under study (designated 'X', 'Y', etc.). Both the *independent* and *interactive* effects of these variables on the dependent variable are studied. These designs are quite complex methodologically (especially if more than two variables are involved), demanding a sophisticated level and techniques of

statistical analysis – scarcely the domain of the novice researcher! The basic model for a
two-by-two factorial design is shown in Figure 7.5.

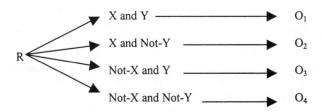

Figure 7.5: Basic model for factorial design

One example of such a design given by Kidder (1981) is an investigation into the interactive
effects of a person's gender and assertiveness on their popularity in a group situation.
Selected 'actors' were primed (unbeknown to subjects in the group) to play the role of a
group member, adopting one of four characteristics: assertive male, assertive female,
submissive male or submissive female. Subsequently, subjects rated each person in the
group (including the 'actor') on a number of qualities, including their popularity. Gender or
assertiveness behaviour alone had no signficant impact on actors' popularity, but the
interactive effect of gender and behaviour did, with assertive males and submissive females
being rated most popular – reinforcing sexual stereotypes.

Boxes 7.2 to 7.4 (further below) illustrate the application of the various true experimental
designs.

Advantages of the true experiment

Due to the rigorous controls exercised and the ability to rule out rival explanations, true
experiments have a much higher *internal validity* than other research designs. Hence
findings may be interpreted as having greater integrity. Also, the true experiment is the most
suitable of any of the research designs for testing hypotheses involving causal relationships.

Limitations of the true experiment

The major weakness of experimental designs is their *external validity*. When an experiment
is conducted in rigidly controlled laboratory conditions, its generalisability to other
populations and settings lacking those controls is suspect. Phenomenologists criticise
experimental designs for the highly artificial environments they create, for divorcing a
phenomenon from its natural setting, where it cannot be observed in its totality: a problem
particularly with the observation of human processes. To help to overcome this limitation,

some researchers will follow up an initial laboratory investigation with field study (as done in the O'Reilly and Roberts (1974) research noted in Box 7.2).

Box 7.2: Example of a complex factorial experimental design

O'Reilly and Roberts (1974) used a series of three 2 x 2 factorial designs to investigate the phenomenon of selective filtration of information in organisational hierarchies. They opted for laboratory experimental simulations rather than field experiments – although some years later these experiments were followed up by a field study (O'Reilly 1978). The basic design involved the interactions of the variables 'favourable information' and 'important information' about the person ('actor', with the variable 'directionality of information flow'. The initial 2 x 2 factorial design was:

Favourable and important information   Unfavourable and important information
Favourable and unimportant information Unfavourable and unimportant information

This was applied to each of the three directions of organisational communication: upward transmission (communication with the boss); downward transmission (communication with subordinates); and lateral transmission (communication with colleagues).

Results indicated that senders filtered out different types of information, depending on the direction of the flow of information and the trust in the receiver. A tendency to pass more favourable and important information upward, and to filter out the negative and unimportant, was noted – management would be denied access to important but unfavourable information. More total information was shared laterally than either upwards or downwards communication, as was more unfavourable information.

Boxes 7.3 and 7.4 present two further examples of true experimental designs.

Box 7.3: Experiments on evaluation of information retrieval systems

One area of information management/information systems research where true experimental designs (laboratory experiments) have been extensively used is in the evaluation of information retrieval systems. The Cranfield (UK) series of experiments from the 1960s established experimental designs for evaluating information retrieval systems (Cleverdon 1962; Cleverdon, Mills and Keen 1966; Foskett 1996).

Components of a traditional information retrieval system experiment include the:

1. *indexing system* – indexing and searching methods and procedures (an indexing system can be human or automated);
2. *collection of documents* – text, image or multimedia documents, or document surrogates (for example bibliographical records);
3. *defined set of queries* – which are input into the system, with or without the involvement of a human searcher; and
4. *evaluation criteria* – specified measures by which each system is evaluated, for example 'precision' and 'recall' as measures of relevance. Recall is the proportion of relevant documents in the collection retrieved in response to the query. Precision is the proportion of relevant documents amongst the set of documents retrieved in response to the query.

In these experiments, it has been found that recall and precision tend to be inversely related (that is, as recall increases, precision decreases, and vice versa). Researchers tend to favour recall over precision, while busy professionals wish to maximise precision.

Traditional online systems based on Boolean logic return document sets with no relevance rankings (although output can be sorted by, for example, date or alphabetically). More recent information retrieval systems based on natural language query processing attempt relevance rankings of system output. However, such rankings relate to closeness of fit to the query statement, and not to human relevance rankings. Precision ratings can be made at specified intervals, for example ratings for precision at ten documents, fifty documents, or 100 documents. Many sophisticated means of generating relevance rankings are under development.

System-oriented experiments for information retrieval system evaluation

These experiments usually involve a very large test collection of documents, a standardised set of queries and associated relevance judgments. Queries are successively batched into the information retrieval system which calculates recall and precision measures for each query.

Box 7.4: The TREC experiments

Perhaps the best known and most extensive of the system-oriented experiments for information retrieval systems evaluation are the recent TREC experiments. (TREC stands for Text REtrieval Conferences, organised by the US-based National Institute of Standards and Technology (NIST)). Annual workshops are intended to foster text retrieval research, based on very large test collections and many universities, research institutions, and industry bodies worldwide participate in the TREC experiments. It is a mammoth experimental research project of global proportions and some significant information retrieval systems research advances have been achieved.

'One of the goals of the TREC conferences has been to support the comparison of IR system performance on a common task of realistic difficulty. Comparisons of IR systems must deal with the possible effects on the IR system performance measure of non-system factors such as: topics; system-topic interactions; supporting hardware and software; additionally, if a human searcher is involved [note that for most of the TREC experiments this has not been the case] searchers' abilities (innate and learned), topic-searcher interactions, searcher-system interactions; various higher-order interactions' (Lagergren and Over 1998, p. 164).

The fundamental research issue arising from the TREC experiments is: Do these systems-oriented laboratory experiments reflect the real-world experience of human searchers? Some of the more recent TREC experiments are designed to address this concern, especially through the 'interactive track' experiments.

Given the diversity and extent of this project, it is not possible to do justice to describing it in this brief introductory text. For further details refer to the NIST Website http://www.trec.nist.gov and to sources such as the ACM SIGIR Conferences on Research and Development in Information Retrieval, where many of these experiments are reported in detail. See Lagergren and Over (1998) for a clear explanation of a very sophisticated TREC-6 experimental design involving nine sites worldwide.

Pre-experimental research designs

Definitions and overview

Pre-experimental designs, as the term suggests, are rudimentary in nature, bearing some similarities to a true experiment, but lacking many of the controls, which makes them very weak methodologically.

These designs utilise neither experimental and control conditions, nor randomisation: hence there is no meaningful comparison. Also, they are unable to overcome the problem of rival explanations. Pre-experimental designs are better avoided where there are alternatives: but often there are no alternatives.

Some particular pre-experimental research designs

One-shot case study

This is the simplest type of pre-experimental design. A person, group, organisation, or object is exposed to something and the effects observed. For example, an organisation that has previously relied mainly on paper-based information systems establishes an intranet. After the system has been fully implemented, observations are made and conclusions are drawn on the impact of the innovation on the organisation – on management-staff relationships, the nature of work, culture, communication patterns, etc. While this is the basis of much everyday reasoning, it has little 'scientific' validity. There are no meaningful comparisons; and many possible sources of rival explanations (for example selection, history). The basic model is depicted in Figure 7.6.

$$X \longrightarrow O$$

Figure 7.6: Basic model for one-shot case study

However, the single-case study does have its place, and is widely used in information systems and information management research. (Case study research was discussed in Chapter 6.)

One-group pre-test/post-test design

The basic model for group pre-test/post-test design is shown in Figure 7.7.

$$O_1 \longrightarrow X \longrightarrow O_2$$

Figure 7.7: Basic model for pre-test/post-test design

In introducing a pre-test prior to the treatment, followed by a post-test, this design is a slight improvement on the one-shot case study. It rules out the problem of selection in that subjects are tested first. However, it does not eliminate other rival explanations. It is also a very weak research design.

Static group comparison

This is a correlational design used in field studies rather than a true experiment. Subjects are divided into groups on the basis of whether or not they possess 'X', the characteristic under study, and observations are subsequently recorded. Randomisation is not used. (This approach was discussed in Chapter 5.)

Advantages of pre-experimental research designs

As pre-experimental designs are weak methodologically, they should be avoided when there are alternatives. However, they may constitute the only option open to the researcher. They are acceptable for an exploratory study, where the researcher wishes to gain insights or gather ideas, and not to generalise to the wider population.

Limitations of pre-experimental research designs

Lacking the controls of a true experiment (that is, randomisation and experimental and control conditions), there are serious threats to internal validity with pre-experimental designs. They provide no meaningful comparison, and are unable to overcome the problem of rival explanations. Also, external validity/generalisability is suspect as samples are not representative.

Quasi-experimental research designs

Definitions and overview

Quasi-experimental research designs are a compromise between the true experiment and pre-experimental designs. Where possible, it is preferable to use a true experiment, but frequently that is not an option, especially in natural settings. These designs are a considerable improvement methodologically on pre-experimental designs. In quasi-experimental designs, groups are formed by deliberate selection, not by random assignment.

Through the use of quasi-experimental designs in field research, it is possible to infer or hint what might be likely causal links, but not to *prove* causality. This is because techniques used are *correlational* in nature: correlation demonstrates that two factors are in some way related, but does not enable us to infer that 'A' caused 'B' – 'B' could have caused 'A'; or both 'A' and 'B' may have been caused by another external factor.

Particular types of quasi-experimental research designs

Pre-test/post-test nonequivalent control group design

This design is a combination of the static group comparison design and a one-group pre-test/post-test pre-experimental design. In combining features of both, it is more interpretable than either. This design includes pre-test information of baseline levels (enabling selection to be ruled out as a rival explanation), and a comparison group. However, like other quasi-experimental designs, the groups are not formed by random assignment, but rather by deliberate selection. The basic model is shown in Figure 7.8.

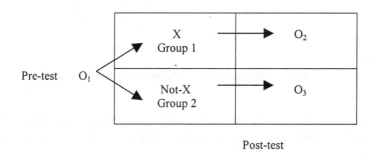

Figure 7.8: Basic model for pre-test/post-test nonequivalent control group design

Porch (1995) used this type of quasi-experimental design to investigate the impact on job satisfaction of introducing an integrated library information management system into her organisation. She identified the introduction of the new system as the independent variable; the consequent changes in job characteristics and the motivating potential of the job, and changes in job satisfaction as the dependent variables; and as moderating variables – expectations of the effects of the new technology on the job, the perceived usefulness of the new technology; prior knowledge, and age, gender and job category. As not everyone in the organisation had access to the new system, Porch was able to set up the 'naturally-occurring' equivalents of an experimental group (those who would use/ used the new system) and a control group (those without access to the new system). She tested job satisfaction using the well-known 'Job Diagnostic Survey' (Hackman and Oldham) instrument. This was applied first before the introduction of the new library information management system (pre-test), and reapplied to the same individuals in both the experimental and control groups after the system had been installed and fully operational for some time (post-test). Changes both within and between the two groups were traced, and conclusions drawn.

This design can also be described as an 'explanatory survey'. See Chapter 5 for a discussion of explanatory surveys and of the constraints on inferring causation with this type of *correlational* study. See also the discussion of Kobasa's (1979) study given in Chapter 5, which exemplifies this type of design.

Interrupted time series design

Interrupted time series designs are an extension of the pre-experimental one-group pre-test/post-test design, using a series of observations/measurements both before and after the treatment condition. Conducted over an extended period (that is, a 'longitudinal' design), the time-series design enables the elimination of maturation and testing as threats to internal validity. With this design, trends in data can be examined before, during and after the treatment. The basic model for this design is shown in Figure 7.9.

$$O_1 \ O_2 \ O_3 \ O_4 \longrightarrow X \longrightarrow O_5 \ O_6 \ O_7 \ O_8$$

Figure 7.9: Basic model for interrupted time series design

A variation on the design is the introduction of a second group as a control, who are tested at the same intervals as the treatment group, but are not exposed to the treatment condition.

Regression-discontinuity design

The regression-discontinuity design builds on the pre-experimental static group comparison design by introducing a series of comparison groups, addressing the issue of selection as a potential rival explanation. It is a 'cross-sectional' design. The basic model is depicted in Figure 7.10.

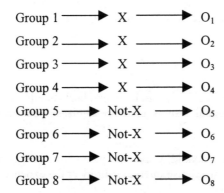

Group 1 $\longrightarrow$ X $\longrightarrow$ O_1

Group 2 $\longrightarrow$ X $\longrightarrow$ O_2

Group 3 $\longrightarrow$ X $\longrightarrow$ O_3

Group 4 $\longrightarrow$ X $\longrightarrow$ O_4

Group 5 $\longrightarrow$ Not-X $\longrightarrow$ O_5

Group 6 $\longrightarrow$ Not-X $\longrightarrow$ O_6

Group 7 $\longrightarrow$ Not-X $\longrightarrow$ O_7

Group 8 $\longrightarrow$ Not-X $\longrightarrow$ O_8

Figure 7.10: Basic model for regression and discontinuity experiments

Advantages of quasi-experimental research designs

In field research (for example an investigation into the social effects of introducing automated ticketing machines on public transport) where it is not possible to use a true experimental design, a quasi-experiment is an option which does permit some hints of causality to be made – but not conclusively proven. While internal validity remains an issue with quasi-experimental designs, their external validity is greater than with the true experiment.

Limitations of quasi-experimental research designs

Compared with the true experiment, the internal validity of quasi-experimental designs is much lower. However, each of the designs just considered does attempt to eliminate particular types of rival explanations.

Conclusion

Researchers use experimental designs when they wish to explore possible causal links between variables. However, there are major constraints on causal inference in research, and there is a trade-off between a researcher's ability to establish definite causal links and to generalise findings to real-life settings. This is the classic conflict between internal and external validity in research design. The laboratory experiment is the design best suited to establishing causation, but it suffers from a limited generalisability to natural settings. On the other hand, the field experiment enables greater generalisation to an external population, but sacrifices the ability to establish causation with any degree of confidence. While it is theoretically possible to maximise both factors by first undertaking laboratory research followed by a field experiment, cost is likely to be a major deterrent.

Discussion questions

- The experiment is often described as the research method best suited to isolating causal links. However, even in experimental designs, there are significant constraints on establishing causation. Discuss.

- There is a trade-off between internal validity and external validity in experimental designs. Laboratory experiments maximise internal validity at the expense of external validity. On the other hand, field experiments maximise external validity at the expense of internal validity. Is it possible for a researcher to maximise both internal and external validity in experimental design? If so, how?

- Detail a scenario, define hypotheses and outline an appropriate experimental design for:

  - a laboratory experiment testing particular human-computer interaction variables; and

  - a field experiment involving the introduction of a new computer system into an organisation, or a new technology into society.

- Consider possible variations to your experimental design (above) given cost and time constraints. How might conclusions which can validly be drawn from experimental results vary from highly sophisticated to much simpler experimental designs?

Further readings

Bickman, Leonard and Rog, Debra J. (eds.). (1998). *Handbook of applied social research methods.* Sage: Thousand Oaks, CA. (Chapter 6 – Boruch, Robert F. Randomized controlled experiments for evaluation and planning; Chapter 7 – Reichardt, Charles S. and Mark, Melvin M. Quasi-experimentation.)

Christensen, Larry B. (1997). *Experimental methodology.* 7th edn. Allyn and Bacon: Boston.

Clarke, Geoffrey M. and Kempson, Robert E. (1997). *Introduction to the design and analysis of experiments.* Wiley: London.

Leedy, Paul D. with contributions by Newby, Timothy J. and Ertmer, Peggy A. (1997) *Practical research: Planning and design.* 6th edn. Merrill: Upper Saddle River, NJ: (See, in particular, Chapter 10 – The experimental study.)

Neuman, William Lawrence. (1997). *Social research methods: Qualitative and quantitative approaches.* 3rd edn. Allyn and Bacon: Boston. (Chapter 8 – Experimental research.)

Sekaran, Uma. (1992). *Research methods for business: A skill-building approach.* 2nd edn. Wiley: New York. (Chapter 5 – Experimental designs.)

Singleton, Royce and Straits, Bruce C. (1998). *Approaches to social research.* 3rd edn. Oxford University Press: New York. (Chapter 7 – Experimentation; Chapter 8 – Experimental designs.)

Yandell, Brian S. (1997). *Practical data analysis for designed experiments.* Chapman and Hall: London.

References for Chapter 7

ACM-SIGIR Conferences on Research and Development in Information Retrieval, for example *SIGIR98: Proceedings of the 21st Annual International ACM-SIGIR Conference on Research and Development in Information Retrieval*, 24-28 August 1998, Melbourne, Australia, eds. W. Bruce Croft, Alistair Moffatt, C.J. van Risjenbergen, Ross Wilkinson and Justin Zobel. ACM Press: New York.

Cleverdon, C. W. (1962). *Aslib Cranfield Research Project: Report on the testing and analysis of an investigation into the comparative efficiency of indexing systems.* Aslib: London.

Cleverdon, C. W., Mills, Jack and Keen, Michael. (1966). *Aslib Cranfield Research Project: Factors determining the performance of indexing systems.* College of Aeronautics: Cranfield, Beds.

Foskett, A. C. (1996). *The subject approach to information.* 5th edn. Library Association Publishing: London.

Kanaga, K.R. and Flynn, M. (1981). The relationship between invasion of personal space and stress. *Human Relations*, **34** (3), pp. 239-248.

Kidder, L.H. (1981). *Selltiz, Wrightsman and Cook's research methods in social relations.* 4th edn. Holt, Rinehart and Winston: New York.

Kobasa, Suzanne C. (1979). Stressful life events, personality and health. *Journal of Personality and Social Psychology,* **37** (1), pp. 1-11.

Lagergren, Eric and Over, Paul. (1998). Comparing interactive information retrieval systems across sites: The TREC-6 Interactive Track Matrix Experiment. In *SIGIR98: Proceedings of the 21st Annual International ACM-SIGIR Conference on Research and Development in Information Retrieval*, 24-28 August 1998, Melbourne, Australia, eds. W. Bruce Croft, Alistair Moffatt, C.J. van Risjenbergen, Ross Wilkinson and Justin Zobel. ACM Press: New York, pp. 164-172.

National Institute of Standards and Technology (US). (1999). [TREC experiments] (online). http://trec.nist.gov/

O'Reilly, C.A. (1978). The intentional distortion of information in organisational communication: a laboratory and field investigation. *Human Relations, 31* (2), pp. 173-193.

O'Reilly, C.A. and Roberts, K.H. (1974). Information filtration in organisations. *Organizational Behavior and Human Performance, 11* (2), pp. 2 53-265.

Porch, Celina. (1995). Planning and implementing your first research project: It's easier than you may think. *Australian Academic and Research Libraries, 26* (2), pp. 86-96.

Tombros, Anastasios and Sanderson, Mark. (1998). Advantages of query biased summaries in information retrieval. In *SIGIR98: Proceedings of the 21st Annual International ACM-SIGIR Conference on Research and Development in Information Retrieval,* 24-28 August 1998, Melbourne, Australia, eds. W. Bruce Croft, Alistair Moffatt, C.J. van Risjenbergen, Ross Wilkinson and Justin Zobel. ACM Press: New York, pp. 2-10.

CHAPTER 8

System development in information systems research

Frada Burstein

Objectives

At the end of this chapter you will be able to:

- recognise the place of system development within the information systems research cycle;

- appreciate the role of system development as a way of theory testing/exploration; and

- understand the difference between system development for practical application and as a tool for research.

Specifics of information systems research

The main aim of conducting information systems research is to '... study the effective design, delivery, use and impact of information technology [IT] in organisations and society' (Keen 1987, p. 3). The study of information systems can be regarded as a multi-disciplinary endeavour (Land 1993; Avison and Fitzgerald 1991).

A set of research methodologies has been explored for use in the general field of information systems research; each being appropriate for different aspects of research depending on the domain and philosophical position of the researcher. Consensus has not been reached on one framework classifying all research approaches suitable for information systems. Attempts at such classifications are usually framed around different research contexts within the 'theory building – theory testing – theory refinement' cycle. On the other hand, from the point of view of the analysis of data about information systems, studies are following both of the major research traditions, that is, positivist and interpretivist (Galliers 1992; Land 1993; Shanks, Rouse and Arnott 1994).

The range of information systems studies requires various approaches, each with its advantages and disadvantages depending on the research focus and application domain. Empirical approaches include case studies, surveys, laboratory and field experiments, and various types of simulation and forecasting on the positivist/scientific side of research, as well as action research and ethnographic studies on the qualitative/interpretive side. These various research approaches allow the capture of a more or less open picture of changes in relation to information systems development and usage in the organisations.

Systems development, a particular research method, has been omitted from most *taxonomies* or classifications of information systems research methods, mainly due to the assumption that system development does not lie within the information systems research domain. The legitimacy of systems development, as a valid research activity within the technical domain of information systems, has been debated extensively and justified by Nunamaker and Chen (1990), Nunamaker, Chen and Purdin (1990-1991) and Parker et al. (1994). Information systems research has been perceived by some as purely a social science thus ignoring the technological side of it. However, this view is changing as more researchers recognise that information systems involve an unavoidable technical component (Cecez-Kecmanovic 1994). Systems development as a research method may bridge the gap between the technological and the social sides of information systems research. This aim can only be achieved by building an application of the proposed theory as an illustration of the 'technical' side information systems domain (Parker et al. 1994).

Systems development approach

Systems development has also been referred to as *engineering* type research also known as *social engineering* (Cecez-Kecmanovic 1994) or *systems development* (Nunamaker, Chen and Purdin 1990-1991; Nunamaker and Chen 1990). It is a developmental and engineering type of research, which falls under the category of applied science (Nunamaker, Chen and Purdin 1990-1991). It is grounded on the philosophical belief that development is always associated with exploration, advanced application and operationalisation of theory (Hitch and McKean 1960).

The research approach may be classified as 'research and development' where scientific knowledge is used to produce '...useful materials, devices, systems, or methods, including design and development of prototypes and processes' (Blake 1978, cited in Nunamaker and Chen 1990, p. 631).

Where systems development fits into the research cycle

In the existing taxonomy of research methods (Neuman 1994; Galliers 1991), a distinction is drawn between basic and applied research. The first is directed towards 'theory building' and contributes to the advancement of the general knowledge of the society. To a certain extent, this kind of research can only be conducted after a field of study has reached a certain level of maturity and has all the parameters clearly defined to be generalisable in a form of an appropriate theory: an established paradigm (Kuhn 1970). Applied research, on the other hand, is targeting a specific problem relating to the introduction or functioning of an information system. In this respect applied research is closer to practice. The result of such research is intended to help practitioners to be better informed about their work environment and do their job better (Neuman 1994).

Building a theory involves discovery of new knowledge in the field of study and can be seen as rarely contributing directly to practice. On the other hand, after the theory is proposed it needs to be tested in the real world to show its validity and to recognise its limitations, as well as to make appropriate refinements according to new facts and observations made during its application. Information systems still represents a relatively new discipline, resulting in a need and place for both types of research. It can be argued that, in any large research project, there are identifiable elements of basic and applied research, usually one followed closely by the other.

Testing can be conducted in more or less natural settings. For this purpose both interpretive and pseudo-scientific approaches can be applied. Interpretive studies represent a less controlled mechanism of applied exploration, whereas experimentation requires a certain level of control over some of the variables under consideration. At least this approach assumes an ability to differentiate between independent, dependent and controlled variables.

In our context of information systems research, the theory proposed may lead to the development of a *prototype* system that is intended to illustrate the theoretical framework. In some more organisation- or society-oriented studies the role of such a system can be played by the existing piece of technology or the process of technology transfer. Thus, systems development becomes a natural, intermediate step linking basic and applied research. In their seminal paper on the role of systems development in information systems research, Nunamaker, Chen and Purdin (1990-1991) argue that systems development represents a central part of a multi-methodological information systems research cycle (see Figure 8.1).

This extended structure, with a systems development component integrated into the research cycle, presents a complete, comprehensive and dynamic research process. It allows multiple perspectives and flexible choices of methods to be considered in various stages of the research process.

We must note here that time limitation is one of the factors to be considered before the decision is made whether systems development can be included in the project. However, if the scope of the prototype is closely monitored to conform to an absolute minimum necessary to illustrate the theory, it is possible to complete one cycle of system(s) development based on the given theory, followed by an evaluation-observation within the time limitations of a student project.

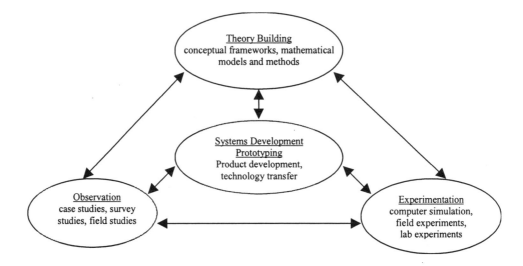

(adapted from Nunamaker, Chen and Purdin 1990-1991, p. 94).

Figure 8.1: A multi-methodological approach to information systems research

Generalised research process model

First proposed in the early 1990s, this systematic approach to information systems research, which includes some systems development, has now been revised and represents the generic research process. As a model, this approach is advocated by the Center for the Management of Information (CMI), University of Arizona (see Figure 8.2). In this case, prototype building takes an equal third part as a mechanism for theory testing and refinement. The central part of the model, *new concept*, evolves through the dynamic feedback loops between various testings of the prototype. The tests are conducted in more or less natural settings (laboratory experiments and field tests) and produce results which are intended to be reflected in the new version of the prototype. On the other hand, the prototype reflects back to the concept under consideration.

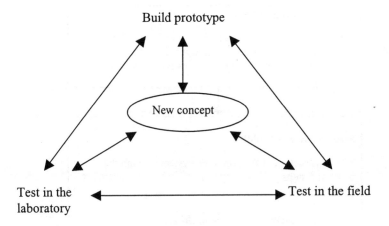

Build prototype

New concept

Test in the
laboratory

Test in the field

(available from http://www.cmi.arizona.edu/)

Figure 8.2: CMI Arizona Research Model

The systems development research procedure

Research methods generally address an existing problem from which a hypothesis is formed and analysed. Analysis may involve prototypical system(s) development to provide proof-of-concept. For fundamental research, this evidence or artifact is important as it becomes the focus for expanding or continuing research (Nunamaker, Chen and Purdin 1990-1991).

The systems development approach denotes a way to perform research through exploration and integration of available technologies to produce an artefact, system or system prototype. Systems development focuses on the theory testing, more than theory building aspects of research, allowing a smooth progression from development to evaluation. It could be thought of as proof-by-demonstration (Nunamaker, Chen and Purdin 1990-1991). On the other hand, it can be useful to consider as part of the exploratory stage of information systems study, when the aim is to observe and evaluate the implications or any other effects of introducing a particular new technology into the organisation. Systems development research process is of an iterative nature, as illustrated in Figure 8.3.

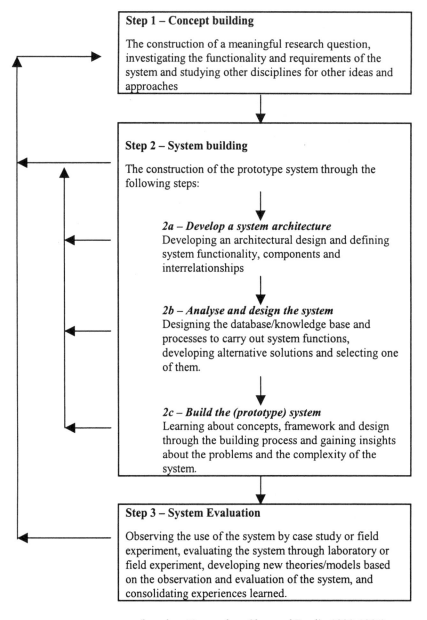

(based on Nunamaker, Chen and Purdin 1990-1991)

Figure 8.3: The systems development method

Thus, a systems development methodology comprises three major steps: concept development; system building; and system evaluation. As is described above, the concept building stage involves some theory building, where the theory can be illustrated by a system. The major difference between this approach as a research method and conventional systems development is that the major emphasis is on the concept that the system has to illustrate, and not so much on the quality of the system implementation. At the beginning of such a project the implementation has to be justified, in terms of whether there is another existing system that is capable of demonstrating the features of the concept under investigation. The evaluation stage of the systems development method is also different from the testing of a commercial system. It has to be done from the perspective of the research questions set up during the concept-building stage, and the functionality of the system is very much a secondary issue.

This approach has been tested in a number of student projects (Sharma 1996; Maynard 1997; Wafula and Swatman 1995; Ngu 1995). Furthermore, following a systems development research cycle, Fung (1997) performed an experimental evaluation in a laboratory experiment setting of the case-based organisational memory system that was developed by Sharma (1996) for her Masters project. The advantage of the approach is that it can be conducted as a sequence of related projects, where each complements the others in a full cycle of theory development and testing throughout the system development.

Systems development research framework is also relevant to information management research. For example, Schauder (1997) reports on research in library-based electronic publishing. This study has been conducted with the aim of evaluating comparative advantages in using CD-ROM and Internet as a media for electronic publishing of Australian materials. This work can be viewed as an example of Step 3 in the systems development methodology. (See Figure 8.3.) The concept under consideration, electronic publishing, has been implemented using two proposed media: INFORMIT CD-ROM publications; and VICNET as an example of Internet-based publishing. The author reviews the results of the experiences gained from these two electronic publishing media. This study can be regarded as a kind of a field test conducted in order to justify the validity and usefulness of the concept. The results feed back into the initial concept development identifying the elements of the communicative transaction associated with this type of publishing. (See Kaufer and Carley (1993).)

Conclusion: The role of system building in information systems research

Research in information systems has been criticised as being too conceptual (Hamilton and Ives 1992; Galliers 1992). However, the concepts under investigation in the information systems study are usually not, by themselves, the main purpose of the research. They rather provide the opportunity to frame the findings in relation to the theories and contribute to the core body of knowledge of the field. Due to its rather applied nature, systems development is essential to prove underlying theories (Nunamaker, Chen and Purdin 1990-1991).

Information systems researchers have argued that it is insufficient that 'a product of IS [information systems] research be *useful* – it must also be *used*' (Parker et al. 1994, p. 198). Hitch and McKean (1960) also stress the interdependence between development and research. The systems development approach allows a link between theory building and applied information systems research. It is also argued that systems development research can be viewed as an example of action research, when the researcher is involved in the construction and testing of a method or an information system in a real-world context (Burstein and Gregor 1999; Baskerville and Wood-Harper 1998).

At the same time, Nunamaker, Chen and Purdin (1990-1991, p. 103) suggest that 'building a system in and of itself does not constitute research' and it is inappropriate for the major contribution of an information systems research project to be some software (Galliers 1993). Where systems are needed as proof-of-concept of an information systems research investigation, development is a valid research activity (Parker et al. 1994). Weber (1987) warns the reviewers of research papers to carefully evaluate the contents of papers describing systems development and design as the major focus. He argues that the design presented in such papers has to be justified by some preliminary basic research, and described in the context of some theory of information systems, or some theory should be used 'to predict the likely success or failure of a design' (Weber 1987, p. 9). Otherwise, such papers cannot be classified as quality research papers.

Nunamaker and Chen (1990) state five criteria for use of systems development as a research methodology in information systems research:

- an important phenomenon can only be studied in the process of system building;

- the result of system(s) building will contribute to the advancement of the information systems theory;

- there are some hypotheses or propositions derived from the theory that require to be experimentally tested through the development process;

- the new system design provides a better solution to the existing problem; and

- some generalised results can be expected from the experiences gained with system building and design (based on Nunamaker and Chen (1990, p. 637)).

Systems development should derive results of practical value to the domain under study, while contributing to theoretical and practical knowledge in the field. The product of information systems research and the lessons learned from development may lead to innovations in the field of information systems as 'knowledge is learning by doing'.

Key summary points

The following summarises the key points raised in this chapter:

- building a system in and of itself does not constitute research;

- development of a prototype is a part of information systems research life cycle;

- building a system is a part of the evolutionary process of research (feasibility assessment); and

- software engineering is a method of systems development research.

Discussion questions

- What are the main advantages of following systems development model research?

- Is it always important for the researcher to establish the most appropriate research approach before the beginning of the project? How will you determine which method is the best for a given situation?

- When in your research project should you decide on whether or not to follow a systems development research approach? Give the reasons for your answer.

- Is it always feasible and advisable to build a system in information systems research? Explain.

Further readings

Cecez-Kecmanovic, D. (1994). Engineering type information systems research: A discussion on its position and quality. In *Proceedings of the 5th Australian Information Systems Conference*. Department of Information Systems, Monash University: Caulfield, Vic., pp. 767-770.

Nunamaker, J., Chen, M. and Purdin, T. (1990-1991). Systems development in information systems research. *Journal of Management Information Systems*, **7** (3), pp. 89-106.

Parker, C., Wafula, E., Swatman, P.M.C. and Swatman P. (1994). Information systems research methods: the technology transfer problem. In *Proceedings of the 5th Australian Information Systems Conference*. Monash University, Department of Information Systems: Caulfield, Vic., pp. 197-208.

References for Chapter 8

Avison, D.E. and Fitzgerald, G. (1991). Information systems practice education and research. *Journal of Information Systems*, **1** (1), pp. 5-17.

Baskerville, R. and Wood-Harper, A.T. (1998). Diversity in information systems action research methods. *European Journal of Information Systems*, **7**, pp. 90-107.

Blake, S.P. (1978). *Managing for responsive research and development.* W.H. Freeman and Company: San Francisco.

Burstein, Frada and Gregor, Shirley. (1999). The systems development or engineering approach to research in information systems: An action research perspective. In *Proceedings of the 10th Australasian Conference on Information Systems (ACIS '99),* Victoria University of Wellington, New Zealand, 1-3 December 1999.

Cecez-Kecmanovic, D. (1994). Engineering type information systems research: A discussion on its position and quality. In *Proceedings of the 5th Australian Information Systems Conference*. Department of Information Systems, Monash University: Caulfield, Vic., pp. 767-770.

CMI Arizona Research Model. (online). http://www.cmi.arizona.edu/

Fung, Soon Meen. (1997). Experimental evaluation of a case-based organisational memory information system. Master of Computing (by Research) Thesis. Monash University, Caulfield, Vic.

Galliers, R. (1991). Choosing appropriate information systems research approaches: a revised taxonomy. In *Information systems research: Contemporary approaches and emergent traditions,* eds. H. E. Nissen, H.K. Klein and R. Hirschheim. Elsevier Science

Publishers B.V.: North Holland, pp. 327-345.

Galliers, R. (1992). Choosing information systems research approaches. In *Information systems research: Issues, methods and practical guidelines,* ed. R.D. Galliers. Blackwell Scientific Publications: Oxford, pp. 144-162.

Galliers, R. (1993). Doctoral information systems research in Britain: A report on the Information Systems Doctoral Consortiums, 1991-1993. *Journal of Information Technology,* **8**, pp. 118-120.

Hamilton, S. and Ives, B. (1992). MIS research strategies. In *Information systems research: Issues, methods and practical guidelines,* ed. R.D. Galliers. Blackwell Scientific Publications: Oxford, pp. 132-143.

Hitch, C.J. and McKean, R.N. (1960). *The economics of defense in the nuclear age.* Harvard University Press: Cambridge, Ma.

Kaufer, David S. and Carley, Kathleen M. (1993). Communication at a distance: The influence of print on sociocultural organization and change. Lawrence Erlbaum Associates: Hillsdale, NJ.

Keen, P.G.W. (1987). MIS research: Current status, trends and needs. In *Information systems education: Recommendations and implementation*, eds. R.A. Buckingham, R.A. Hirschheim, F.F. Land and C.J. Tully. Cambridge University Press: Cambridge, pp. 1-13.

Kuhn, T. S. (1970). *The structure of scientific revolutions.* 2nd edn. University of Chicago Press: Chicago.

Land, F. (1993). The information system domain. In *Information systems research: Issues, methods and practical guidelines,* ed. R.D. Galliers. Blackwell Scientific Publications: Oxford, pp. 6-13.

Maynard, Sean. (1997). A multiple constituency approach to DSS evaluation. Master of Computing (by Research) Thesis. Monash University: Caulfield, Vic.

Neuman, W. L. (1994). *Social research methods: qualitative and quantitative approaches,* 2nd edn. Allyn and Bacon: Needham Heights, Ma.

Ngu, Daniel. (1995). Knowledge modelling for intelligent decision support. Honours thesis. Monash University: Caulfield, Vic.

Nunamaker, J.F. and Chen, M. (1990). Systems development in information systems research. In *Proceedings of the 23rd Hawaii International Conference on Systems Science.* IEEE Computer Society Press: Los Alomitos, Ca, pp. 631-639.

Nunamaker, J., Chen, M. and Purdin, T. (1990-1991). Systems development in information systems research. *Journal of Management Information Systems,* **7** (3), pp. 89-106.

Parker, C.,Wafula, E., Swatman, P.M.C. and Swatman, P.A. (1994). Information systems research methods: The technology transfer problem. In *Proceedings of the 5th Australian Conference on Information Systems.* Monash University, Department of Information Systems: Caulfield, Vic., pp. 197-208.

Schauder, Don E. (1997). Publishing on CD-ROM and Internet: Experiences from two library based enterprises. (online). http://educate1.lib.chalmers.se/IATUL/proceedcontents/abs196/Schauder.html

Shanks, Graeme, Rouse, Anne and Arnott, David. (1993). *A review of approaches to research and scholarship in information systems.* (Working Papers Series). Department of Information Systems, Monash University: Caulfield, Vic.

Sharma, Ramita. (1996). Knowledge acquisition for case-based decision support: A hierarchical classification approach. Master of Computing (by Research) Thesis. Monash University: Caulfield, Vic.

Wafula, E.N. and Swatman, P.A. (1995). Merging FOOM and MOSES: A semantic mapping from object-Z to structural object-oriented diagrams. In *Proceedings of the 6th Australian Information Systems Conference (ACIS '95).* University of Western Australia: Perth, pp. 27-30.

Weber, R. (1987). Toward a theory of artifacts: a paradigmatic base for information a systems research. *Journal of Information Systems*, **Spring,** pp. 3-19.

CHAPTER 9
Action research
Majola J.H. Oosthuizen

Objectives

At the end of this chapter you will have a better understanding of:

- philosophies on which action research is based;

- nature of the action research method;

- what is involved in rigorous action research; and

- techniques used in action research.

The philosophy of action research

While action research can be explained from the perspective of many philosophies, this chapter explains it primarily from the perspectives of hermeneutics and action science. Hermeneutics is defined as:

> hermeneutic, *adj*. interpretative; explanatory.
> hermeneutics, *n*. the science of interpretation, esp. of the Scriptures (*Macquarie dictionary* 1996, p. 820).

Action research is a hermeneutical or interpretive approach (Galliers 1992). The terms 'hermeneutical' and 'interpretive' could be used as synonyms (Phillips 1992). The first is derived from Greek, the second from Latin. Hermeneutics was initially driven by the need to interpret Scriptures, but gradually came to be used in a wider context:

> In short, then, hermeneutics came to be seen as the study of the interpretation and understanding not only of texts, but also of human actions and customs and social practices (Phillips 1993, p. 103).

Action research could be seen as a hermeneutical approach concerned with the study of human actions and social practice. Within social sciences, action research could be seen to belong to the critical social sciences stream of philosophies, of which action science (Argyris, Putman and Smith 1985) is one. A key difference between critical science and other philosophies of social science is that it is necessary for the researcher to participate in the action (Galliers 1992, p. 157), while other social science philosophies require that the researcher must have a detached, unbiased observer role. The action researcher could also search for knowledge as observer, but he or she will also be actively involved in the bringing about of certain practical outcomes (Foster 1972), particularly those that provide practical benefits to the client (Galliers 1992). The search for practical benefits to the client is frequently a main reason why action research is chosen as a method.

The cyclic nature of action research (further described below), is another core characteristic. Lewin (1946) is attributed as possibly the first writer who explicitly proposed the use of the cyclic action research approach, as a means to simultaneously solve problems and to generate new knowledge (Marrow 1969).

Sources of action research

The action research approach has been applied in many fields, such as in organisations and organisational behaviour, community development, schools, agriculture, architecture and environmental planning (Deschler and Ewert n.d.). Applications in the various fields resulted in several traditions of action research, each with its own writers and descriptions (Brown 1993; Selener 1992). Some of the texts that provide an overview of action research are by Whyte (1964; 1991), Kemmis and McTaggart (1982) and Stringer (1996). Some of the texts that describe action learning, which is similar but more concerned with action as opposed to research, are by Revans (1983), Pedler (1991), Schon (1991), Dixon (1994), and Argyris and Schon (1996).

A number of Internet communities exist (see Dick 1992), which focus on action research. The description of action research which follows is primarily based on the Action Research and Evaluation On Line (AREOL) course material of Dick (1997a-o). Dick's Internet listserver (ARLIST-L) (Dick 1997) is one of the primary means by which action researchers, scholars and practitioners from all over the world can communicate with one another.

The nature of action research

Action research has a two-fold focus: action in practice and knowledge generation through rigorous research. It is sometimes shown as:

Action research = action + research.

Action research is often intended to bring about change of practice, while creating knowledge at the same time. These combined characteristics make it useful for exploratory research to bring about improvement of practice, or to propose new solutions to practical problems.

Action research is usually carried out in discrete cycles, where later cycles are used to challenge, support and refine insights and results from previous cycles. When the approach is used appropriately, this cyclic feature of action research can be used not only to propose theory, but also to test theory. However, like case studies, action research is usually concerned with single situations, for example, a single group or company. Therefore, although the approach can generate theoretical propositions that go beyond single situations, action research is seldom seen as an appropriate approach to test the general applicability of theories.

Action research is critically reflective. The need for reflection exists in times when current action does not produce the desired results, and change is needed. This is why action research is often concerned with change in practice. The need for critical reflection is the reason why action research is cyclic: it calls for a process that has reflection as a fundamental part of each cycle. In its most basic form, the action research cycles can be illustrated as shown in Figure 9.1.

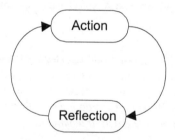

Figure 9.1: The most basic action research cycle

Note that reflection is based on experiences of action, and that the whole constitutes a learning process. Such a process is particularly useful in situations where effective nominal theory for practice is absent. In these situations the action research cycles function like mini-experiments in practice. Through reflection on previous action a new theory of the form 'if I do X, then Y will occur' is proposed, which is then applied in practice, and tested, in a cyclic manner. In each cycle, the result indicates whether the theory worked, and thus if it can be used as basis for further refinement, or if it needs to be changed.

This cyclic approach of knowledge generation and testing allows the process to remain flexible. There is no reason why a cycle should use the same methods as previous cycles; the action of every new cycle is simply based on the best possible action that could be proposed after reflecting on the previous cycles. In this sense, action research as research methodology is different from other research methods, where is it expected that the method is designed in detail, in advance, and used throughout the research project. This does not mean that deliberate and detailed planning are excluded from action research. In fact, the action research cycle is often proposed to contain multiple elements, such as shown in Figure 9.2 where planning is part of the cycle.

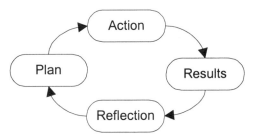

Figure 9.2: A typical action research cycle

Some writers, such as Pedler (1991), point out that steps, such as planning, action and observation, are action in themselves, and therefore each of them could also be followed by reflection. However it is not so easy, and sometimes artificial, to separate such steps in practice. It is important that deliberate reflection goes on throughout action research. To ensure this, reflection ought to be scheduled *at least* once after the main action, for every formal action research cycle.

The techniques used within action research also influence the nature of the action research cycles (some of the major techniques are outlined below). For example, the Delphi approach, outlined in Chapter 12, typically uses only a few, but very distinct cycles. In contrast, when the dialectic approach is used, the individual cycles are many and hardly visible, being embedded in the communication between people. The dialectic approach, which is introduced later, is based on communication with an emphasis on the identification and resolution of differences.

A final fundamental characteristic of action research is that it is concerned with the improvement of practice. Here the issue to draw attention to is that the choice and contribution of participants will determine the extent to which practice is captured and improved. Like other participants, the researcher will work hard to contribute to solutions. Because action research is concerned with real practice, it is important that the stakeholders are sufficiently represented. Dick (1997f) lists the informants, interpreters, planners, implementers, facilitators, researchers and recipients as functions that participants could have. This list provides ideas of stakeholders that could be involved. In practice, some participants could take on many roles.

The selection of people to be involved in action research should, and usually does, receive special attention. To better manage action research projects, professional action researchers develop skills related to human interaction issues, such as in conflict and communications management. The concern of the action researcher with human interaction issues is a distinguishing feature of action research when compared with many other research methods.

Rigorous action research

The previous section described the nature of action research. This section discusses how action research can be carried out in a *rigorous* manner, to generate reliable and valid knowledge.

In discussing rigour in action research, Dick (1997m) proposed a framework, which divides the action research process into seven components (see Figure 9.3). Rigour should be applied to each of these components and to their relationship to one another.

The framework positions the action components (A and D) as concerned with intervention, while the research components (B and E) are concerned with understanding and knowledge. Action research projects should address both interests simultaneously.

The framework further distinguishes between the action research strategies (A, B, and C), and the day-to-day implementation issues thereof (tactics D, E, and F). For example, in the action research described in Box 9.1 below, main strategies of the research projects were the scheduling of cycles that involve deliberate and documented action and reflection; the using of multiple measures to achieve rigour; and the building of a causal model of the findings, which was simulated and the results compared with reality. At the same time the day-to-day process involved communication, contributions, judgment and decisions by, with, and about real and busy professionals. It was found that these short-term tactical issues demanded more attention than the higher level strategic issues, and that they were critical in the overall success of the projects.

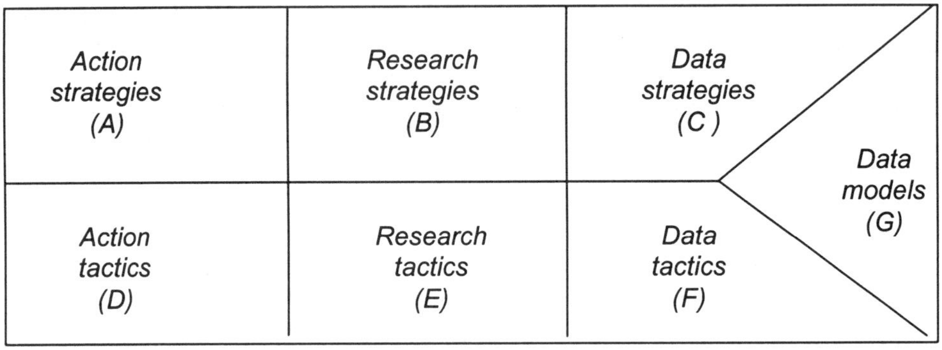

Action strategies (A)	Research strategies (B)	Data strategies (C)	Data models (G)
Action tactics (D)	Research tactics (E)	Data tactics (F)	

(Dick 1997m)

Figure 9.3: Components of the action research process

Both action and research generate knowledge and information, which could be called data (C and F). An important challenge for action researchers is to capture this data in some way or another. For example, in the action research, reported in Box 9.1 every major cycle resulted in a formally distributed report, while minor cycles were recorded in minutes of meetings, email, and specially created documents. There was an emphasis on documenting understanding and subjecting it to scrutiny.

Finally, the insights from the action research projects must be presented in ways that are conveniently understandable to humans, for example in the form of frameworks or models (G). The research projects in the example included a number of formal and informal presentations to people at various levels in the organisation, in meetings up to two days long. In those meetings, managers and staff could question the understanding and make further recommendations.

Rigour should be applied to the components of the framework, from a research as well as an intervention perspective. From the intervention perspective, rigour is typically framed as, 'How do we know that the insight into practice and the solutions that you suggest are valid and appropriate in practice?' From a research perspective it is typically framed as, 'How do we know your theorisation is valid?'

Box 9.1: Example of action research to investigate cognitive processes underlying strategy development

The aim of the research was to investigate the nature of strategy development processes within a single large mining company, with the purpose of providing systems to enable effective strategy development. To improve validity of insights, four independent projects were carried out over a period of 18 months (which is quite long for graduate action research projects), to investigate the processes:

Scenario building – investigation of strategy development processes without involvement of computer modelling.

Third party model use – investigation of computer modelling to develop strategy, which was originally done by a third party consulting company.

Modelling based analysis – development of computer models for strategy development, with emphasis on formal analysis.

Modelling based on expert participation – development of computer models for strategy development, with emphasis on expert participation rather than formal analysis.

Each of these projects was concerned with different products and involved different participants. Each also went through multiple cycles, and sometimes cycles within cycles. The researcher participated actively, alongside company participants, in all of these activities. The main tasks of the researcher were to ensure the research process systematically went through cycles which involved critical reflection, and to record observations and insights from each cycle.

As mentioned above, details of the action research process can seldom be planned systematically and up front, as is usually the case with experiments concerning natural laws. This is because action research is a process through which solutions and insight are generated in an explorative manner. Participants (including the researcher) must remain responsive to new insights that are gained through action and reflection, and new methods may be used at each stage of the process, as appropriate.

Although professional action research also strives for rigour, the approach is somewhat different from that of the natural sciences. In summary, Dick (1997g) proposes six ways through which rigour can be improved in action research projects:

- use each cycle to disconfirm emerging interpretation;

- critique and refine methods at each cycle;

- collect data and interpretations in each cycle, for testing in later cycles;

- search for and address divergent data;

- use the literature as sources of possible disconfirmation; and

- subject the changes resulting from the process to disconfirmation.

Dick (1997j) discusses these issues in much more detail. The action research, outlined in Box 9.1, applied the following measures:

- *The viewing of participants' action as a primary criterion* – the client's willingness to act on conclusions is an indication of validity and desirability from the perspective of the client (Argyris, Putman and Smith 1985). In the study the client's investment in resources and time was very significant, which indicated a high degree of validity from the perspective of the client.

- *The use of continuous seeking of disconfirming evidence* – in the study the insights and interventions were of strategic importance to the company researched, and high calibre people were employed as managers and business analysts to address this area. Little chance existed to get any strategic recommendation accepted, unless such recommendations were seen to be valid, and to add significant value.

- *The use of different methods of observation and interpretation* – the study used many methods of communication, evaluation and data presentation, as indicated above. In addition, the insights were incorporated into a system dynamics model of the subject domain, in order to simulate and review the logic and consequences.

- *The use of different informants* – the study involved independent and geographically dispersed business units, departments, and participants, thereby ensuring that a wide range of perspectives was taken into account.

- *Multiple case studies* - the action research involved four independent projects and four independent industries, thereby effectively increasing the number of instances researched.

- *The asking of different questions for equivalent information* – the four projects of the study approached the issue researched from four different angles.

- *The use of different researchers* – many of the participants of the study were involved in company strategic development in a serious way, and they regularly questioned insights and solutions of their own accord.

- *The comparison of results with the literature* – throughout the study, the literature was researched extensively, to validate ideas and to find better solutions.

- *The collection, explication, and reflection on data in each cycle, to allow continuous scrutiny* – the study enforced processes to consistently capture and store information for each cycle.

- *The use of multiple cycles* – the study involved twenty-one major cycles, which often contained many minor cycles.

As these measures show, even though some would argue that it is harder to achieve rigour in action research than in more conventional methodologies of research, the use of multiple measures help to increase the rigour, and thus the validity of the research findings. In research the issue is not so much if the findings are valid, but rather if they are seen to be valid.

Techniques that can be used in action research

The previous section described basic action research *strategies*. This section briefly outlines some *techniques or tactics* that can be used in action research. For a more detailed discussion of the techniques, please consult the references.

It is important not to see these techniques as alternative action research methods, because each cycle ought to address the issues investigated in the most appropriate manner. Therefore the action researcher must build competencies in various techniques that could be used in the action research process. That said, the action researcher is confronted by a general attitude in research, which expects consistency in techniques. For that reason it is often advisable to break a study up into a number of projects, and to be consistent in the use of techniques for each project.

Convergent interviewing

Dick (1990; 1997l) describes convergent interviewing as an information collection technique that can be used when the researcher is unsure what information needs to be collected. This technique directs focus on the issues that are important.

Typically, it starts with a single broad question from the interviewer to the interviewee. Then the interviewer simply tries to let the interviewee talk for as long as possible, typically for an hour or so. This should give the interviewer an idea of what is important and what not. From this point similar interviews are conducted with further interviewees. During later interviews, the interviewer explores for explanations on issues where interviewees disagree. Where the interviewees agree, the interviewer tries to find disconfirming views. In this manner the interviews converge on issues of importance. They seek to resolve disagreements and strengthen views by trying to disconfirm them. Initially the content is unstructured, but it gradually converges on specific issues. The convergent interview process itself, however, is structured.

Delphi, face-to-face

The Delphi technique is described in Chapter 12. Dick (1997b; 1997k; 1997l) describes a version thereof, which is not the usual mailed survey approach through which experts make forecasts, but a face-to-face approach. He suggests that principles of Delphi can be used in facilitated face-to-face meetings, for example to build understanding and consensus among different disciplinary groups. To illustrate, individuals can be asked to propose answers to certain issues. Those answers are listed and fed back to a wider group. Disagreements can then be discussed in small groups and results fed back to the wider group. The whole group can then discuss the issues and decide on priorities. Based on the results individuals can reconsider their individual answers, and the process continues until a high degree of consensus is reached while a wide range of information has been considered in the process. Alternatively, the skilled facilitator can use principles of Delphi to mimic the Delphi process while the group physically remains together.

Dialectics

Dialectical – or hard consensual – approaches aim at consensus by focusing on *disagreements* and trying to resolve them. For example, one person may say: 'I claim [so and so]', to which the response is, 'I do not agree, but I am interested. Please explain more'. Dick (1997k) suggests dialectical approaches as pursuing three goals:

- to provide honest information, directly communicated;
- to strive to understand what others say; and
- to use disagreement to identify where more information is needed.

In essence, the dialectic approach welcomes disagreement as a way to generate better information on which decision making can be based. To achieve this, the researcher and participants actively try to create situations that avoid defensive behaviour. Since defensive behaviour is the usual behaviour of people (Argyris and Schon 1996), special processes are required to achieve these goals, such as those described by Argyris and Schon (1996) and Dick (1997k).

Evaluation

The evaluation literature is extensive, as references to Patricia Rogers (Dick 1997o), Marcia Conner (Dick 1997n) and the AREOL bibliography (Dick 1997a) indicate.

Dick (1997m) suggests that evaluation methods could sometimes be used to carry out action research, and action research could sometimes be used to carry out evaluation. Within the context of job appraisal, for example, Dick proposes that most people would rather do a good job than a bad job. However, the connotation attached to evaluation or appraisal is often negative. Action research could be used as an approach to generate mutual understanding and to work towards better solutions, rather than to focus on judgment.

Focus groups

The structured focus group technique (Dick 1990; 1997c; Krueger 1988; Morgan 1988; Stewart and Shamdasani 1990; Babbie 1992) is described in Chapter 15. It is an exploratory interview technique, which is similar to convergent interviewing discussed in a previous section. A main difference between these techniques is that focus groups will concentrate on one or more predetermined issues or questions (such as how well a new product is expected to sell), whereas convergent interviews *identify* such issues or questions. Both techniques start with relatively open-ended questions, but proceed to address those questions in a structured way. The two approaches can often be used in a complementary manner. The main aim of structured focus groups is thus to collect information: it is not an approach used to get consensus or agreement.

When used in action research, the focus group technique requires participation. Dick (1997c) recommends that the facilitator should emphasise that all participants must have time to think and opportunity to state their own views, even if those views do not agree with the mainstream view. Debate is discouraged, because it may hinder people from volunteering information. The process could be carried out in phases (or cycles), including creating awareness and preparation; introduction of specific issues and views; collection of contextual information; interpretation of information; and integration of views. One of the main advantages of focus group techniques is that they quickly and efficiently explore specific issues.

Group feedback analysis

Group feedback analysis (Dick 1997d; 1997i; Heller 1969) typically involves a pre-compiled questionnaire to which participants respond in face-to-face settings. After collation of the results, the participants will typically assist with the interpretation, planning and improvement of the insights. It is better than surveys, primarily because it involves and encourages feedback from the participants. Generally group feedback analysis is not recommended for situations where serious conflicts exist between participants.

'Option-one-and-a-half'

The option-one-and-a-half technique (Dick 1997e) is a dialectic technique where agreement is created out of disagreement. It is used when there are two or more solutions, and using the best of the existing options develops a new solution. Essentially the process lists the options, then it lists the advantages and disadvantages of each option, from which a final solution is developed. Various techniques can be used within each of the phases of the process.

Search

There are many techniques under the generic name of 'search', including futures search, search workshops, or search conferences. Dick (1994; 1997h) describes a particular version of search, being a one-day technique for community planning. In that version the aim is to develop a public shared vision for people who work together. The process begins with plans to work towards that vision. The workshop is structured and typically goes through the following steps:

- Introduction and overview
- Review of the community history
- Development of a shared vision

- Taking account of wider influences
- Identifying stakeholders
- Strengthening the shared vision
- Identifying key plans
- Setting up working parties (Dick 1994; 1997h)

This technique is very similar to strategic planning approaches used for decades. A useful contribution of Dick's description is that it outlines the actual tactics used during such meetings.

Conclusion

Action research is a methodology that is concerned with knowledge and improvement of human action. In the example of action research discussed in this chapter, for example, it was used to investigate strategy development, and also to see how certain solutions could affect that action. Action research is an approach that develops knowledge and solutions in a cyclic manner, where each cycle is used as an opportunity to reflect on the validity of theories and effectiveness of solutions based on field experience in the preceding cycles. That insight is then used to proceed with action in the next cycle.

Action research is concerned with purposeful human action. Purposeful human action cannot be assumed to follow stable patterns, as in natural science. This is because humans react in changing ways to a changing world based on their perceptions and value systems, which also change. Action research builds understanding about this dynamic environment.

A consequence of the dynamic environment is that knowledge about the purposeful human action must be validated, if possible: at the time of action, where it happens, by those involved in, or affected by, the action. Stable knowledge can be built when the same theories appear to hold true from cycle to cycle, from situation to situation, from time to time, and from group to group. But even then, action research should be seen as potentially building transferable knowledge, rather than generalisable knowledge.

Discussion questions

- Why is the researcher's participation in the intervention process important in action research?

- How can action research be made rigorous?

- As research methods, how do experiments compare with action research?

- Why does action research (and action science) focus on specific situations and not on general laws?

Further readings

Argyris, C., Putman, R., and Smith, D. M. (1985). *Action science: Concepts, methods and skills for research and intervention*. Jossey-Bass: San Francisco. (Compares the different philosophies of science, explaining action science in that context.)

Phillips, D. C. (1993). *Philosophy, science and social inquiry: Contemporary methodological controversies in social science and related applied fields of research*. Pergamon Press: New York. (Discusses various paradigms of social science, and how they relate.)

References for Chapter 9

Argyris, C., Putman, R. and Smith, D. M. (1985). *Action science: Concepts, methods and skills for research and intervention*. Jossey-Bass: San Francisco.

Argyris, C. and Schon, D.A. (1996). *Organizational learning II*. Addison-Wesley: Reading, Ma.

Babbie, E. (1992). *The practice of social research*. 6th edn. Wadsworth: Belmont, Ca.

Brown, L. D. (1993). Becoming a PAR practitioner. In *Profiles of participatory action researchers*, eds. J. Forrester, J. Pitt and J. Welsh. Einaudi Center for International Studies, Cornell University and Department of City and Regional Planning: Ithaca, NY.

Deschler, D. and Ewert, M. (n.d.). *Participatory action research: Traditions and major assumptions*. Cornell University: Ithaca, NY.

Dick, B. (1990). *Convergent interviewing*, Version 3. Interchange: Brisbane, Qld.

Dick, B. (1991). *Helping groups to be effective: Skills, processes and concepts for group facilitation*. Interchange: Brisbane, Qld.

Dick, B. (1992). Links to action research (and other) resources elsewhere. (online).
http://elmo.scu.edu.au/schools/sawd/ari/links.html

Dick, B. (1994). *Search: A participative community planning process.* 6th edn.
Interchange: Brisbane, Qld.

Dick, B. (1997). Arlist-L: Action research mailing list. (online).
http://www.scu.edu.au/schools/sawd/ari/arlist.html

Dick, B. (1997a-o). *Action research and evaluation online (AREOL), Archives*:

(1997a). Action learning bibliography. (online).
http://www.scu.edu.au/schools/sawd/arr/al_biblio.html

(1997b). Face-to-face delphi. (online).
http://www.scu.edu.au/schools/sawd/arr/delphi.html

(1997c). Structured focus groups. (online).
http://www.scu.edu.au/schools/sawd/arr/focus.html

(1997d). Group feedback analysis. (online).
http://www.scu.edu.au/schools/sawd/arr/gfa.html

(1997e). Option one-and-a-half. (online).
ftp://ftp.scu.edu.au/www/arr/options

(1997f). Participative processes. (online).
http://www.scu.edu.au/schools/sawd/arr/partproc.html

(1997g). Rigor in action research. (online).
http://www.scu.edu.au/schools/sawd/arr/rigour.html

(1997h). Search. (online).
ftp://ftp.scu.edu.au/www/arr/search

(1997i). Action research and evaluation online (AREOL), session 05: Achieving participation. (online).
http://www.scu.edu.au/schools/sawd/areol/areol-session05.html

(1997j). Action research and evaluation online (AREOL), session 06: Achieving rigor. (online).
http://www.scu.edu.au/schools/sawd/areol/areol-session06.html

(1997k). Action research and evaluation online (AREOL), session 07: Collecting and analyzing data. (online).
http://www.scu.edu.au/schools/sawd/areol/areol-session07.html

(1997l). Action research and evaluation online (AREOL), session 08: Convergent interviewing. (online).
http://www.scu.edu.au/schools/sawd/areol/areol-session08.html

(1997m). Action research and evaluation online (AREOL), session 10: Evaluation as action research. (online).
http://www.scu.edu.au/schools/sawd/areol/areol-session10.html

(1997n). Recommended learning, training, and development books by Conner, M. L. (online).
http://www.scu.edu.au/schools/sawd/arr/trdbooks.html

(1997o). Meta-evaluation bibliography. (online).
ftp://ftp.scu.edu.au/www/arr/meta-eval_bib

Dixon, N. (1994). *The organizational learning cycle: How we can learn effectively.* McGraw-Hill: London.

Foster, M. (1972). An introduction to the theory and practice of action research in work organizations. *Human Relations*, **25** (6).

Galliers, R. (ed.) (1992). *Information systems research: Issues, methods and practical guidelines*. Blackwell Scientific Publications: Oxford.

Heller, F. (1969). Group feedback. Analysis: A method of action research. *Psychological Bulletin*, **72**, pp.108-117.

Kemmis, S. and McTaggart, R. (1982). *The action research planner*. Deakin University: Waurn Ponds, Vic.

Krueger, R.A. (1988). *Focus groups: A practical guide for applied research*. Sage: Newbury Park, Ca.

Lewin, K. (1946). Action research and minority problems. *Journal of Social Issues*, **2**, pp. 34-46.

The Macquarie dictionary. (1987). 2nd rev. edn. Macquarie Library: Chatswood, NSW.

Marrow, A.J. (1969). *The practical theorist: The life and work of Kurt Lewin.* Basic Books: New York.

Morgan, D.L. (1988). *Focus groups as qualitative research.* Sage: Newbury Park, Ca.

Pedler, M. (ed.) (1991). *Action Learning in Practice.* 2nd edn. Gower: Aldershot, Hants.

Phillips, D.C. (1992). *The social scientist's bestiary: A guide to fabled threats to, and defences of, naturalistic social sciences.* Pergamon: New York.

Phillips, D.C. (1993). *Philosophy, science and social inquiry: Contemporary methodological controversies in social science and related applied fields of research.* Pergamon Press: New York.

Revans, R.W. (1983). *ABC of action learning,* Chartwell Bratt: Bromley, UK.

Schon, D.A. (1991). *The reflective practitioner.* Basic Books: New York.

Selener, D. (1992). Participatory action research and social change: Approaches and critique. Unpublished doctoral dissertation. Cornell University: Ithaca, NY.

Stewart, D.W. and Shamdasani, P.N. (1990). *Focus groups: Theory and practice.* Sage, Newbury Park, Ca.

Stringer, E.T. (1996). *Action research: A handbook for practitioners.* Sage: Thousand Oaks, Ca.

Whyte, W.F. (1964). *Action research for management.* Irwin-Dorsey: Homewood, Il.

Whyte, W.F. (1991). *Participatory action research: New forms of participation in industry and culture.* Sage: Newbury Park, Ca.

CHAPTER 10
Ethnography
Solveiga Saule

Objectives

At the end of this chapter you will be able to:

- understand the major differences between positivist and interpretivist philosophical frameworks within ethnographic study;

- describe the particular attributes of constructivist, critical theory and post-modern philosophical frameworks within ethnographic study;

- articulate the differences between post-positivist, constructivist, critical theory and post-modern philosophical frameworks; and

- discuss the issues of validity in relation to the subjectivity of the researcher and the researched, and the ways in which they are influencing ethnographic philosophical frameworks.

Introduction

Whereas the goal of natural sciences is to proffer scientific explanations of phenomena and events, the goal of the social sciences is to grasp and understand the meaning of social phenomena, social groupings and events (Schwandt 1998, p. 223). Both positivist and interpretivist ethnographic study is used to elucidate aspects of people's lives and make sense of social and/or cultural phenomena. This chapter will discuss both positivist and interpretivist approaches to ethnographic study, with an emphasis on the latter. (Basic concepts related to positivist and interpretivist approaches to research are discussed in Chapter 2.) The emphasis in this chapter is on the theoretical underpinnings of ethnography. The practical aspects and examples are included in Chapter 16.

Ethnographers study people in their everyday contexts and utilise the medium of the text to describe and theorise on the nature of the topic they are studying. Experimental conditions developed by the researcher are not used within interpretivist ethnographic study, as is the case with some positivist approaches to the study of behaviour, culture, community and identity. Instead, interpretivist ethnographers observe, study and analyse the actions and behaviour of people as they live and work in their natural environments, in order to contribute to ethnographic literature and theory.

By evaluating the words of the people being studied in their natural environment, and analysing and theorising upon the various systems of knowledge constructed within the confines of a social grouping, the ethnographer is able to provide what Geertz (1973) describes as a 'thick description'. Geertz first used this expression when he stated: 'Culture is not a power, something to which social events, behaviours, institutions, or processes can be causally attributed; it is a context, something within which they can be intelligibly – that is thickly – described' (p. 14). Within this 'thick description', the contradictions, complexity and multiplicity of realities, as they are articulated by the studied and as they are observed and analysed by the ethnographer, are presented.

Many ethnographic researchers work towards developing theory regarding the object of study. Theory in this context does not imply the conventional use of the word theory, where theory 'predicts' and 'controls'. Instead, ethnographic literature provides a 'contribution to public dialogue about a particular topic' (Hammersley 1992, p. 15) that does not present the 'truth' about a particular phenomenon, but an interpretation of an event, community, behaviours, or social grouping. As ethnographic studies are not a 'science' in conventional terms, the strategic approaches cannot be uniformly predetermined. Thus, ethnographic researchers develop different frameworks that shape how they will conduct a study, analyse the data, and present it in its final form. Concomitantly, interpretations about what ethnography can and should be, and critiques of these interpretations, have developed since the first ethnographic studies of the colonial period evolved.

This chapter will look at the various frameworks[1] that have been developed in the twentieth century, with a focus on the last thirty years. Positivism, post-positivism, constructivism, critical theory, and postmodernist ethnography will be discussed in detail. It will also

---

[1] The term 'frameworks' in the case of sciences and the humanities signifies assumptions, norms, values and traditions that create, perpetuate and institutionalise particular forms of knowledge within a particular field of study (Stanfield 1998, p. 346).

discuss the problem of validity and the subjectivity of the researcher and the researched, to elucidate the predominant issues within ethnographic writing today.

Positivist approaches to the analysis of culture and social phenomena

Ethnographic research in the modern era rose to the fore during the colonial period with the ostensibly scientific study of the cultures of 'strange peoples' living in the colonial outposts. These studies were carried out under the guise of anthropological research and were used to discern the cultural systems, social structures and organisations of tribal peoples. They were also used as attempts to account for the origins, histories, and multiplicity of races, cultures and civilisations that existed (Vidich and Lyman 1998, p. 47). Within the developed world, ethnographic study emerged in the early twentieth century at the University of Chicago. It was used to study the subaltern and immigrant communities existing in Chicago at the time (Hammersley 1990, p. 3). The use of ethnographic research then branched out into other social sciences, including education, social work and communications, as culture emerged as a new 'problematic object of description and critique' (Clifford 1986, p. 3).

Ethnographers were initially positivist in outlook, and adopted a realist framework. It was held that there was one reality 'out there' to be realised (Guba 1990, p. 19), that was free of the influences of time and context, subjective interpretations of reality and human agency. Consequently, positivists asserted that through a scientific and rigorous analysis, universal truths could be discerned that lay beneath the superficial diversities of different cultures. The validity or quality of an inquiry was determined by the conventional benchmarks of scientific 'rigour'. Internal validity (the appropriateness and applicability of the methodology used); external validity (whether the data can be generalised and the theory can be utilised for similar phenomena); and reliability (quality of the research being carried out) are the bases on which a positivist ethnographic study were judged (Guba and Lincoln 1998, p. 213).

Positivists also believed that, as scientists responsible for the illumination of the truths behind human activity and behaviour, they approached research as neutral and objective observers. The background of the observer was purported to have no influence on the outcomes of the study. The subjectivity of the observer, including the observer's own history, political outlook, and relationship with the people and/or phenomena being researched, were consequently not accounted for, nor considered a problem. Positivists did not feel that, as researchers engaging in empirical study, their own life histories could colour their choice of methodology, data analysis and strategy of theoretical development.

Within anthropology, texts written by Malinowski (1922), Mead (1960) and Bateson (1972) are prime examples of ethnographic study where the culture under study is presented as timeless, and representative of that culture's 'essence'. In these texts, the ethnographers portray themselves as objective and distant observers of the culture. Data are presented as a direct reflection of an indisputable reality, rather than the ethnographer's interpretation of a constructed reality.

Post-positivism developed after the Second World War. It rejected the professedly scientific and universalist approach towards the study of cultures and peoples as carried out by positivists. Post-positivists believed that, while there was a reality 'out there', the ways in which individuals and social groups interpreted a particular reality were multiple and dependent on the variables of environment, a social grouping's history, and resources. There was therefore not a singular truth that could be brought to light by rigorous and scientific study, although there was one reality to be discerned. Post-positivism opened up the way to the interpretivist approach to ethnographic study.

Interpretivist philosophical frameworks

Contrasting positivist and interpretivist attributes

The flexibility of interpretation inherent in the canon that reality 'is constructed' has inevitably lead to the development of different beliefs in how ethnographic study should be carried out, its goals in undertaking analysis, its attributes, and its relationship to society. Constructivism and critical theory will be discussed in the next section, as they are prime examples of the different ways in which ethnographic research has come to be theorised.

The advent of interpretivism instigated a number of changes in the philosophical attributes of ethnographic research. First, interpretivists prefer to elucidate local stories over grand theories. Their primary goal is to understand the social actor's definitions, interpretations, and understandings of a situation and/or event (Schwandt 1998, p. 221). The actors being studied are recognised as individuals who construct meaning and, hence, have their own interpretations of reality. 'That is, particular actors, in particular places, at particular times, fashion meaning out of events and phenomena through prolonged, complex processes of social interaction involving history, language, and action' (Schwandt 1998, p. 222).

Second, interpretivism considers the context in which a particular event or phenomenon occurs to be integral to ethnographic study. Positivists tend to ignore context by selecting a particular subset of variables with which to carry out analysis while obscuring other variables from consideration that could, if considered, alter the findings of a research project (Guba and Lincoln 1998, p. 195). Interpretive approaches do not separate meaning from the 'facts' of a phenomenon. Facts have little weight within an interpretive ethnographic study. The ways in which these facts are interpreted by individuals and social groupings are the central categories of study. Interpretivist philosophy posits that facts cannot be independent of context as all reality is perceived through interpretation. Hence, facts cannot be collected and tested against an objectively determined hypothesis because the facts cannot exist outside of a subjectified context (Guba and Lincoln 1998, p. 199).

Third, as briefly mentioned in the first section, interpretivists recognise the role that the ethnographer plays in the development of an ethnographic text. Along with those being studied, it is accepted that ethnographers, too, approach ethnographic study as individuals with histories, and philosophical and political attitudes towards life and study which will dictate a particular set of political, moral, ethical and cultural values within the context of the research. Interpretivists reject categorically the positivist's assertion that social phenomena and culture can be studied and analysed with scientific neutrality and objectivity.

Three predominant philosophical frameworks within ethnographic study are constructivism, critical theory and post-modern ethnography. These are discussed in the next section, together with the questions of validity, and the subjectivity of the researcher and the researched.

Constructivism

Constructivists believe that reality is constructed through discourse; what we take to be self-evident truths are in fact the products of complicated discursive practices (Schwandt 1998, p. 236), where individuals construct reality through communicating with others. Guba (1990, p. 25) states: 'Reality exists only in a mental framework (construct) for thinking ...' which is expressed and articulated through a variety of modes of social organisation and interaction, such as language, ritual, religion, morality and politics. Constructivists maintain that each individual possesses sentiments about what is true. This notion of 'truth' guides individuals in their continuing interpretation of events, social phenomena, and the behaviours of other people.

Such an approach to ethnographic study has three important implications. First, it is accepted that a theory cannot adequately and categorically explain the nature of a given phenomenon or the presence and activities of a social grouping. Since reality exists only in the minds of each individual, and each individual's perception of what is real will differ from others, reality itself is pluralist and relativist and cannot be pinned down. Thus, ethnographic interpretations of the reality of a phenomenon can be multiple and will often conflict. One truth will not exist at any point. Rather, 'truth is a matter of the best-informed and most sophisticated construction on which there is consensus at any given time' (Schwandt 1998, p. 243).

Second, constructivists recognise that the researcher cannot be objective. The divide between the researcher and the subject of research is tremendously blurred (Guba 1990, p. 26). Despite this blurring of boundaries, constructivists encourage the researcher to maintain a semblance of partiality within the study to increase the validity of the study. As the subjectivity of the researcher cannot be avoided, constructivists believe that it is necessary for researchers to make their potential influence on the interpretation of the narrative explicit in the ethnographic text, thus allowing the reader of the text to have an understanding of the researcher's background and position.

Third, constructivists believe that it is only through the researcher's interaction with those being studied that the nature and shape of social constructs can be elucidated (Guba and Lincoln 1998, p. 207). They use an inductive approach to methodology, listening to the issues addressed by the participants in the study, and building analysis and theory from that.

Constructivists engage in participant observation practices, outlined in Chapter 16 and use methods such as grounded theory to construct an ethnographic research text. In short, constructivists work with the people being studied through a dialectic of analysis, critique, and reanalysis (Schwandt 1998, p. 243).

Critical theory

Critical theorists share similarities with constructivists in that they believe that reality is interpreted by social actors as individuals or within social groupings. However, they diverge philosophically from constructivists because of their identification with historical realism. They believe that, although reality is constructed, a history of repression determined by patriarchal, ethnocentric, agist and other social stratification systems influences the ways in which people choose, and are able, to construct their own realities (Denzin and Lincoln 1998, p. 187). When undertaking ethnographic study and writing ethnographic texts critical theorists use:

- the emancipatory aspects within the philosophies of feminism (Duran 1991; Fonow and Cook 1991);

- ethnic and racial studies (Collins 1990; hooks (sic) and West 1991; Stanfield 1998);

- anti-colonialism (Spivak 1988);

- post-modernism (Brown 1995; Van Maanen 1995); and

- Marxism (Nelson and Grossberg 1988).

The adherence to emancipatory politics means that their interpretation of their own roles as writers of culture differs from constructivists and others working within interpretivist frameworks of ethnographic study.

Critical theorists write value-laden texts, where notions of impartiality and objectivity are entirely absent. They believe that ethnographic literature should not simply describe and construct theory that reflects a particular social and/or cultural phenomenon. 'Critical theorists seek to produce transformations in the social order, producing knowledge that is historical and structural, judged by its degree of historical situatedness and its ability to produce praxis or action' (Denzin and Lincoln 1998, p. 187). Researchers not only have the responsibility of ensuring they are accountable for representing the people being studied fairly and forthrightly. Nor can the ethnographic work merely be a source of 'thick description', where the text reflects the words, interpretations and actions of the social actors involved. They must also incorporate an emancipatory narrative into the text. Thus, investigators will have an obvious and strong influence on the data analysed as they approach the ethnography from an overt ideological stance.

Four main problems occur within critical theory ethnographies. First, Hammersley (1990, pp. 67-69) believes that the emancipatory model of critical theory suffers 'from too narrow a conception of the appropriate audience for research' as well as the range of topics that are judged to be of importance. Only those who fit under the category of 'oppressed' are deemed worth studying.

Second, critical theory loses much of its validity as an authentic account or interpretation of a phenomenon because of its ideological approach. Hammersley (1992) asks the poignant question: At what point is the line drawn within the ethnographic text to distinguish between political insight and political prejudice? (p. 15) At what point within critical theory does an ethnographic text become diatribe for a political movement and/or ideal, rather than a scholarly look into the culture of a social grouping?

Third, Fine (1998, p. 152) wonders about the potential for the maintenance of stereotypes within critical theory. By stating that there are particular disadvantaged groups which need to be given a voice through critical theory, those groups which may not be visible to the ethnographer's eye may remain invisible. Also, the complexities and contradictions that exist in any social grouping may be ignored in order for the researcher to write a 'good' emancipatory ethnographic text.

Fourth, many critical theorists write that knowledge about a particular social group can only be realised and articulated by members of the community itself (Spivak 1988; Omolade 1994). Subscribing to this belief means that it is only individuals from within a community, be it a lesbian community or an African-American community, who are able to write for and about that community. The need for validity and rigour of analysis becomes lost, and the possibility of qualified individuals who are removed from a social grouping contributing to ethnographic analysis is no longer possible.

Triangulation

A paradox exists within ethnographic research. How does one create objective theory through the study of subjective human experiences? The answer to this question is that an 'objective science' of subjective human experiences cannot exist. Instead, ethnographers attempt to develop dense and widely scoped texts whose validity can be ensured through the use of triangulation.

All of the frameworks within interpretivist ethnographies utilise triangulation. Triangulation (discussed in Chapter 2) is a practice that uses a range of techniques and extracts, ideas, and concepts from a variety of frameworks. This encourages the validation of an ethnographic text as it emphasises the use of multiple methods and theoretical constructs (Guba 1990, p.

23) thus adding rigour, breadth, and depth to a study (Denzin and Lincoln 1998, p. 4). Four different modes of triangulation are commonly used. First, data triangulation allows the ethnographer to access a variety of data sources for the study. Second, ethnographers use several different researchers and/or evaluators. Third, multiple theories and/or perspectives are adopted to interpret a single set of data. Fourth, multiple methods are undertaken to study a single problem or phenomenon (Janesick 1998, p. 46). Although triangulation will not prove one hundred percent effective in establishing valid ethnographic texts, it does show a text's readers and the ethnographer's peers that a degree of rigour has been applied to the amalgamation, analysis and writing up of the data.

Continuing critiques of the main philosophical frameworks within interpretivist ethnographic research

Despite attempts to encourage a level of scientific rigour in interpretivist ethnographies, there are still issues raised in regard to the validity of ethnographic texts, the subjectivity of the ethnographer and of the individuals and/or social groupings under study. These issues will be discussed in this section.

The proof of validity

Geertz (1973, p. 5) believes that the goal of anthropology is to act as an 'interpretive science in search of meaning, not an experimental science in search of laws'. Within an interpretivist framework ethnographies are not objective narratives but subjectified accounts of culture. Within the social sciences the quality and validity of an ethnographic study may be hard to gauge because there does not exist a quantifiable and literal mechanism through which to conduct research. Hammersley (1990, p. 73) states: 'We can never be absolutely certain about the validity of any knowledge claim'.

Consequently, ethnographic texts are often criticised for not being scientific enough in methodology and philosophical framework (Hammersley 1990, p. 3). This largely stems from the fact that there does not exist an over-arching standard of evaluation. Interpretivists do not attempt to validate a study on standards established by the scientific, positivist framework, which as mentioned previously, have standards of internal and external validity. Instead, interpretivists use notions of trustworthiness and authenticity.

Ethnographic writers must rely on persuasiveness and utility rather than 'scientific proof' in arguing their position (Denzin and Lincoln 1998, pp. 187-202). They need to write in a creative fashion, utilising Geertz's (1973) notion of 'thick description', rather than writing in a dry fashion that merely conveys facts and figures. The ethnographers must be critically subjective (Reason 1998, p. 280). Along with providing evidence of having successfully used triangulation, they must explain in the text their own perceptions of the roles they played in amalgamating the data, as well as their own thoughts on the ways in which they may have or may not have influenced their study. Finally, it is important to note that each particular branch of the social sciences will have a certain set of criteria to determine the validity of an ethnographic text. These criteria will be grounded in the canonical texts that a particular community believes to be integral to its mission. What is used as a set of criteria in one community may not be considered cogent in another (Altheide and Johnson 1998, pp. 288-289). It is up to the researcher to query the elements of these criteria, and to write the ethnographic text accordingly.

Issues of authorship and the subjectivity of the researcher

In the past thirty years, interpretivist ethnographers have debated the influences of political, cultural, ethical, and social outlooks on the ways in which researchers will approach, undertake, and write up ethnographic studies. While schools such as the critical theory school of ethnography actively encourage the participation of the researcher within the research process, other schools, such as the constructivist school encourage the researcher to pursue a certain level of impartiality. Despite substantive dialogue regarding this issue, writers on ethnographic methodology are still debating this topic.

Although interpretivist ethnographic practices recognise the subjective nature of ethnographic study, the influence of such filters as race, class, gender, and ethnicity are still not adequately accounted for. Yet it is these categories which integrally affect the ways in which a situation or community is interpreted. Writers, such as Spivak (1988) and hooks (sic) (1988) believe that ethnographers cannot represent, in any form, the voices of the 'Other', as they are personified in the studied. Instead, studies conducted on social groupings and particular cultural practices can only be undertaken by people residing within that particular community.

As mentioned in the case of critical theorists, for ethnographers, in general, this is also not a viable solution to the problem of representation. Instead, a more considered and moderate stance needs to be taken. As Fine (1998, p. 142) states:

> As researchers we need to position ourselves as no longer transparent, but as classed, gendered, raced and sexual objects who construct our own locations, narrate these locations, and negotiate our stances with relations of domination.

By acknowledging themselves as authors of texts, and by making apparent their own histories within ethnographic texts, the authors become visible and public (Denzin 1998, p. 317). This makes them bear more responsibility for the ways in which the information is presented and data interpreted. Van Maanen (1995, p. 3) suggests that in making themselves publicly known within ethnographic texts, authors/researchers reinforce the validity of their findings. He states: 'It is ... the ethnographer's direct personal contact with others that is honoured by readers as providing a particularly sound basis for reliable knowledge'.

The subjectivity of the researched

Concomitant with the stance that there does not exist a set of truths waiting to be discovered through ethnographic study, is the fact that those who are being studied will not be entirely representative of the phenomena and/or social grouping under analysis. Nor are they presenting themselves in their entirety. Subjects being studied cannot be presented in an objective or holistic fashion. Instead, they are able to only articulate part of the story, as they see it, and wish the interviewer to witness. They can only offer accounts or stories of their own interpretations of events. Thus, there is the problem of how the ethnographer decides whose data will be sought out and/or used for the purposes of the research text? At what point should there be a retreat from analysis and interpretation of data, and acceptance as 'fact' of the words of informants, if at all? (Fine 1998, p. 152).

The utilisation of different techniques (that is, triangulation) will bring out different aspects, interpretations and viewpoints of a phenomenon. This is a central way in which to deal with the potential problems arising regarding the validity of the information provided by informants within a study that is interpretive in approach.

The issues of validity, subjectivity and authority of the author, and the subjectivity of individuals being studied has led many ethnographers to look for new ways of undertaking ethnographic research. Post-modern ethnography, which will be discussed in the next section is a newly emerging framework through which many researchers are attempting to deal with the problems of ethnographic research as outlined above.

Post-modern ethnography

Denzin (1998, p. 314) states that within the ethnographic field, some researchers are questioning the assumed authority of the ethnographic text. He describes the core of this sensibility as one in which there is 'doubt that any discourse has a privileged place, any method or theory a universal and general claim to authoritative knowledge'. Within post-modern ethnographies, the researcher no longer 'observes' as an outsider. Post-modern ethnographic texts explicitly write the ethnographer into the narrative. Researchers divorce themselves from any residual notions of objectivism, embracing instead a philosophy of 'creativity' and 'personalisation' (Denzin 1998, p. 321) and complete subjectivity. Post-modern ethnographers engage in dialogue over monologue, where they interact and become a part of the community they are working in (Tyler 1986, pp. 126-127). They immerse themselves into the field of study and the lives of the subjects. After acquiring a great understanding of their subjects, they will, through rigorous effort, produce a contextualised reproduction and interpretation of the stories told by the subjects. Each ethnography will ultimately 'present an integrated synthesis of experience and theory. The final interpretive theory is multi-voiced and dialogical. It builds on native interpretations and in fact simply articulates what is implicit in those interpretations' (Vidich and Lyman 1998, p. 80).

Within post-modern ethnography, the text is regarded merely as a piece of writing. 'It cannot be said to either present or represent ... an unmodified and unfiltered record of immediate experience and an accurate portrait of the culture of the other' (Vidich and Lyman 1998, p. 78). Authors lose all authority over their particular area of study. The author is merely contributing to a discourse that may or may not exist regarding that particular topic of study.

The ways in which the author chooses to contribute to this discourse within a particular field of knowledge has broadened within post-modern ethnographic writing. 'Experimental ethnographies' are being explored by some researchers (see Clifford 1986; Richardson 1998). Such experimental ethnographies include confessional ethnography, where researchers narrate stories in which they play the central protagonists. In this type of narrative, authors discuss how they came to observe the cultures studied. Self or auto-ethnographies are also utilised. Within these narrative forms authors write about their own culture, the distinctions between the researcher and the researched completely disappearing via this process (Van Maanen 1995, pp. 9-11).

Other forms of experimental writing include poem form, writing from different subject positions, and collaborative writing, where the ethnographer writes a narrative together with the group being studied (Richardson 1998, pp. 366-367).

Conclusion

Interpretivist ethnography, which is now the predominant form, is concerned with the telling of stories of culture, as interpreted by ethnographers, through which highly contextualised and localised theory is cultivated.

Denzin (1998, p. 315) states that the age of a putative value-free social science is over. The aim of social research is to capture the character and construct of a phenomenon, which can only be achieved by first-hand contact with events, individuals, and social groupings. This aim cannot be achieved by the inferences made from what people do in artificial settings. Rather, social events and processes need to be explained in terms of their relationship to the context in which they occur. Ethnographic study is not just concerned with presenting the 'truth' about a particular phenomenon, cultural event and/or grouping. Rather, it has become a process of the researcher interpreting the ways in which individuals and groups interpret their own realities. Further discussions of the techniques used by ethnographers, and examples of ethnographies/participant observations can be found in Chapter 16.

Discussion questions

Controversies within ethnographic study still remain, particularly with the advent of post-modern ethnography. Questions arise, including:

- To what extent should an ethnographic text concern itself with theory building in contrast to providing thick descriptions of social phenomena and events?

- What responsibilities do ethnographers have towards the people they study?

- What responsibilities do ethnographers have to the reader?

- When does a narrative of culture no longer fit the perimeters of an ethnographic text, a question particularly poignant for post-modern ethnographers?

Further readings

Altheide, David L. and Johnson, John M. (1998). Criteria for assessing interpretive validity in qualitative research. In *Collecting and interpreting qualitative materials,* eds. Norman K. Denzin and Yvonna S. Lincoln. Sage: London, pp. 283-312.

Denzin, Norman K. and Lincoln, Yvonna S. (1998). *The landscape of qualitative research: Theories and issues.* Sage: London.

Hammersley, Martyn. (1990). *Reading ethnographic research: A critical guide.* Longman: London.

Vidich, Arthur J. and Lyman, M. (1998). Qualitative methods: their history in sociology and anthropology. In *The landscape of qualitative research: Theories and issues,* eds. Norman K. Denzin and Yvonna S. Lincoln. Sage: London, pp. 41-110.

References for Chapter 10

Altheide, David L. and Johnson, John M. (1998). Criteria for assessing interpretive validity in qualitative research. In *Collecting and interpreting qualitative materials,* eds. Norman K. Denzin and Yvonna S. Lincoln. Sage: London, pp. 283-312.

Bateson, Gregory. (1972). *Steps to an ecology of mind.* Ballantine: New York.

Brown, Richard Harvey. (ed.). (1995). *Postmodern representations: Truth, power, and mimesis in the human sciences and public culture.* University of Illinois Press: Chicago.

Clifford, James. (1986). Introduction: Partial truths. In *Writing culture: The poetics and politics of ethnography,* eds. James Clifford and George E. Marcus. University of California Press: Berkeley, Ca, pp. 1-26.

Collins, Patricia Hill. (1990). *Black feminist thought: Knowledge, consciousness and the politics of empowerment.* Unwin Hyman: Boston.

Denzin, Norman K. (1998). The art and politics of interpretation. In *Collecting and interpreting qualitative material,* eds. Norman K. Denzin and Yvonna S. Lincoln. Sage: London, pp. 313-344.

Denzin, Norman K and Lincoln, Yvonna S. (1998). Introduction: Entering the field of qualitative research. In *The landscape of qualitative research: Theories and issues,* eds. Norman K. Denzin and Yvonna S. Lincoln. Sage: London, pp. 1-34.

Duran, Jane. (1991). *Toward a feminist epistemology.* Rowman and Littlefield: Savage, Md.

Fine, Michelle. (1998). Working the hyphens: Reinventing self and other in qualitative research. In *The landscape of qualitative research: Theories and issues,* eds. Norman K. Denzin and Yvonna S. Lincoln. Sage: London, pp. 130-155.

Fonow, M. and Cook, J. (eds.). (1991). *Beyond methodology: Feminist scholarship as lived research.* Indiana University Press: Bloomington, In.

Geertz, Clifford. (1973). *The interpretation of cultures.* Basic: New York.

Guba, Egon. (1990). The alternative paradigm dialog. In *The paradigm dialog,* ed. Egon G. Guba. Sage: London, pp. 17-27.

Guba, Egon G. and Lincoln, Yvonna S. (1998). Competing paradigms in qualitative research. In *The landscape of qualitative research: Theories and issues,* eds. Norman K. Denzin and Yvonna S. Lincoln. Sage: London, pp. 195-220.

Hammersley, Martyn. (1990). *Reading ethnographic research: A critical guide.* Longman: London.

Hammersley, Martyn. (1992). *What's wrong with ethnography? Methodological explorations.* Routledge Press: London.

hooks, bell (sic). (1988). *Talking back: Thinking feminist, thinking black.* Between the Lines: Toronto.

hooks, bell (sic) and West, Cornell. (1991). *Breaking bread: Insurgent black intellectual life.* South End Press: Boston.

Janesick, Valerie J. (1998). The dance of qualitative research design: Metaphor, methodolatry and meaning. In *Strategies of qualitative inquiry,* eds. Norman K. Denzin and Yvonna S. Lincoln. Sage: London, pp. 35-55.

Malinowski, B. (1922). *Argonauts of the Western Pacific.* Routledge and Kegan Paul: London.

Mead, Margaret. (1960). *Coming of age in Samoa: A psychological study of primitive youth for western civilisation.* Mentor: New York.

Nelson, Cary and Grossberg, Lawrence. (eds.). (1988). *Marxism and the interpretation of culture.* University of Illinois Press: Chicago.

Omolade, Barbara. (1994). *The rising song of African American women.* Routledge Press: New York.

Reason, Peter. (1998). Three approaches to qualitative research. In *Strategies of qualitative inquiry,* eds. Norman K. Denzin and Yvonna S. Lincoln. Sage: London, pp. 261-291.

Richardson, Laurel. (1998). Writing: A method of inquiry. In *Collecting and interpreting qualitative materials*, eds. Norman K. Denzin and Yvonna S. Lincoln. Sage: London, pp. 345-371.

Rosaldo, Renato. (1989). *Culture and truth: The remaking of social analysis.* Beacon Press: Boston.

Schwandt, Thomas A. (1998). Constructivist, interpretivist approaches to human inquiry. In *The landscape of qualitative research: Theories and issues,* eds. Norman K. Denzin and Yvonna S. Lincoln. Sage: London, pp. 221-259.

Spivak, Gayatri Chakravorty. (1988). Can the subaltern speak? In *Marxism and the interpretation of cultures,* eds. Cary Nelson and Lawrence Grossberg. University of Illinois Press: Chicago, pp. 271-313.

Stanfield, John. (1998). Ethnic modelling in qualitative research. In *The landscape of qualitative research: Theories and issues,* eds. Norman K. Denzin and Yvonna S. Lincoln. Sage: London, pp. 333-358.

Tyler, Stephen A. (1986). Post-modern ethnography: From document of the occult to occult document'. In *Writing culture: The poetics and politics of ethnography*, eds. James Clifford and George E. Marcus. University of California Press: Berkeley, Ca, pp. 122-140.

Van Maanen, John. (1995). An end to innocence. In *Representation in ethnography,* ed. John Van Maanen. Sage: London, pp. 1-35.

Vidich, Arthur J. and Lyman, M. (1998). Qualitative methods: Their history in sociology and anthropology. In *The landscape of qualitative research: Theories and issues,* eds. Norman K. Denzin and Yvonna S. Lincoln. Sage: London, pp. 41-110.

CHAPTER 11
Historical research
Graeme Johanson

Objectives

After reading this chapter, you will be able to:

- describe what history is, and what data it requires;

- explain how the intellectual tools of a historian operate;

- identify research situations appropriate to the use of historical method; and

- understand history's main benefits.

This chapter does not amount to a comprehensive do-it-yourself manual. It is more in the style of a strategic plan.

All around us

The nature of time ensures that history 'is'. We are its makers as well as its products. Whether we act freely and independently, or in reaction without choice, or for mixed reasons, we cannot escape it. History affects our daily lives all the time. It engages us by means of the decisions which we make, when based on our past experiences, and by means of our assumptions about the nature of our future, about what is probable or what is desired.

Historians are simply purposeful researchers who concentrate their energies on motives, experiences, behaviours, fears and hopes more than most. They hold a mental magnifying glass over individuals and societies, and specialise in recording and passing on what they observe upon close examination. History is a continually-updated, methodical description and recording, a stylish explanation of trends and events. It has many uses, as examples in this chapter will indicate.

In the practice of information management and information systems, and their related occupations, history manifests itself in the nurture of cultural heritage and is also embedded in daily routines. This is well demonstrated in Bennett (1994). The effects of decisions made by professionals in these fields are cumulative, and what was done in the past can determine what is possible in the immediate future. For example, a study of a collection of information, in a library, an office, or on a desktop, will reveal much about the origins of the data, the purpose of its creation, the likely impact of the current use of the information, and its probable lifespan. Such a study was carefully undertaken in related histories by Bridge (1986) and Talbot (1992).

The accumulated historical knowledge can help identify future patterns of use of information by an individual, group, and/or organisation. A systems analyst will be assisted by an information audit which provides this type of historical analysis. A thorough discussion of key aspects of this process is found in Markley (1996). Whether the systems are traditional publications, personal networks or far-reaching electronic ones, systems designers need to understand the origins and patterns of information flows in order to make them useful. This is very clearly shown in a landmark analysis sponsored by the Australian government on Australia as an information society (House of Representatives 1991).

Further discussions which indicate the nexus between history and information management and systems can be found in Campbell-Kelly and Aspray (1996); Garrison (1979); Higgs (1998); Jones (1997); Katz (1998); Kelly (1977); Morrison and Talbot (1985); Stieg (1992); and Wiegand (1989).

In the next section I describe the origins and nature of historical data and the researcher's relationships with it. Then I explain what evaluative criteria a historian uses to critique evidence. This is followed by a discussion of the usefulness of historical research generally. Questions to encourage further discussion are at the end of the chapter.

In this chapter I do not cover every aspect of every research process. Many of the methods mentioned elsewhere in this book are ones that a historian employs consistently. One crucial example is the formulation of a hypothesis, to guide the historian's thinking, analysis, and findings. Historians hypothesise all the time, but this chapter does not deal in detail with the importance of creating hypotheses. Many of the questions set out in the section on 'critiquing the evidence' could form part of formal historical hypotheses, if changed from stark questions into propositions to be tested against evidence.

Evidence

Every researcher uses data, but the historian – like the lawyer – usually calls it 'evidence'. It is fundamental to historical research, and is always of the past. Its quantity and complexity creates dilemmas. It occupies the attention of the historian as researcher a great deal more than the time which many other researchers devote to sifting relevant evidence. The evidence may defy existing codes; it may be full of enormous surprises. Early in the research process, the historian aims to describe all connected situations, and then to explore all logical explanations for any links between them. The possibilities are very large to start with. The research focus narrows later on, as slabs of evidence are chosen carefully for analysis.

Evidence may originate in many places, and consist of quite different things. It can be tangible objects, such as coins or credit cards; records of economic and social relationships, for example, trading; invisible processes, like incurring debt; unspoken rules, like limited liability; institutions, like market-places and stock exchanges; abstractions, like a cash flow; or theories or systems of thinking, like 'free trade' or a 'command economy'. Any of this evidence can be used in special ways by the historian.

The historian will try to imagine the likely ways that participants in past experiences were thinking and feeling. Obviously it is rarely possible to examine all the evidence involved, often for very practical reasons. Some evidence will have disappeared, or never be disclosed. An eyewitness to an accident may walk away nonchalantly, oblivious to the significance of his inner observations, or how they fit into the complete jigsaw of all evidence of the scene. Yet the historian still wants to try to make sense of the whole puzzle. Participants' thoughts may have to be deduced from what others observed about behaviours at the accident. Knowledge of the psychology of perception and observation should assist the historian in this instance. The intense interest of the historian in human motives and behaviours makes history overlap a lot with the principles that lie behind researching biography.

Some evidence will be omitted selectively by the historian after deliberation. Repetitive confirmation of an accepted piece of common knowledge, for example, becomes superfluous. It is unlikely that a historian will need to remind modern computer scientists that all computers derive their fundamental coded mathematical basis from the hypothetical Universal Turing Machine, invented in 1936.

Other evidence will be overlooked inadvertently upon a cursory examination, but will be reintegrated into mainstream historical commentary after considered reflection. Some evidence is mulled over many times. Evidence provided by modern DNA tests on old, organic samples is an example of re-examining old data with new tools.

Some history is more fashionable than others. Sometimes politicians, or others within an interest group, seek to suppress evidence in order to propagate their own narrow interpretations of the past. They manage to foster and sustain a predetermined sampling of evidence for posterity. Excessive emphasis on men's achievements is an example of recently-acknowledged bias which diminishes women. Manipulators of evidence seek to control attitudes and opinions about the past in order to shape minds for the future. Most Japanese history texts like to focus on economic successes and to side-step records of the evils perpetrated by Japan's imperial armies in the 1930s to 1940s.

We delegate to certain groups and organisations the responsibility of keeping or destroying our historical evidence. Collecting and caring for evidence, and weeding it, are part of the professional duties of curators, custodians, librarians, archivists, recordkeepers, and others. The desires to nurture or to destroy suggest an intrinsic power in the evidence itself. Thus, family historians may be specially interested in skeletons in the closet, while public relations experts are concerned above all else to maintain images unsullied by human error or character taint.

The value of evidence changes over time, as do the purposes for collecting and using it. Videos taken of family members today may become just historical records of fashion (as worn by unidentified individuals) to generations in the future. Contemporary medical files of individual patients in Iceland collected now by local doctors will become part of a gene archive sold by the Icelandic government to private researchers of the future.

In this section I have described the characteristics of data used by the historian, including an explanation of the great range of evidence used, and the process of its identification. Evidence is collected for different purposes and used differently at different times. Once a historian has tried to locate all extant evidence on a topic, then evaluative criteria are applied to it. It is subjected to a series of intellectual assessments and, herein, lies the heart of a historical 'method'.

Critiquing the evidence

Now I proceed to identify criteria that historians use, and to describe their roles. In real life, of course, a historian uses a full armoury of intellectual weapons to capture and subdue the past, not one weapon at a time. I separate them in this section for purposes of clearer description, but some criteria overlap.

An internal contradiction exists in the mind of historians. It is that they are themselves a product of their times, and they are constrained by what they are able to know here and now. Confusion can arise from the existential fact that different participants tell different stories about a single event. Some stories contradict others. Nevertheless, constants remain in this maelstrom of competing accounts. Normally three basics can be identified: a comprehensive body of apposite evidence; a strong human desire to hypothesise about the relationships between the past and the present; and social benefits that derive from publicly airing all the differing voices.

The flexibility caused by the vagaries and preoccupations of the times in which the historian lives is counterbalanced by a high level of stable interest in important facts. Facts are anchors, run-of-the-mill propositions, pieces of linguistic shorthand, which we all agree to use daily – whether we are historians or not – to describe past reality. Different perspectives create different views of facts, and of the usefulness of them. Yet on the whole common agreement makes for consistency and continuity.

It is time to describe what a historian does with the heritage of facts. What are the key intellectual attributes that a historian brings to research? The learnt skills of history can be applied to a wide range of non-historical projects. The six roles described here are very powerful when used in combination and they summarise historical methodology. The sequence described below implies a progression in the research process.

Detective

By definition all of the historian's data is of the past, as noted, but any of it may need to be held up to the light for closer inspection. Historians have a mental check-list of questions. They might ask: what evidence is left after the event? If some evidence is not available, how much information is required to indicate a change of circumstances? How much will show a sudden, catastrophic event? A process of identification begins any search, then a tentative reconstruction of activity, events, structures, processes. Where is the key evidence likely to be found? How complete is it? What gaps are there? Are the gaps accidental or intentional? What form was the evidence in before? What form is it in now? How can it be laid out carefully today for reinterpretation? Who should be entrusted with testing it? Are appropriate experts available? Box 11.1 gives an example of the uses of detection by the historian.

Box 11.1: Detecting in action

Detecting questions come into play in a study of the library of Alexandria, Egypt, on the Mediterranean Sea, one of the 'seven wonders' of the ancient world. There is reliable evidence of famous Greeks visiting it in the fourth century B.C. to acquire knowledge of astronomy, science, mathematics, librarianship, linguistics, medicine and theology. Visits conferred great cultural status, so many aspirants claimed in autobiographies to have travelled to Alexandria, even though they had not. The writings in Greek and Latin of some with firsthand knowledge – Herodotus, Plato, Theophrastus, and Eudoxus – are reliable in naming those who really did make the pilgrimage.

People are always curious to know why the well-known books met their end after about 400 years. The causes of demise illustrate certain benefits of detection skills. In 48 B.C. Gaius Julius Caesar allied with Cleopatra in a civil war against her brother Ptolemy XIII. This alliance is well documented in official histories of the time. As a battle tactic Caesar set fire to Ptolemy's fleet of ships in the harbour, but the fire spread from the dockyards and destroyed the library, we are told by the historians Plutarch, Livy and Seneca. Whether Caesar was aware of the threat to the main library, we do not know. A branch library in Alexandria survived until 391 A.D. when the Christian, Roman Emperor Theodosius I ordained its destruction on the grounds that it was a threatening pagan institution. Egyptian eyewitnesses recorded its demolition.

Nine centuries later, during the time of the Crusades, yet another fable emerged. This fabrication, designed to slander Muslims, asserted that an Arab general destroyed the entire collection of Alexandrian manuscripts by using them as fuel to heat his baths. Many of them had already been destroyed by the Crusaders' own religious predecessors!

Thus the bulk of the extant evidence about the library was, as a whole, first and secondhand accounts, thirdhand commentaries by writers who had read visitors' accounts, and manuscript copies of the books in other collections outside Egypt. We owe almost all of our modern knowledge of classical Greeks to the rare copies dispersed from Alexandria around Europe. None of the estimated 543,000 volumes survived at the port city. None of the library buildings survived. No architectural drawings survived. The fire and razing took care of that. Overall the evidence has been ferreted out well after the destruction and pieced together again by modern historians and archaeologists. The writers who do mention the sad events of 48 B.C. and 391 A.D. pass over them quickly as coincidental to other more important events in their own lives.

Sceptic

Having identified likely clues, the historian is led to ask how reliable the evidence is. Once found, can it be depended on? How credible were the producers of the data, and the distributors of it? How extensively was it distributed? How carefully have the curators of the evidence selected it for storage? Has the data been corrupted over time? In what ways? By whom? Who had a vested interest in ensuring its survival or disappearance? What parts of it have gone missing? Box 11.2 provides an example of the need to question the reliability of the evidence.

Box 11.2: Example of the historian acting as sceptic

The leader of China from 1949, Mao Zedong promoted his country through radical modernisation. Mao read in order to liberate himself from his restrictive peasant background. His favourite books were the history and literature of Chinese dynasties, European philosophers and political treatises. He told other communists that books taught him at the age of thirty how he should guide his kin through revolution to throw off feudal and imperial oppression. His Chinese literary inheritance stretched back 3,800 years continuously. No other written culture had survived for as long.

He also attempted to censor it for modern consumption, expunging parables that conflicted with his own ideals. He objected to allowing his people access to selected literature which he believed romanticised non-Communist causes or ancestors. From 1966 to 1968 his Red Army killed four million Chinese and destroyed entire libraries, museums, art galleries, temples, and pagodas. Fiction by Shakespeare, Shelley and Shaw was burnt.

A Western historian has difficulty finding truthful sources about Mao's reading habits in retrospect, even his English favourites. If we consult the few available biographies written in Chinese, an official bias overwhelms us. We are entitled to remain sceptical about their omission of details. During the 'Cultural Revolution', Chinese who wanted to read unapproved literature had to do so in secret, and a flourishing black market traded Western 'corruption'. One reader who escaped as a refugee from China in the late 1960s remembers purchasing an illegal copy of a French novel secretly, tearing off its cover, and replacing it with 'The selected works of Mao Zedong' to disguise it.

From the 1920s Mao wrote ideological tracts, and lyric poetry. When the first printing of 'The selected works of Mao Zedong' occurred, eighty million copies were circulated, along with fifty-seven million copies of his poems. Mao became a cult hero, in China and elsewhere. His publications assumed mythical status. Official tributes to Mao are nothing more than crude hagiographies. Western historians have no entrée to official government records of his life, if they are kept. His image as a dedicated reader and great writer has been 'revised' officially by later Chinese leaders numerous times since his death in 1975.

Attributor

Mao's life story is a recent reminder that the historian needs to know who created the evidence, and why? To whom is it attributed? Where did it come from originally? How remote is it from its source? Is its context lost? What did the data mean to its creator, and its original audience? Is its meaning still complete? If it were presented to an audience today, would it be understood and believed fully? Has the meaning changed? Who has copied it, used it, and for what purposes? Are these surrogates trustworthy? Box 11.3 presents an example of the problems of attribution.

Box 11.3: Purposes of attribution

An example of the historian's role as attributor is found in the story of the Rosetta Stone, the most viewed object today in the British Museum, London. The problems in this case are not bias and self-aggrandisement, but lost languages and survival of evidence. The data served several quite different purposes at separate times.

In 196 B.C. the priests of King Ptolemy V of Egypt issued a decree honouring him. The papyrus decree was copied onto a black basalt slab in three languages – hieroglyphic, demotic, and Greek – for preservation. The stone itself became lost in rubble, and the message on the decree was forgotten for many centuries. The original meaning of the text is inconsequential today.

In 1799 French soldiers, who had invaded Egypt, dug up the stone slab near the town of Rosetta while building a military fort. The stone had been used for nothing more than building material. The Greek language was understood still, only fragments of demotic were known, and the meaning of hieroglyphics had been lost completely.

The three texts on the stone – assumed to contain the same message – were examined by French and English scholars for fourteen years before they managed to decode them in 1822. Fortunately there was sufficient overlap in the surviving fourteen lines of damaged hieroglyphic, thirty-two lines of damaged demotic, and fifty-four lines of damaged Greek, to permit unequivocal elimination of alternative meanings. The fixedness of the inscription on stone made tampering after 196 B.C. unlikely.

The historian attributed much to the Rosetta Stone. Its different contexts, uses and meanings had to be traced and explained. As a result, intense interest in classical civilisations attracted research funding from European monarchs and governments. The text on the Stone – when used as a codebreaker – assumed significance far beyond its original, intended purpose. Serious modern study of Egyptian history can be dated to the deciphering, when all other hieroglyphics became translatable.

Verifier, clarifier

Verifying involves internal checking by the historian. Is evidence internally consistent? We need to know, for instance, whether it is a deliberate hoax. Is the evidence typical of the evidence emanating usually from the scrutinised source? Was the creator of the evidence regarded as reliable at the time by contemporaries? Are there other witnesses who agree with the accounts recorded via the primary source? Has the evidence been reviewed since its creation? Is it confirmed from outside sources? Does one piece of evidence corroborate others? Have people twisted the evidence over time to their own ends? Have exaggerations, distortions, or legends grown up around it, which had no place in the original context? Have the later glosses destroyed the meaning or impact intended by the original creator? Box 11.4 tries to summarise a complex illustration.

Disentangler

The next set of questions is about unravelling. Looked at in its entirety, the historian asks, what does all the evidence mean? How easily are the boundaries of its meaning defined? To whom should it have meaning? Was it intended to remain unambiguous or secret for ever? How different is the audience for the evidence now, compared with the original, intended audience? Which mix of modern interpretations of the evidence is most likely to be true, on the balance of probabilities? Can the evidence be disentangled sensibly, or is it just too much of a mish-mash to make any sense? Who today is interested in knowing about the plethora of meanings attached to the evidence? An example of the process of disentanglement is presented in Box 11.5.

Storyteller, explainer

The culmination of historical research is often the resolution of a hypothesis. Towards the end of the evaluative process, the researcher asks whether the original hypothesis can be accepted, or whether it should be reviewed? In the case of the cave paintings it is extremely difficult to draw a firm conclusion. This uncertainty itself comprises a sort of 'conclusion'.

The historian has a duty to describe and explain the past as accurately as possible in the present, to show why we are, what we are, where we are. The evidence should be selected and connected as a story which appeals in its telling – stimulating excitement, fear, respect, understanding and awe. Whether it is presented in the form of the spoken word, film, printed text, music, picture, multimedia, or other means, it should be both entertaining and instructive.

Box 11.4: Who verifies what?

A twenty-three year old actor decided to deceive the American public on Hallowe'en, 1938. He used all the rules of verification, corroboration and clarification to turn truth on its head. He fooled millions. Orson Welles broadcast across the USA on the CBS radio network that Martians were invading. In fact he and his scriptwriters had adapted H.G. Wells's science fiction novel 'War of the Worlds' into a radio play. Today you can listen to the entire broadcast on the Internet, with the voices of the original actors – and decide for yourself how realistic you think it sounds!

Today it is simply entertainment. In 1938, however, in a world on the precipice of a catastrophic war, the public mood was paranoid. Although Welles warned during the broadcast that it was just a play, people ran into the streets in panic, telephoned CBS and the police, or rushed to their shotguns on the farms. The story aroused too many fears for it to be heard 'just' as entertainment.

To make the play more realistic, Welles acted the role of a professor of astronomy at Princeton University's observatory, another colleague acted as a news announcer from the CBS radio station they were in, corroborating reports of explosions on Mars followed by observations of an object falling onto a farm in New Jersey. Another acted as a farmer being interviewed, while 'police' and anxious 'spectators' butted in. An imaginary Brigadier General declared martial law as the Martians blasted the farm with deadly heat rays from their landing craft.

The drama continued to unfold with great imaginative skill. If a historian were assigned the task of trying to document a real Martian invasion, he or she would search for and identify the types of evidence that Welles provided. The realistic tone of Welles's characters, their plausible personalities, the accessibility of the medium (popular radio) and the mass audience contributed to his play being accepted at face value.

These things would also contribute to an acceptable historical account of an extraterrestrial landing. In effect, Welles was mimicking the historian. Journalists do so commonly. Cleverly Welles adopted the role of verifier, providing constant 'checks' on the authoritativeness of his separate fictionalised sources, as they participated, whilst also attempting to supply corroboration by reporting the situation through the eyes of different 'observers'.

Box 11.5: Example of disentanglement

Many dilemmas are posed by the oldest known paintings in the world, in Palaeolithic caves in southern Europe, Siberia, north America, and north-western Australia. Radiocarbon dating and other forms of dating establish some of these images as about 35,000 years old.

The images on the walls show many animals – humans as hunters of bison and deer, a rhinoceros, mammoths, fish, oxen, kangaroos, snakes, horses and ibexes. The pictures imply that the regions around the caves were sufficiently fertile to support life on a large scale. Fertility probably encouraged dense settlement. Some of the well-proportioned prey depicted on the walls of the caves are pockmarked with holes made from thrown spears, suggesting hunting practice.

When caves were first 'discovered' in Europe in 1879, no-one believed that the ancient peoples were talented enough to paint the murals themselves. Then more caves in different regions were found in the 1940s, and dating became more precise in the 1950s. New theories about the meanings of the paintings emerged.

Some were straightforward, some far-fetched. Some took the pictures at face value, seeing in them the daily struggle of humans against nature, while others found magic, sorcery, sexual conflicts, concealed psychic needs, and mysterious 'sparks of consciousness' in them. An art historian is fascinated to work out the painting techniques but also finds aesthetic genius in them, a special style. The background of the viewer affects which tangle of evidence is seen first, and which meanings unravel thereafter.

The story should synthesise the best of the evaluated evidence to demonstrate the authenticity of the links in the chain of causation. The historian presents cause and effect in the form of 'most likely' explanations – not as absolute truths. Universally-valid generalisations from historical research across time and space rarely hold water. Deduction – moving logically from a generalisation about the past to a particular instance in the present – is usually not attempted extensively by historians. It is too foolhardy. Chance plays too great a part. The level of 'proof' in history is on the balance of probabilities, as in fact it is in most disciplines.

In this section I have described six main intellectual activities of the practising historian. All the roles involve testing and interpreting the evidence in order to arrive at a viable explanatory narrative.

Uses of history

What are some important uses of history?

Obviously a research student employs some of the principles outlined above, whether the topic is purely historical or not. Almost all research projects involve a mixture of different disciplinary methods. It is normal for a researcher to explain the origin of any topic, and reasons for initial interest in it. This introduction may vary from short to drawn out. It is common for all researchers to acknowledge the value of prior work. In each of these cases, historical background is crucial.

Historians use hypotheses as working tools, not to arrive at hard-and-fast guidelines for future human behaviour. History can demystify ignorance about the past, make some sense of real chaos, help civilise societies, nurture reflective decision making, assist in contemporary problem solving, and provide moral insights. This is a formidable list of possible achievements.

The insights of historians are original, taking local, contemporary values into account, and enabling future generations to get inside the heads of their close ancestors, to understand their thinking and decisions, to admire their achievements and to avoid their pitfalls in the future. People promote their own culture, beliefs, and morals, often too stridently, while they always lean on their own past heavily, perhaps without due acknowledgment. The historian tries to make us understand the angle and weight of that lean, and its props. The historian describes, explains and invigorates previous knowledge and useful experiences which permeate our individual and collective lives.

This brief final section has described how the skills of the historian can be applied in several contexts, in research, decision making and problem solving generally. Historical research will succeed in the future so long as it promises a fuller appreciation of what mattered in the past.

Discussion questions

- How different is the method of the historian from the mental models used by: the sociologist; psychologist; journalist; lawyer; systems analyst; publisher; biographer; and financier?

- Write down three hypotheses worthy of testing by historical method, and describe what types of evidence a historian would need to test them.

- Imagine a real-life problem that could not be assisted at all by historical research methods.

- Imagine an event in the workplace which could only be researched properly by using historical method.

- Describe one situation which could be researched feasibly by using three different research methods, and explain which one method would be the best for researching one nominated part of the described situation.

Further readings

Barzun, Jacques and Graff, Henry F. (1992). *The modern researcher*. Houghton Mifflin: Boston.

Carr, E.H. (1985). *What is history?* Penguin: Harmondsworth.

Southgate, Bev. (1996). *History: What and why? Ancient, modern, and postmodern perspectives*. Routledge: London.

References for Chapter 11

Bennett, J.M. (ed.). (1994). *Computing in Australia: The development of a profession*. Hale and Iremonger: Sydney.

Bridge, C. (1986). *A trunk full of books*. Wakefield: Nestley, SA.

Campbell-Kelly, Martin and Aspray, William. (1996). *Computer: A history of the information machine*. Harper Collins: New York.

Garrison, Dee. (1979). *Apostles of culture: The public librarian and American society, 1876-1920*. Macmillan: New York.

Higgs, Edward. (ed.). (1998). *History and electronic artefacts*. Clarendon: New York.

House of Representatives Standing Committee for Long Term Strategies. (1991). *Australia as an information society: The role of libraries and information networks*. AGPS: Canberra.

Jones, T. (1997). *Carnegie libraries across America: A public legacy*. Wiley: New York.

Katz, Bill. (1998). *Cuneiform to computer: A history of reference sources*. Scarecrow Press: Lanham, MD.

Kelly, T. (1977). *Books for the people: An illustrated history of the British public library*. Deutsch: London.

Markley, Robert (ed.). (1996). *Virtual realities and their discontents*. John Hopkins University Press: Baltimore, Md.

Morrison, E. and Talbot, M. (1985). *Books, libraries and readers in colonial Australia: Papers from the Forum on Australian Colonial Library History, 1984*. Graduate School of Librarianship: Monash University: Clayton, Vic.

Stieg, M.F. (1992). *Public libraries in Nazi Germany*. University of Alabama: Tuscaloosa.

Talbot, M. (1992). *A chance to read: a history of the Institutes Movement in South Australia*. Library Board of South Australia: Adelaide.

Wiegand, W.A. (1989). *An active instrument for propaganda: The American public library during World War I*. Greenwood: New York.

CHAPTER 12
The Delphi method
Kirsty Williamson

Objectives

At the end of this chapter, you will be able to:

- describe the characteristics which set the Delphi method apart from other methods;

- understand the historical origins of the method;

- describe how the method works; and

- understand the types of research questions/situations for which the method can be used.

Introduction

It was difficult to decide where the Delphi method should be placed in a book which is attempting to treat 'methods' separately from 'techniques'. The 'Delphi method' is often termed the 'Delphi technique'. The decision was made to include the chapter in the 'methods' section because Delphi provides a design for undertaking research, which is underpinned by theoretical explanation. This makes it more than just a data collection mechanism. The technique for data collection most used in the Delphi method is the self-administered questionnaire.

The following two views of the Delphi method are found in the literature. The first is a more general definition, but Linstone and Turoff (1975), who are key names in the 'Delphi' literature, believed that it provides a good summary of both the method and its objective:

> Delphi may be characterised as a method for structuring a group communication process, so that the process is effective in allowing a group of individuals, as a whole to deal with complex problems (Linstone and Turoff 1975, p. 3).

The second definition is more specific:

> The Delphi technique of futures research is an attempt to use the science – rather than the art – of prophecy by gathering a consensus of experts' opinions using several rounds of questionnaires or interviews, and providing controlled feedback of results between rounds as a means of forecasting future trends (Sproull 1988, p. 240).

This definition may be rather misleading in that the consensus is not 'gathered', but rather is 'developed' through providing feedback from each round of questionnaires. (The use of interviews is not common.)

The founders of the Delphi method, Dalkey and Helmer of the Rand Corporation (1963, cited in Gupta and Clarke 1996, p. 186), stated that the primary purpose of the Delphi method is to: 'obtain the most reliable consensus of opinion of a group of experts ... by a series of intensive questionnaires interspersed with controlled opinion feedback'.

Below is a description of the way a Delphi study usually proceeds. The steps are illustrated by the process used to undertake a Delphi study in the late 1970s. The study focused on the information needs of older people and the major sources of information used to meet those needs. It was also concerned with the need for new and different kinds of library services and what form these might take. The purpose was to provide a basis for future library services for older people (Williamson and Stayner 1980). The Delphi method was chosen in order to include as many people who worked with the aged as possible (in the then cities of Ringwood and Croydon in Victoria). The chosen group was too big for a face-to-face meeting, but not large enough to provide a suitable sample for a survey. It seemed that the indirect *discussion* of a Delphi study would be a good method for investigating the research questions. Although the study took place twenty years ago, its methods and findings are still relevant.

Steps in a Delphi process

1. A panel of experts in the field under study is set up. In the Williamson and Stayner (1980) study, twenty-nine people who worked with older people formed the panel. They included aged care workers, district and geriatric nurses, ministers of religion, and the branch librarians of the Ringwood and Croydon libraries.

2. The panel is sent a first-round questionnaire.

3. The results from the first-round questionnaire, together with a summary of the comments and arguments given by respondents in support of their answers, are incorporated in a second round questionnaire and the original questions are repeated. With the Williamson and Stayner (1980) study, bar charts were used to show the way the panel had answered each question. An example is how important the panel considered each of the information needs listed – from very important, on a Likert scale, to very unimportant. See Figure 12.1 for the bar chart and arguments presented for the topic.

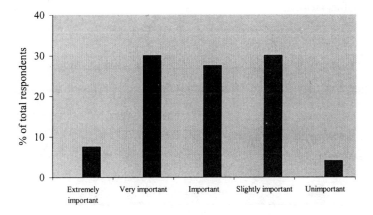

COMMENTS:

Information on consumer products is important:

- So that elderly people are not robbed.
- Because of limited finance usually available to the elderly.
- Products need to be chosen to maintain health and quality of life and assist elderly to remain in their own homes.
- Choice of products is often an immediate need.

Information on consumer products is of limited importance:

- Consumer products are low on any list of priorities.
- Most elderly have most consumer needs already.

Figure 12.1: Consumer products: Results from first round questionnaire

4. Each respondent thus has an opportunity to reconsider his or her own view in the light of other views of the panel, and to answer the original questions again. In the Williamson and Stayner (1980) study, enough panel members changed their answers to most questions to make the panel responses close to consensus positions after the second round. Figure 12.2 shows the change which occurred for the topic.

5. Further rounds may be conducted on the same basis. With the Williamson and Stayner (1980) study, it was not considered necessary, or practical, to undertake a third round.

There are many variations on this basic model, especially through the sophisticated technology now available to researchers. See, for example, Turoff and Hiltz (1997) and discussion later in this chapter.

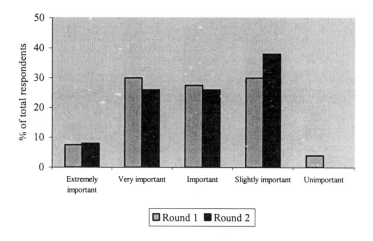

Figure 12.2: Consumer products: Results from first round and second round questionnaires

According to the literature (see the reference list, particularly *The Delphi technique* (n.d.)) the following are key elements of Delphi studies:

- a panel of experts is used for obtaining data;

- data are collected in writing;

- there is a systematic attempt to produce a consensus of opinion, as well as identify opinion divergence;

- the composition of the panel is not disclosed and there is no direct interaction between participants. There is a guarantee of anonymity of both the experts and their specific judgments and statements throughout the exercise;

- there are at least two or more rounds between which a summary of the results of the previous round is communicated to, and evaluated by, the participants. Participants are permitted to review and revise their judgments, and their reasons for them after reading those of their peers; and

- it is most common for a consensus to develop, but if this does not occur, the divergence of views and the reasons for them become clear.

Historical perspectives

As noted, the Delphi method was developed by the Rand Corporation in the 1950s. Most of its early uses were in the military and industrial fields. Since many of the early Delphi studies used the method to make forecasts of future occurrences, the name was first applied by some people at Rand as a joke, which was not entirely appreciated by its founders, Olaf Helmer or Norman Dalkey (Turoff and Hiltz 1997). The joke was that in Greek mythology, the famous Greek oracle, Pythia, 'performed' at Delphi where the temple sacred to the god Apollo was built. When Pythia was consulted, she would utter weird sounds as in a frenzy, much in the way that the witches in Shakespeare's Macbeth intoned: 'Double, double, toil and trouble ...'. At Delphi, temple priests interpreted these to the public, and thus they were able to exert considerable influence over the future actions of cities, as well as private individuals, who sought the oracle's advice.

The Delphi method as developed has been used both to predict the future and evaluate alternative courses of action (Reilly 1973, p. 188). However, the method has not been without its critics. For example, Busha and Harter (1980) saw the Delphi method as not having a sound theoretical base and of achieving results which are often less than spectacular.

When a Delphi study is appropriate

According to Linstone and Turoff (1975, cited in Buckley 1994, p. 160) usually one or more of the following properties of the research problems or questions lead to the need for employing Delphi:

- the problem does not lend itself to precise analytical techniques but can benefit from subjective judgments on a collective basis;

- the individuals who need to contribute to the examination of a broad or complex problem have no history of adequate communication and may represent diverse backgrounds with respect to experience and expertise;

- more individuals are needed than can effectively interact in a face-to-face exchange;

- time and cost make frequent group meetings infeasible;

- the efficiency of face-to-face meetings can be increased by a supplemental group communication process;

- disagreements among individuals are so severe or politically unpalatable that the communication process must be refereed and/or anonymity assured; and/or

- the heterogeneity of the participants must be preserved to assure the validity of the result – avoidance of domination by quantity or strength of personality ('bandwagon effect').

In the case of the Williamson and Stayner (1980) study about the library and information needs of older people, most of the above points were applicable. What was particularly interesting was that several panel members commented that they found the study professionally interesting and valuable. At that time, many of the professional respondents concerned with the aged had little contact with others working in the area. It was a chance to become acquainted with the views of others, without the time and travel needed for face-to-face meetings, which would be ineffective, anyway, with such a large number of people involved.

Uses of the Delphi method

According to Gupta and Clarke (1996, p. 185), the Delphi method has been extensively used in planning, policy analysis, and long-range forecasting, in both the public and private sectors. It has also been used in a range of fields, including education and library and information studies. Buckley (1994, p. 159) saw the real value of the method as assisting with technological change: 'With a plethora of emerging new technologies and initiatives to choose from, the Delphi techniques may serve as a worthwhile tool for choosing which to implement'. For an extensive bibliography of theory and applications of the Delphi method, see Gupta and Clarke (1996). Two examples of how the method has been used in the fields of information management and systems are in Box 12.1. Both are cited by Buckley (1994, pp. 160-161). Another example is provided by Winzenried (1997).

Advantages and disadvantages of the Delphi method

As with all other research, regardless of the method, a Delphi study must have clear objectives. The questions to panels must be clear, carefully analysed, and the feedback needs to be accurately based on results. The lists of advantages and disadvantages are based on the assumption that the Delphi study is rigorously carried out and that the method is suited to an investigation of the research questions.

Box 12.1: Examples of Delphi studies in information management

1. Wilson (1975) was interested in research priorities in social welfare library and information work and undertook a 'modified' Delphi study to investigate these. He sent a questionnaire to eighty-one practitioners in the field of social welfare as well as librarians, information officers, and research workers. The analysis of the questionnaire showed that the social welfare workers saw citizens' information and the internal organisation of information services in social services departments as the important problem. On the other hand, librarians appeared to attach more importance to the effectiveness of existing information services and to user needs (p. 256). The respondents to the questionnaire were then brought together for a forum during which a consensus was achieved on research priorities. Wilson's conclusion that face-to-face interaction for the second 'round' is likely to achieve a 'stronger consensus' (p. 258) seems unfounded, given that he did not test the extent of consensus which could be achieved with the traditional Delphi approach of a second round questionnaire.

2. Otto (1982) undertook a Delphi study of the role of the academic librarian in the twenty-first century, especially in relation to library education. At the time of his study, he was therefore looking ahead twenty years. This was a very rigorous study, involving 153 participants who were librarians, library school administrators and library school faculty and three rounds of questionnaires. As with the Wilson (1975) study a consensus was reached with some exceptions. Otto emphasised the role of the Delphi method for providing a basis for planning, which was also the rationale for the Williamson and Stayner (1980) study. In Otto's words, 'It is the handle, if you will, by which we may steer the future itself' (Otto 1982, p. 86). In other words, Otto stressed his belief that the consensus of opinion of experts is stronger than individual opinion.

Advantages

- Delphi elicits responses from experts who bring knowledge, authority and insight to the issues involved;

- the systematic bringing together of expert views in several rounds to reach consensus provides a stronger basis for decision than do individual judgments (Buckley 1994, p. 163);

- experts can be gathered from all over the world and are not limited to a geographic region;

- the process also provides a cooperative learning exercise for the experts involved. (Gupta and Clarke (1996, p. 186);

- it allows respondents to modify their answers without the pressure of face-to-face interaction. Thus the effect of strong personalities and people of higher status is avoided;

- it allows for the exploration and review of the assumptions, information or opinions leading to different assessments;

- controlled feedback and anonymity help panellists to revise their views without publicly admitting that they have done so. They are thus encouraged to take up a more personal viewpoint rather than a cautious institutional position (Gupta and Clarke 1996, p. 186);

- by giving respondents the chance to consider the answer and reasons of other respondents and to modify their own answers, a consensus of opinion may emerge. The degree of divergence of opinion, if any, and the reasons for it, can be gauged;

- experience has shown that in Delphi applications there is an increasing convergence in the opinions of respondents from iteration to iteration. Where accuracy of response can be checked, it seems to increase with iteration. (Williamson and Stayner 1980, p. 189);

- the process is relatively inexpensive to organise and administer; and

- it is one of the few forecasting methods that has a fair to good prediction accuracy over different time horizons – short-term, medium, and long range (Gupta and Clarke 1996, p. 187).

Disadvantages

- Delphi studies can be slow and time consuming, although the advent of the computer and the Internet has helped in this respect;

- the lack of the stimulation of face-to-face interaction can be a negative factor. A successful 'brain-storming' session often produces momentum and enthusiasm which can stimulate new, creative ideas;

- the researcher, or the respondents themselves, may misunderstand the written inputs of panel members;

- there is also scope for the researcher, who is the only one who sees all the answers of the participants, to manipulate the feedback so that it reflects his or her own views, rather than providing an impartial account;.

- the panel of experts can be too homogeneous or like-minded, thus producing a skewed data set (*The Delphi Technique* n.d.);

- there can still be a 'bandwaggon' effect due to the 'lack of independent response after the first round because of feedback of results to respondents ...' (Sproull 1998, p. 240); and

- anonymity can encourage a lack of accountability for responses.

The role which technology can play

It is now common for Delphi studies to be undertaken using a computer and the Internet. Turoff and Hiltz (1997) say that 'it is actually easier to accomplish this using a computer system than it has been with paper and pencil based Delphi studies'. They talk about the 'round' structure and the need to limit the physical size of any pencil and paper survey as placing severe constraints. 'Hence paper and pencil Delphis are usually limited by the "top down/bottom up" dichotomy rather than allowing more complete parallel entry to any aspect of the problem' (Turoff and Hiltz 1997). They give the example of a single Delphi which might explore, on the first round, 'goals' (a top view) and specific 'consequences' (a bottom view).

> Relating goals to consequences requires developing the relationships inherent in alternative actions and states of nature. These would be put off to a later round. In the computerised environment individuals could be free to tackle any aspect of the problem according to personal preference (Turoff and Hiltz 1997).

With computer-based Delphis, there are more options available with regard to anonymity.

> This allows the other members of a group to obtain more understanding of why specific individuals are agreeing or disagreeing with certain concepts. For example, knowing all the arguments a person has made about accepting or rejecting a given position allows people to better tailor what needs to be said to perhaps change an individual's viewpoint. It also allows the expression of more complex individual viewpoints. This coherency is hard to observe or utilise when everything is anonymous (Turoff and Hiltz 1997).

In computer-based Delphi studies, researchers often make it clear to respondents that they do not need to respond to every question and that responses can be at any time, rather than as part of a 'round'. This continuous feedback can create design and structural problems.

The Delphi method was initially designed for pen and paper and the method needs to be refined to take into account the very flexible ways of undertaking it which are now possible.

Conclusion

The Delphi method is less well known than most of the other methods covered in this book. Nevertheless, it can be very useful if research questions require educated perspectives on the future. It can also be useful where prediction is not involved, particularly for some planning and policy questions. The advent of the Internet has considerably broadened the possibilities of undertaking international Delphi studies with ease. The need for rigour and a systematic approach is just as vital in this new, more flexible environment.

Discussion questions

- What factors should be considered in deciding whether to choose the Delphi method to undertake research?

- What issues or problems in the field of information management and systems would be appropriate for an investigation using the Delphi method?

- Assume that your research questions are suited to data collection using either focus groups or the Delphi method. Discuss the proposition that: The advantages of using the Delphi method outweigh the disadvantages.

- In a Delphi study conducted on the Internet, how can the researcher coordinate the research in a systematic way?

Further readings

Buckley, Christopher C. (1994). Delphi technique supplies the classic result? *The Australian Library Journal*, **43** (3), pp. 158-164.

Sproull, Natalie L. (1988). *Handbook of research methods: A guide for practitioners and students in the social sciences*. Scarecrow Press: Methuen, NJ.

Turoff, Murray and Hiltz, Starr Roxanne. (1997). Computer based Delphi processes. (online).
http://eies.njit.edu/~turoff/Papers/delphi3.html

References for Chapter 12

Buckley, Christopher C. (1994). Delphi technique supplies the classic result? *The Australian Library Journal*, **43** (3), pp. 158-164.

Busha, Charles H. and Harter, Stephen P. (1980). *Research methods in librarianship: Techniques and interpretations*. Academic Press: Orlando, NY.

Dalkey, N. and Helmer, O. (1963). An experimental application of the Delphi method to the use of experts. *Journal of the Institute of Management Science*, **9**, pp. 457-467, cited in Gupta, U.G. and Clarke, R.E. (1996). Theory and applications of the Delphi technique: A bibliography (1975-1994). *Technological Forecasting and Social Change*, **53**, pp. 185-211.

The Delphi technique and its uses in social science research. (An updated revision of Strauss, H.J. and Zeigler, L.H. The Delphi technique and its uses in social science research. *Journal of Creative Behavior*, **9**, pp. 253-259.) (online). http://www.psych.ucalgary.ca/CourseNotes/PSYC413/Assignments/LabManual/proj2/sandz..html

Gupta, U.G. and Clarke, R.E. (1996). Theory and applications of the Delphi technique: a bibliography (1975-1994). *Technological Forecasting and Social Change*, **53**, pp. 185-211.

Linstone, Harold A. and Turoff, Murray. (eds.). (1975). *The Delphi method: Techniques and applications*. Addison: Reading, Ma.

Otto, Theophil. (1982). The academic librarian of the 21st century: Public service and library education in the year 2000. *The Journal of Academic Librarianship*, **8** (2), pp. 85-88.

Reilly, Kevin D. (1973). The Delphi technique: Fundamentals and applications. In *Targets for research in library education*, ed. Harold Borko. American Library Association: Chicago, pp. 187-199.

Sproull, Natalie L. (1988). *Handbook of research methods: A guide for practitioners and students in the social sciences*. Scarecrow Press: Methuen, NJ.

Turoff, Murray and Hiltz, Starr Roxanne. (1997). Computer based Delphi processes. (online). http://eies.njit.edu/~turoff/Papers/delphi3.html

Williamson, Kirsty and Stayner, Richard. (1980). Information and library needs of the aged. *The Australian Library Journal*, **29** (4), pp. 188-195.

Wilson, T.D. (1975). Research priorities in social welfare library and information work. *Journal of Librarianship*, **7** (4), pp. 252-261.

Winzenried, Arthur. (1997). Delphi studies: The value of expert opinion bridging the gap – data to knowledge. In *Information rich but knowledge poor? Emerging issues for schools and libraries worldwide*, eds. Lynne Lighthall and Ken Haycock. International Association of School Librarianship: Vancouver, BC.

Section 3: Techniques

Introduction

The third section, Chapters 13 to 16, describes techniques used for data collection. Techniques are defined as the means by which data are gathered and samples selected. Techniques discussed in this section include questionnaire design, interviewing, focus groups and ethnographic techniques, including participant observation.

CHAPTER 13
Research techniques: Sampling
Kirsty Williamson

Objectives

At the end of this chapter you will be able to:

- define the terms used to describe sampling and samples;

- describe different types of sampling;

- understand the concept of random sampling;

- understand how decisions about the type of sample to be used should be matched to the purpose of the research and the specific research questions to be investigated; and

- understand the limitations of non-probability samples, especially in relation to generalisations.

Introduction

This chapter is the first in a series of chapters intended to introduce you to a range of different techniques which are used in research. The approach used here is somewhat different from that used by most writers of 'research methods' texts, who usually deal with 'techniques' as an integral part of specific methods. The rationale for taking the approach of introducing techniques separately from methods, is that most of the techniques can be used in more than one method. For example, sampling is relevant to almost all research methods.

Since an important goal of this book is to assist you to be critical users of research, there is an emphasis on the salient points to notice when evaluating how well a technique has been used. In the case of sampling the term 'random sampling' is probably the most misused in the research literature. It is very important that you understand the definition of random sampling and that you are also able to judge when researchers have understood and applied it correctly. It is also important to understand when results can be generalised and when they cannot (which is related to sampling) and to understand the terminology of sampling, for example, how a population differs from a sample.

Sampling is very important in both quantitative and qualitative research. Positivist and interpretivist research '... may have very different ideological roots but there is a common concern in ensuring that respondents are *representative*' (Payne 1990, p. 23). Most 'research methods' books for the social sciences, or for a related field, include information on sampling. Examples of references are: Alreck and Settle (1995); Babbie (1992); Black and Champion (1976); Burns (1990); Busha and Harter (1980); Henry (1990); Kalton (1983); Payne (1990); Powell (1997); Tanner (1995). The question of appropriate sample size is a perennial one. A number of authors deal with it, but Henry (1990) devotes a whole chapter to it and Australian Bureau of Statistics (1990, pp. 26-29) and Fowler (1993, pp. 33-35) provide useful discussions.

Definition of terms

Key terms used in sampling are defined below.

- *Population* – a complete set of all those elements (people, institutions, for example) which have at least one characteristic in common and which a researcher wishes to study, for example all Victorian academic librarians. (In the selection of a population for a study, considerations are: size, costs in time and money, and accessibility.)

- *Population stratum* – a subdivision of a population based on one or more specification, for example all Victorian academic librarians under the age of thirty.

- *Element* – an individual member or unit of a population. Each academic librarian would be an element of the population of academic librarians.

- *Sample* – a selection of elements from the total population to be studied. A sample is any part of the population, whether it is representative or not. (A sample is usually drawn because it is less costly and time consuming to survey than is the population; or it may be impossible to survey the population.)

- *Case* – an individual member or element of the sample.

- *Sampling frame* – the list of elements from which the sample, or some part of the sample, is selected.

- *Parameter* – a measure descriptive of a population characteristic.

- *Statistic* – a measure descriptive of a sample characteristic. *Sampling error* concerns the degree to which the sample characteristics approximate the characteristics of the population. (This only applies to probability sampling.)

Types of sampling

Sampling is used when it is not possible to include the whole of a population in a research project, for example, all Australian academic librarians. It is also important to realise that it is not always necessary to select a sample. It may be possible to use the 'population', for example, all of Year 8 students in a small high school. In a survey of Moorabbin Citizens Advice and Aid Bureau Williamson (1986) used a population: the aim being to survey *all* the users during a two month period

If you do need to select a sample, there are two basic types: probability and non-probability.

Probability sampling

With probability sampling (where random sampling fits), the probability or likelihood of the inclusion of each element of the population can be specified. In true probability sampling, each element must have an *equal* and *independent* chance of being included in the sample. For example, if the population is 10,000, then each element must have a 1/10,000th chance of being drawn. It is therefore important that the parent population be known. If a researcher says that a random sample was selected, then you, as critic, need to check on the likelihood that the sample conforms to the standard definition.

The main advantage of probability sampling is that the resultant sample is considered to be *representative*. One strongly influential school of thought is that, only when a sample is considered to be representative in this sense, is it possible to generalise to the population from which the sample is drawn. This is also something a critic should look for. Does a researcher, who has not selected a random sample, make broad generalisations from the research findings, when those findings really only apply to the participants in the research? Or does the researcher generalise to a population from which the sample was not selected at all?

Inferential statistics are used to determine how closely the sample represents the parent population – in other words, the amount of sampling error. Sampling error has to do with the degree to which the sample characteristics approximate the characteristics of the population. In general, the smaller the sample, the greater the sampling error. Conversely, the larger the sample, the smaller the sampling error. That is why larger samples are considered preferable.

There are several types of probability sampling.

Simple random sampling – this gives each element in the population an equal and independent chance of being included in the sample. It also makes the selection of every possible combination of elements equally likely. For example, if you have a sampling frame, listing a population of 500 elements (for example 500 names of academic librarians, each allocated a number from one to 500), and you draw a simple random sample of fifty from that population, you would be as likely to include the academic librarians numbered one and three as those numbered two and four or one and two.

Simple random sampling can be done by:

- *a fishbowl draw* – where numbered slips of paper, representing each element of the population, are put into a large container. The main disadvantage of this method is that it is very unwieldy with a large population. Imagine identifying, listing, and allocating a number to, every academic librarian in Victoria (that is, setting up the sampling frame), and then writing each number onto a separate slip of paper. These need to be placed in a container large enough to hold them. The numbers have to be well mixed and, as each number is drawn out and ticked off on the sampling frame, it must be placed back in the container and mixed in again. This is done so that the number of slips in the container (and the chance of each element being selected) remain constant. For example, if forty-five out 500 numbers are removed, the chance of the forty-sixth element being selected is one in 455 and not one in 500 as was the case with the first element selected.

- *random number tables* – which are continuous row/column sequences of numbers, not appearing in any particular order and where no number appears more frequently than any other. It is possible to use a random starting point, and then work across or down the numbers to select the required sample.

- *computer-determined random sampling* – where a computer program numbers the elements in the population (which have been, first of all, listed by the researcher), generates its own series of random numbers, and prints the list of elements selected.

Stratified random sampling – this is where the population is first divided into groups or categories. Independent random samples are then drawn from each group or stratum. The strata should be defined in such a way that each element appears in only one stratum. For example, if 'age' and 'sex' are important variables for your sample of academic librarians, you might decide to divide your sample into the following groups:

Males aged 20 to 39	Females aged 20 to 39
Males aged 40 to 59	Females aged 40 to 59
Males aged 60+	Females aged 60+

How this example would be used where a proportionate stratified random sample is required is explained below.

- *Proportionate stratified random sampling* is used to obtain a sample which will have specified characteristics in exact proportion to the distribution of those characteristics in the population. Table 13.1 shows a possible distribution of the example above.

Academic librarians	No. in population	No. in sample
Males aged 20 to 39	50	5
Males aged 40 to 59	100	10
Males aged 60+	40	4
Females aged 20 to 39	70	7
Females aged 40 to 59	150	15
Females aged 60+	90	9
Totals	500	50

Table 13.1: Distribution using proportionate stratified random sampling

When you select a stratified random sample, each category (for example males aged twenty to thirty-nine) is treated as a separate population and a random sample is selected accordingly. The necessary information about your initial population is, of course, a requirement.

The advantages of such a sample are that representativeness, in relation to your population, is enhanced. (Sampling error is reduced.) Proportionate sampling also requires fewer cases to give a specified degree of accuracy. However, there is little point in taking this trouble if you have a large random sample, likely to be representative anyway.

- *Disproportionate stratified random sampling* is where the strata of the sample are not necessarily distributed according to their proportionate weight in the population from which they are drawn. It may be that the researcher wants some strata over-represented. It may be that some strata are so small as to be in danger of being barely represented in the total sample. For example, in surveying school students, it might be considered important to include relatively higher proportions of students with disabilities.

Note that there are problems with statistical tests with disproportionate stratified random samples. When some strata are represented more heavily than others, a certain amount of bias enters.

In critiquing research, one thing to look for is whether a researcher, who has not stratified the sample, points out the differences between the proportions of key groups (such as age groups) in the sample and in the population. It gives an indication of how closely the 'sample' represents the 'population' for key variables. This should often be done, whether a sample is randomly selected or not. (See Box 13.1 for an example of a comparison between proportions of key groups in a sample and a population.)

Box 13.1: Example of a comparison between proportions of key groups in a sample and a population

In a study of the information, communication and telecommunications needs of older adults, first mentioned in Chapter 1, Williamson (1995) built a special sample of 202 older Victorians. This is called a purposive sample, described further below. In doing so it was important to indicate how closely the sample reflected the Victorian population of older people, with regard to key variables such as 'sex' and 'age'. It was reported that:

The sample consisted of 202 people, aged sixty and over, of whom 87 (43.1%) were males and 115 (56.9%) were females. At the time of the 1991 Census, 44% of the Victorian population aged sixty and over were males and 56% were females – very close indeed to the sample proportions (Williamson 1995, p. 100).

With regard to age, the following table was included:

Sample respondents by age

Age group	No. of respondents	% of respondents	1991 Vic Census %
60 to 74 (young aged)	146	72.3	70.1
75 to 84 (old old)	44	21.8	23.5
85+ (very old)	12	5.9	6.4
Total	**202**	**100.0**	**100.0**

In comparison with the 1991 Census, the 'young aged' group was slightly over-represented in the sample and the other two groups slightly under-represented.

Systematic sampling – this technique involves taking every nth element from a list until the total list has been sampled. For example, if we were to alphabetically list 500 academic librarians and select every tenth on the list, we would end up with a sampling ratio of 1:10 and a sample of fifty.

Differences of opinion exist about the classification of this method, that is whether it can be called probability or non-probability sampling. Powell (1997, p. 68) says that most consider this method as reliable and accurate as simple random sampling, as long as the list is randomly or alphabetically and not hierarchically arranged. However, Black and Champion (1976) believe that, because systematic sampling ignores all persons between every nth element (which means that not every combination of elements has an equal chance of being selected), it is not probability sampling.

Cluster sampling (or *area sampling*) – this is used at times when large populations are studied – or large geographic areas. The technique involves dividing a population into clusters or groups and then drawing a sample from these clusters, for example randomly selecting two schools from each Department of School Education region of Victoria. Care needs to be taken that the diversity of the population is reflected in the clusters.

Non-probability sampling

This is used when the investigator is interested only in obtaining a sufficient number of elements to satisfy research objectives. There are important limitations on generalisation from the findings.

Accidental sampling – the researcher simply selects the cases at hand, for example people on a street corner, patrons as they enter or leave a library.

Purposive sampling – this is used when it seems impossible to select a random sample and/or it is important to include specific groups in a sample. This was precisely the situation with the Williamson (1995) study discussed above. In that case a random sample was not possible because the study was dealing with an age group where a proportion of the population are mentally and physically unable to participate in field work lasting four to six hours. Therefore a sample which was 'balanced' on a range of variables, for example sex, age, education, income, location (or place of abode), was built. Box 13.1 indicated the extent to which this purposive sample reflected the Victorian population at that time with regard to the variables sex and age.

Note that no matter how strongly you believe your purposive sample to be typical, there is no way of ensuring that it is representative in the probability sense.

Snowball sampling – this is where individual or people in an organisation identify their friends or associates to participate in a study. In their turn, these people nominate other possible participants. It is partly through 'snowball sampling' that a purposive sample can be built.

Incomplete sampling – if a large percentage of cases do not respond or participate in a study, then assurance that the sample is representative of the population is lost, even though the sample may have been selected randomly. An incomplete population list will also not give a probability sample.

Sample selection in positivist and interpretivist studies

Probability sampling or random sample selection is often used in positivist research. If a researcher wishes to generalise from a sample to the population from which it has been selected, the sample must be randomly selected, as described above. Sometimes it will be impossible to select a random sample, or the response rate is so low that the sample must be considered 'incomplete'. In this case there is a limitation on the generalisations that can be made: the findings can only be regarded as fully applicable to the sample involved.

While it is theoretically possible to select randomly a sample for an interpretivist study, most researchers prefer to select a purposive sample. When you can only manage a small sample, as is usually the case with qualitative research, you need to include representatives of all the important sub-groups and personal characteristics which might be of interest in your study. This is also referred to as *theoretical sampling* which is related to the concept *of theoretical saturation* which comes from grounded theory as described by Glaser and Strauss (1967). With theoretical saturation, sampling continues until each category of investigation is saturated (or no new or relevant data is emerging from a particular category).

Conclusion

'Random sample' is one of the most misused terms in the research lexicon. It is very important to understand this term, and to use and apply it correctly. Random sampling gives each element in the population (from which the sample is chosen) an equal and independent chance of being selected.

For research to be useful, it is not essential to have a random (or probability) sample. With qualitative research, it will usually not be possible or necessary. While research using purposive or other forms of non-probability samples is completely acceptable, it is crucial to remember the limitations to the generalisations which can be made to the population from which the sample has been drawn.

Discussion questions

- What are the differences between probability and non-probability samples?

- What is a random sample? What difficulties does the selection of a random sample present to the researcher?

- For what type of research should a researcher select a random sample?

- What are the considerations to be taken into account when building and using a purposive sample?

Further readings

Henry, Gary T. (1990). *Practical sampling*. Sage: Newbury Park, Ca.

Payne, Philip. (1990). Sampling and recruiting respondents. In *Research methods in library and information studies,* ed. Margaret Slater. Library Association: London, pp. 23-43.

References for Chapter 13

Alreck, Pamela L. and Settle, Robert B. (1995). *The survey research handbook. Guidelines and strategies for conducting a survey.* Irwin: Burr Ridge, Il.

Australian Bureau of Statistics. (1990). *An introduction to sample surveys. A user's guide.* Australian Bureau of Statistics: Victoria.

Babbie, Earl. (1992). *The practice of social research.* 6th edn. Wadsworth: Belmont, Ca.

Black James A. and Champion, Dean J. (1976). *Methods and issues in social research.* Wiley: New York.

Burns, Robert B. (1990). *Introduction to research methods in education.* Longman Cheshire: Melbourne.

Busha, Charles H. and Harter, Stephen P. (1980). *Research methods in librarianship: Techniques and interpretations.* Academic Press: Orlando, NY.

Fowler, Floyd J. (1993). *Survey research methods.* Sage: Newbury Park, Ca.

Glaser, Barney G. and Strauss, Anselm L. (1967). *The discovery of grounded theory: Strategies of qualitative research.* Aldine de Gruyter: New York.

Henry, Gary T. (1990). *Practical sampling.* Sage: Newbury Park, Ca.

Kalton, G. (1983). *Introduction to survey sampling.* Sage: Beverly Hills, Ca.

Payne, Philip. (1990). Sampling and recruiting respondents. In *Research methods in library and information studies,* ed. Margaret Slater. Library Association: London, pp. 23-43.

Powell, Ronald. (1997) *Basic research methods for librarians.* 3rd edn. Ablex: Norwood, NJ.

Tanner, Kerry. (1995). *Research designs: An introduction for students of the Master of Business (Information Technology) at RMIT and at Singapore Institute of Management.* RMIT Department of Information Management and Department of Business Computing: Melbourne.

Williamson, Kirsty. (1986). Information seeking by users of a Citizens Advice Bureau. *The Australian Library Journal*, **35** (4), pp. 197-195.

Williamson, Kirsty. (1995). Independent learning and the use of resources: VCE Australian studies. *Australian Journal of Education*, **39** (1), pp. 77-94.

CHAPTER 14
Research techniques: Questionnaires and interviews
Kirsty Williamson

Objectives

At the end of this chapter you will be able to:

- understand the different types of questionnaires and interviews;

- understand the considerations needed for good design of both questionnaires and interviews;

- describe the qualities of good interviewing and good interviewers;

- describe the advantages and disadvantages of using each technique; and

- understand when it is appropriate to use questionnaires, rather than interviews, and vice versa, in a research project.

Questionnaires

Introduction

The most common research instrument is almost certainly the self-administered questionnaire. It is principally used to collect quantitative data, but open-ended questions can be used for qualitative data. It is most closely associated with the survey to the point that many people call the instrument a 'survey', rather than a 'questionnaire'. This is not strictly correct, because a survey is a particular research design, the major instrument for which is usually the questionnaire. On the other hand, a questionnaire can be used in a range of different ways and as part of a number of different research designs. For example, questionnaires might be used to collect some quantitative data to supplement other, qualitative data collection techniques in a case study, to provide demographic data for subjects in an experiment, or as one of the techniques used in ethnography/participant observation.

Questionnaires have been used frequently in the information management/librarianship field, especially to try to understand the needs of library users and to evaluate library services. In the information systems field, questionnaires can be used during information systems development and implementation. They are particularly helpful in identifying potential system users' information and processing requirements in situations where there are large numbers of users at different sites and in helping gather information about user satisfaction with systems and about system use. A large systems development project at an Australian utility included a national survey of its customer service centre staff to obtain information about their requirements for a proposed system to support their sales and marketing activities. Later, after the system had been installed at most sites, questionnaires were used in conjunction with focus groups to gather information about usage patterns because of concerns that the systems were under-utilised. A number of factors affecting usage were identified, including some relating to the functionality of the system itself and others relating to training and system implementation issues.

Since everyone has some experience in filling in questionnaires, the common attitude is that questionnaires are easy to develop. On the contrary, they are not simple to design and require specialised knowledge. There are myriad references available which cover questionnaire design. Most discussions of 'survey methodology' include a section on questionnaire design. Coverage is included in Alreck and Settle (1995); Australian Bureau of Statistics (1990); Babbie (1992); Bell (1993); Best (1970); Black and Champion (1976); Burns (1990); Busha and Harter (1980); Martyn and Lancaster (1981); Moser and Kalton (1971); Powell (1997); *Questionnaire design* (n.d.); and Tanner (1995). Oppenheim (1966), although quite old now, is still a very useful text. In the research field, many of the fundamentals remain unchanged, so that older references often remain quite useful. This applies to questionnaire design. Many of the listed references have examples of questionnaire questions. There is also a section in Chapter 5 of this book, about Internet surveys which is relevant.

When is the use of a self-administered questionnaire appropriate?

- A self-administered questionnaire is appropriate when its purpose is easily explained in print and when the instructions and questions to be asked are straight forward.

- Because they are relatively cheap (compared with interviews), questionnaires allow a larger sample, as well as a wider geographical distribution of the sample, and the collection of a large amount of data in a relatively short time. They are therefore useful in quantitative research, for example, if the researcher wants a breadth of data from a random sample from which to make generalisations to a population. Questionnaires are also simple to administer and easy to analyse (compared with data from interviews).

- With some topics of a personal nature, the anonymity of the self-administered questionnaire can encourage respondents to provide frank, truthful answers. There is not the embarrassment of disclosing information to a stranger.

- Questionnaires are not appropriate if complex in-depth data are required, or where it is important to allow respondents to modify and develop their initial opinions (that is, for qualitative research).

Types of questions

Before constructing individual questions, it is important to decide on the kind of information required to fulfil the research objectives. If the researcher does not have an extensive understanding of either the issues to be investigated in the questionnaire, or of the target population, it is a good idea to undertake some exploratory interviews with typical respondents. This usually results in a much better understanding of what questions to ask, the categories which need to be offered for specific questions, and the responses which might be expected from a specific target group.

Typical questionnaire questions can be classified in different, but sometimes overlapping, ways.

Factual questions – these are straight-forward questions which give respondents a number of categories from which to choose answers which are correct for them. For example:

Are you a member of the Lamington Public Library?   YES [ ]
                                                        NO [ ]

With questions of fact, it is best not to place too much strain on people's memories. Questions relating to recent events are likely to elicit more reliable answers.

Opinion questions – opinions are often measured by a Likert scale. For example:

Are you satisfied with the Lamington Public Library? Circle only one number on the scale.

1	2	3	4	5
Very satisfied	Satisfied	Undecided	Unsatisfied	Very unsatisfied

Note that the numbers used in the above example provide easy pre-coding. (See Chapter 17 on data analysis.) You need either to use 'numbers' or 'boxes' consistently.

Closed questions – respondents are presented with a number of possible categories of response, which should **always** include an 'other' category. For example:

Why do you use the Lamington Public Library? (Tick as many boxes (categories) as are applicable.)

1. To borrow books   [ ] 1 2 9 0

2. To borrow other materials, for example, videos   [ ] 1 2 9 0
   Please specify all other materials borrowed, including videos, if applicable

   _____

   _____

3. To read newspapers or other materials in the library   [ ] 1 2 9 0

4. To use data bases on CD-ROM   [ ] 1 2 9 0

5. To use the Internet   [ ] 1 2 9 0

6. To bring your children   [ ] 1 2 9 0

7. To attend the classes or other functions held in the library [ ] 1 2 9 0

8. To use the photocopying facilities   [ ] 1 2 9 0

9. Other. Please specify all your other uses.   [ ] 1 2 9 0

   _____

   _____

The advantage of closed questions is that they provide frames of reference which guide respondents' replies. This may clarify the concepts used and make clear the kinds of answers sought. They also make for much easier analysis.

The numbers on the right of the boxes are pre-coding which will explained in Chapter 17

Open questions – these allow respondents to reply in their own words. For example:

In your own words, describe your level of satisfaction with the Lamington Public Library.

_____

_____

The advantage of open questions is that they allow respondents to qualify their responses rather than choose categories which may not express their situations or views precisely. If respondents do not understand the question, or the response categories, or are uninformed on the topic, this will become clear. They enable the collection of qualitative data, to supplement the quantitative data.

Disadvantages of questionnaires

- *Difficulty in securing an adequate response.* Response rates tend to be much lower than when the interview method is used. While certain strategies, for example, follow-up mailings and careful attention to questionnaire design, may result in a higher response, response rates to mailed questionnaires seldom exceed 50% and rates between 15% and 50% are common.

- *Difficulty in obtaining responses from a representative cross-section of the target population.* Non-respondents may differ in characteristics from respondents. Questionnaires may be difficult for the less well educated, or people with language problems or other disabilities, to complete. They are also inappropriate for young children. Reasons for non-response are difficult to gauge.

- *Lack of opportunity for respondents to qualify answers or for researchers to probe for further information.* The former is particularly important if respondents perceive questions to be ambiguous, or feel they do not quite fit into any of the categories offered. The latter means that most questionnaires do not uncover causes or reasons for respondents' attitudes, beliefs and actions.

- *Lack of opportunity to control how and when the questionnaire is answered.* Researchers cannot be sure that respondents have been conscientious about filling in their responses.

- *Lack of opportunity to acquire supplementary observational data.* There is usually no personal contact between the researcher and the respondent.

- *Complex data cannot be collected.* Questions must be simple and straight-forward. Even then, there is a possibility of misinterpretation of the questions by the respondent.

Hints for good questionnaire design

- The appearance and arrangement of the questionnaire are vital. The forms should be attractively and clearly presented. Spacing is very important. For hints on good presentation, see *SC1101: Introduction to data collection and analysis* (1998).

- Take great care in deciding on the questions to include. Unless you have an excellent grasp of your subject, it is a good idea to do some exploratory interviews with individuals typical of your likely respondents first. Then, select those questions that are essential to accomplish the objectives of your study. Don't make the questionnaire too long.

- Group items logically, in coherent sections, that is, those that deal with a specific aspect of the topic, or that use the same response options. Try to link sections smoothly. Wherever possible use consistent response options, for example, numbers to circle or boxes to tick. Ask sensitive, personal questions later in the questionnaire.

- Give clear instructions at the beginning of the questionnaires and wherever needed throughout. Only use questions applicable to a sub-category of respondents if essential. Make sure instructions are crystal clear.

- Avoid bias in questions and in alternatives for answering closed questions. *Exhaustive* and *mutually exclusive* alternatives are needed. Always include an 'other ... please specify' category.

- Ask clear, simply worded, unambiguous questions which are free from jargon. Three types of questions to avoid:

  - Double-barrelled questions, each part of which may require a different answer, for example, 'Do you do press-ups and eat porridge first thing in the morning?' The answer might be that you eat porridge, but only in the winter, and you never do press-ups.

  - Statements which contain negatives (with which respondents are to 'agree' or 'disagree'), for example, 'I never lie' or, 'I do not have a full-time job'. (Think whether you could answer 'yes' or 'no' to these.)

  - Hypothetical questions. Where respondents have not actually experienced particular situations, they are less likely to know, reliably, how they would react to them.

There are also numerous small points to watch: clearly number questions and pages; arrange the place where respondents mark their answers close to the question, to avoid mistakes; put the word, 'over', on the bottom of the front side of a page, if questions appear on both sides; put the name and address of the person to whom the form should be returned, even if a stamped, addressed envelope is included; request that respondents check their questionnaires before returning them in good time; thank them for their participation; and offer to send them a short report of the findings.

Piloting the questionnaire

This is absolutely essential. You need to try out the questionnaire with typical respondents. The best way to do this is to have the questionnaire filled in, and then to sit with pilot respondents and discuss their interpretations of questions; any problems of understanding which they had; and any improvements in wording which they would recommend. For this process you should not use the same respondents as will take part in the survey proper.

Obtaining a high response rate

There are a number of ways to encourage high response rates:

- include a stamped, addressed envelope;

- use polite follow-up cards or letters to remind the respondent of the importance of the questionnaire and the need to return it. (Phoning, if practical, is even more effective.);

- a suggested deadline is a good idea; and

- personally typed letters on official letterhead tend to increase return rate.

Critiquing questionnaires

The sections above have given you a great deal of detail about when it is appropriate to use questionnaires in research and what to look for in terms of good questionnaire design. This can be used to analyse both the appropriateness of the use of a questionnaire in a piece of published research, and the standard of the particular questionnaire involved. In particular you should seek an indication that a questionnaire has been piloted with typical respondents, that questions are clear and unambiguous, and that the presentation of the questionnaire is of a sufficiently high standard to ensure reliable responses.

Interviewing

Introduction

Mostly seen as a technique for collecting qualitative data, interviewing can be used in a range of different methods. It is one of the techniques frequently used in case studies; it can be used to supplement survey data; and also in experimental design. Interviews are used in a survey if the information sought is complicated and it is therefore difficult to ask questions simply in a self-administered questionnaire. Given that personal contact is mandatory with interviews, it is also often easier to obtain a higher response rate using this technique.

Interviewing in interpretivist or naturalistic research aims at understanding people from their own point of view. Fidel (1993, p. 219) uses terms such as 'nonmanipulative', 'noncontrolling', 'open' and 'flexible' to describe the approach to data collection. Highly structured interviews, where 'the questions and answer categories have been predetermined' (Minichiello et al. 1990, p. 19, cited in Gorman and Clayton 1997, p. 125), which are really only survey questionnaires administered by interview, would therefore be excluded. Exploratory and other in-depth interviews, on the other hand, are very appropriate in interpretivist methods. Exploratory interviews can be very useful in the early stages of most research projects. Unless a researcher has a very good understanding both of the types of participants who will be involved in the study, and of the content, it is useful to undertake some exploratory interviews with typical participants.

For interviewing in interpretivist research, see Gorman and Clayton (1997); Mellon (1990); Patton (1990); Sandler (1992); and Slater (1990). Most of the references listed for 'questionnaires', above, also include sections on 'interviews'. The standard social sciences texts all contain sections on interviewing.

Types of interviews

Structured (standardised or scheduled) – with these each respondent is asked exactly the same questions. The sequence of the questions is also fixed. Unless there is some freedom for respondents to express their own views, unconstrained by the researcher's agenda, this is simply a survey questionnaire administered by interview.

Structured interviews are used where it is important to be able to compare results across respondents: for a survey, for a number of respondents within a case study, or for multi-site case studies. There can be the flexibility for individual expression within a more formal structure.

It is important to note that if a structured interview schedule is used, it must be tested in the same way as a self-administered questionnaire.

Unstructured (non-standardised, non-scheduled, or in-depth) – with this approach each answer basically generates the next question. This type of interview is useful for exploring a subject or for gaining insights into people (the kind of exploratory interview, mentioned above). Unstructured interviews are sometimes used in case studies to collect extensive data from key people. These are the interviews which are seen as wholly acceptable in interpretivist research. They are also often used before compiling a structured interview schedule or a self-administered questionnaire.

Semi-structured – these interviews have a standard list of questions, but allow the interviewer to follow up on leads provided by participants for each of the questions involved. The semi-structured interview is closer to the unstructured, in-depth interview, than to the structured, standardised form.

The purpose of in-depth interviewing is basically '… to capture the respondent's perspective on a situation or event under study' (Mellon 1990, p. 55). This is in keeping with the central precepts of interpretivism. As Slater (1990, p. 114) says, '… the respondent is allowed, in fact, encouraged, to talk expansively on the main subject, raising topics within it in any order s/he wishes'.

Usually in-depth interviews are tape recorded (with the permission of the interviewee). Slater (1990, p. 114) says that 'the more fully and accurately any interview can be recorded in the respondent's own words, the better analysis and conclusions will be'. Tape recording of interviews also avoids the disruption to interviews which results from the need to take notes.

Both structured and unstructured interviews have been used extensively in both information management and information systems. Issues concerned with the introduction of new technology into libraries and with information seeking behaviour are only two of the many research areas in which interviews have been used in information management. Both unstructured and structured interviews are often used during information systems development to gather information about potential users' requirements for a proposed system. Unstructured interviews allow users to articulate their specific concerns and needs while structured interviews are useful for detailed or specific information about current operations and future requirements. Unstructured interviews were used extensively for requirements gathering in a project to develop a module of an EIS (Executive Information System) to monitor and report on the financial and physical performance of the projects undertaken by a government authority. Senior and middle-level executives were asked about their program monitoring and reporting needs in a relatively informal interview process. It was felt that executives would lose interest in the project if obliged to participate in a formal process, that they would not have time to attend formal meetings, and that the overheads involved in organising committees and formal meetings would slow down the process and lead to a loss of interest in the project.

Advantages of interviews

- Perhaps with the exception of telephone interviews, for which it is often difficult to recruit participants, there is almost always a better response rate than for mailed questionnaires. This is because of the personal contact required to set up interviews. Usually it is possible to achieve response rates of 80 to 85%, compared with response rates for mailed questionnaires which rarely exceed 50%, and can be as low as 15%.

- Complex and complete responses are more likely because probing can be used, and explanation and clarification can be provided to the respondent. The interviewer can attempt to ascertain that the respondent has understood and interpreted the questions in the way intended by the researcher. The numbers of 'don't knows' and non-responses are usually quite small.

- The interviewer has the opportunity to observe the respondent and perhaps his or her living conditions. Even standardised interviews allow for discussion before and after the formal interview, and this can add to the understanding of the respondents' viewpoints. The validity of information can also be checked on the basis of a respondent's non-verbal cues.

- Face-to-face interaction assists in the establishment of rapport and a higher level of motivation amongst respondents. The interviewer can be a powerful stimulus – more powerful than words on paper.

- Interviewers can *control* the context of the interview to some extent and try to ensure that respondents concentrate on the issues at hand.

- Interviews are useful in obtaining responses from people who are unable to fill in questionnaires, for example the aged, young children, the illiterate, and some groups with disabilities.

- Interviews can provide much richer data than self-administered questionnaires. Research reports are enhanced by the opportunity to quote the actual words of respondents.

- Unstructured interviews allow for flexibility in questioning and the follow up of interesting leads.

Disadvantages of interviews

- Interviews are expensive in time and money, and this limits the number and geographic location of respondents who can be included.

- Interviewer and inter-interviewer variability can be a problem, especially where interviews are used as an alternative to self-administered questionnaires, or where comparisons are to be made across respondents. In these cases, there is a need for an emphasis on consistency in the way questions are asked. Even the same interviewer may vary in the tone of voice used to ask questions, in responses to answers, and in the use of probes.

- Related to this, there can be threats to validity and reliability because of 'interviewer effect'. Apart from the variation in interviewer techniques, mentioned above, factors which may bias an interview include the personal characteristics of the interviewer (such as age, sex, educational level, race, and experience at interviewing); and the opinions and expectations of the interviewer, if those are made known consciously or unconsciously. The result may be a desire on the part of the respondent to answer in a way considered to be socially acceptable to the interviewer.

- Unstructured interviews can be difficult to record and analyse. As mentioned above, usually in-depth interviews are tape recorded (with the permission of the interviewee). The problem associated with this is that the tapes need to be transcribed, a very time consuming and expensive task.

Qualities of interviewers

Interviewers should be neutral and dispassionate, but at the same time personable, empathetic and enthusiastic so that participation is encouraged. Body language is important. Interviewers must be acceptable to the respondent. Characteristics such as sex, age, race, social class, manner of dress and speech may play a part in whether a respondent will consent to be interviewed, and on their level of cooperation during the interview. With a touch of humour the cartoon from the *New Yorker* in Figure 14.1 illustrates not only the need for clear questions, but also the potential problem of cultural and attitude differences between interviewers and interviewees.

Accurate reporting is essential, which means that interviewers must be competent in this regard. They need to be observant and perceptive (for example, hunches should be recorded). Where comparisons across respondents are to be made, interviewers need to be trained to minimise inter-interviewer variability.

With regard to the in-depth interviewing used in interpretivist research, the respondent should do most of the talking, although a good interviewer will be in control of the situation at all times. It is important for interviewers to avoid 'conversational traps' which include the desire to express their own opinions, to display their knowledge about the topic, to argue with respondents or attempt to persuade them to their point of view (Mellon 1990, p. 55).

"Next question: I believe that life is a constant striving for balance, requiring frequent tradeoffs between morality and necessity, within a cyclic pattern of joy and sadness, forging a trail of bittersweet memories until one slips, inevitably, into the jaws of death. Agree or disagree?"

Figure 14.1: How not to conduct interviews

Slater (1990, p. 114) says that 'in the classic depth interview, apart from reminding the respondent that he or she is still interested, the interviewer tries not to intervene much, until the final mopping up stage'. Given that a good interviewer should never interrupt, the complex tasks of interviewing requires: 'remembering what has been said, remembering what you want to know more about, and remembering what general areas need to be covered' (Mellon 1990, p. 55).

In summary interviewing, whether as part of quantitative or qualitative research, is not as straight-forward as it may seem. It requires considerable thought and preparation, not only with regard to the questions to be asked, but also in relation to a wide range of issues which may have an effect on the quality of the data which is collected.

Discussion questions

- When is it appropriate to use a self-administered questionnaire?

- What are the features of a well designed questionnaire? And of a poorly designed one?

- What are the advantages and disadvantages of using a structured interview rather than a questionnaire?

- What are the qualities of good interviewers and good interviewing where a structured interview schedule is used and answers across respondents are to be compared?

- What makes for good interviewing in interpretivist or naturalistic research?

Further readings

Bell, Judith. (1993). *Doing your research project.* 2nd edn. Open University Press: Buckingham, pp. 75-90. (Chapter 7 - Designing and administering questionnaires.)

Mellon, Constance. (1990). *Naturalistic inquiry for library science: Methods and applications for research, evaluation and teaching.* Greenwood Press: New York, pp. 37-49.

Powell, Ronald. (1997). *Basic research methods for librarians.* 3rd edn. Ablex: Norwood, NJ, pp. 83-104.

References for Chapter 14

Alreck, Pamela L. and Settle, Robert B. (1995). *The survey research handbook. Guidelines and strategies for conducting a survey.* Irwin: Burr Ridge, Il.

Australian Bureau of Statistics. (1990). *An introduction to sample surveys. A user's guide.* Australian Bureau of Statistics: Victoria.

Babbie, Earl. (1992). *The practice of social research.* 6th edn. Wadsworth: Belmont, Ca.

Bell, Judith. (1993). *Doing your research project.* 2nd edn. Open University Press: Buckingham.

Best, John W. (1970). Preparing and administering the questionnaire. In *Research in education.* 2nd edn. Prentice-Hall: Englewood Cliffs, NJ, pp. 170-171.

Black James A. and Champion, Dean J. (1976). *Methods and issues in social research.* Wiley: New York.

Burns, Robert B. (1990). *Introduction to research methods in education.* Longman Cheshire: Melbourne.

Busha, Charles H. and Harter, Stephen P. (1980). *Research methods in librarianship: Techniques and interpretations.* Academic Press: Orlando, NY.

Fidel, Raya. (1993). Qualitative methods in information retrieval. *Library and Information Science Research,* **15**, pp. 219-247.

Gorman, G.E. and Clayton, Peter. (1997). *Qualitative research for the information professional: A practical handbook.* Library Association Publishing: London.

Martyn, John and Lancaster, F. Wilfred. (1981). *Investigative methods in library and information science: An introduction.* Information Resources Press: Arlington, Va.

Mellon, Constance. (1990). *Naturalistic inquiry for library science: Methods and applications for research, evaluation and teaching.* Greenwood Press: New York.

Minichiello, V. et al. (1990). *In-depth interviewing: Reaching people.* Longman Cheshire: Melbourne, cited in Gorman, G.E. and Clayton, Peter. (1997). *Qualitative research for the information professional: A practical handbook.* Library Association Publishing: London, p. 125.

Moser, C.A. and Kalton, G. (1971). *Survey methods in social investigation.* Heinemann: London.

Oppenheim, A.N. (1966). *Questionnaire design and attitude measurement.* Heinemann: London.

Patton, Michael Quinn. (1990). *Qualitative evaluation and research methods.* 2nd edn. Sage: Newbury Park, Ca.

Powell, Ronald. (1997). *Basic research methods for librarians.* 3rd edn. Ablex Publishing: Norwood, NJ.

Questionnaire design. (n.d.). (online). http://www.cc.gatech.edu/classes/cs6751_97_winter/Topics/quest-design/

Sandler, Mark. (1992). Qualitative research methods in library decision-making. In *Qualitative research in information management*, eds. Jack D. Glazier and Ronald R. Powell. Libraries Unlimited: Englewood, Co, pp. 187-200.

SC1101: Introduction to data collection and analysis (1998). (online) http://www.deakin.edu.au/~agoodman/sci101/lect17.html

Slater, Margaret. (1990). Qualitative research. In *Research methods in library and information studies,* ed. Margaret Slater. Library Association: London, pp. 107-127.

Tanner, Kerry. (1995). *Research designs: An introduction for students of the Master of Business (Information Technology) at RMIT and at Singapore Institute of Management.* Department of Information Management and Department of Business Computing, RMIT: Melbourne.

CHAPTER 15
Research techniques: Focus groups
Kirsty Williamson

Objectives

At the end of this chapter you will be able to:

- describe the characteristics of focus groups;

- understand something of the historical origins and uses of focus groups;

- understand the wide range of contemporary uses of focus groups, including the ways in which they can be combined with other techniques;

- describe the advantages and disadvantages of focus groups in comparison with other methods and techniques; and

- understand the issues which are involved in designing successful focus groups.

Introduction

What is a focus group? The following two definitions are found in the literature:

> A focus group is a carefully planned discussion designed to obtain perceptions on a defined area of interest in a permissive, non-threatening environment ... conducted with approximately 7 to 10 people by a skilled interviewer (Krueger 1994, p. 6).

> The contemporary focus group interview generally involves 8 to 12 individuals who discuss a particular topic under the direction of a moderator who promotes interaction and assures that the discussion remains on the topic of interest (Stewart and Shamdasani 1990, p. 10).

Apart from the fact that Krueger emphasises 'a permissive, non-threatening environment', these two definitions are similar. The literature (see reference list at the end of this chapter) highlights the following key characteristics of focus groups:

- groups consist of seven to twelve people with certain characteristics in common in relation to the topic;

- focus groups are conducted in series;

- participants are reasonably homogeneous and unfamiliar with each other;

- focus groups collect qualitative data regarding perceptions, feelings and opinions, in participants' own terms and frameworks of understanding – about products, services, issues or opportunities;

- data and insights are produced through group interaction in an interview process;

- focus groups have a discussion focused on a small number of issues related to a predetermined topic; and

- it is the researcher who determines the topic and has a distinctive role as moderator of the discussion.

Setting up focus groups

Once it has been decided that focus groups are a suitable way of collecting data, the next stage is to set up the groups. Steps to follow in doing this are outlined below. The design of focus groups is discussed further, towards the end of the chapter. Illustration is provided from the recent experience in the Monash University and Charles Sturt University research group, ITNR (referred to in Chapter 2). ITNR undertook a project on the potentialities of online services for blind and vision-impaired people.

- *Decide on the type of participants who are suited to help answer the research questions.* In the case of the ITNR research, participants were needed who were either blind or vision-impaired themselves, or knew a lot about the needs of blind and vision-impaired people. They also needed to understand about online services, especially the Internet, and their possibilities. Because the research was concerned about the differences of access of country and city people, it was decided to set up a city focus group in Melbourne, Victoria, and a country focus group in Wagga Wagga, New South Wales.

- *Use contacts to find suitable participants.* ITNR contacted the major associations for the blind and vision-impaired in Melbourne and Wagga Wagga. Some of the participants in each of the focus groups were people from the organisations which work with blind and vision-impaired people. The ITNR experience was that it is often not easy to recruit suitable participants. For the Melbourne focus group there were eight participants; in Wagga Wagga there were only five. However, the latter group seemed to work better because of the smaller size and the greater degree of intimacy created by a smaller table.

- *Organise a suitable venue for each focus group* – one that is centrally located and easy to find.

- *Decide on the length of time for the focus groups*, and inform your participants as you contact them. The ITNR focus groups were about one and a half hours.

- *Carefully work out the questions you will ask.* Make sure you put a time limit on each question. It is easy to spend most of the focus group on the earlier questions, and to leave insufficient time for later ones.

It is important, with focus groups, to find participants who are likely to have opinions about the topic of your research. If you want to discuss library services, you might form focus groups of various types of library users. Or you might decide to have one group of non-users to try to understand why they do not use library services and what might change this.

Uses of focus groups

In recent years, focus group research has been '... carried out by psychotherapists and counsellors, community developers, consumer affairs professionals, small businesses, and lawyers, among others' (Widdows, Hensler and Wyncott 1991, p. 353). Focus groups have been particularly used in market research because they enable producers, manufacturers and sellers to understand the thinking of consumers.

Focus groups are used to collect qualitative data. They are particularly appropriate when the goal is to explain how people regard an experience, idea, or event (Krueger 1994, p. 8). They have many points in common with individual interviews: both are suited to probing topics in depth and in a variety of ways. They are both also useful to '... the interviewer who is trying to develop a working understanding of the respondent's views in the respondent's own terms, and in relation to how the respondent integrates these views into an overall perspective' (Reviere 1996, p. 58). The choice of an individual or group interview will depend on a number of factors including whether the topic is impersonal enough to be posed to a group and whether there is benefit to be derived from hearing the issue discussed in a group setting (Reviere 1996, p. 61).

Morgan (1997, p. 17) says that: 'The simplest test of whether focus groups are appropriate for a research project is to ask how actively and easily the participants would discuss the topic of interest'. However, just because a focus group is workable does not mean to say that it is the preferred technique: other possible qualitative techniques need to be evaluated. For example, participant observation, discussed in Chapter 16, would be the preferred choice if a naturalistic setting is required, including the ability to observe a variety of types of interaction and behaviour. (Focus groups are limited to verbal interaction and self-reported data.) Individual interviews would be preferred where the goal of the research is to gain an in-depth understanding of each person's opinions and experiences. Just as individual interviews can be used as a component of participant observation/ethnography, so can focus groups, provided they are one of a set of techniques used in the natural setting.

Krueger (1994) writes of the value of focus groups for client needs assessment by service providers, and for evaluating social programs in an era where accountability is the buzz word:

> Focus groups can provide ... information about perceptions, feelings, and attitudes of program clients. The procedure allows professionals to see reality from the client's point of view (Krueger 1994, p. 9).

Moreover, focus groups can be used to gain relatively fast reaction in areas perceived as needing improvement or change (Hart 1995, p. 280).

When focus groups are considered appropriate, there is a variety of ways in which they can be used:

- as a self-contained technique, the results of which can stand on their own;

- for preliminary or exploratory research prior to the use of other, usually quantitative techniques – see first example in Box 15.1;

- as a follow-up procedure after other, usually quantitative techniques, have been used – see second example in Box 15.1;

- in combination with a quantitative technique, such as a questionnaire, where one is seen as complementary to the other; and/or

- as a fully complementary technique with another qualitative technique such as individual interviews or as *one* of the techniques used in participant observation/ethnography or in a case study.

In a list which partly overlaps with the points above, Stewart and Shamdasani (1990, p. 15) present a list of uses of focus groups:

- obtaining general background information about a topic of interest – see first example in Box 15.1;

- generating research hypotheses that can be submitted to further research and testing using more quantitative approaches;

- stimulating new ideas and creative concepts;

- diagnosing the potential for problems with a new service or product;

- generating impressions of products, programs, services, institutions, or other objects of interest;

- learning how respondents talk about the phenomenon of interest. This, in turn, may facilitate the design of questionnaires, survey instruments, or other research tools that might be employed in more quantitative research; and/or

- interpreting quantitative results previously obtained – see second example in Box 15.1.

Box 15.1: Examples of the use of focus groups in information management and systems

1. In information systems research, a focus group was used to identify key issues related to the development of a data warehouse. The purpose of the focus group, which was conducted at Monash University in 1997 (Shanks and O'Donnell 1997), was to obtain background information so that the strengths and weaknesses of a new concept could be determined (second point in the first list and first point in the second list). The focus group had ten members and was conducted in two consecutive sessions. Each session had the same members, due to the difficulty of recruiting appropriate subjects. The group identified a number of important features of data warehousing, as well as a number of important factors associated with the business case for data warehousing. The group participated in the development of an evolutionary process model for data warehousing and identified key issues for data warehousing.

2. An example from information management where focus groups were used to interpret quantitative results previously obtained (seventh in the second list and third point in the first list) comes from Markey (1992, p. 87). The project was titled Online Computer Library Center (OCLC) project and investigated online catalogue use, nationwide in the USA. The focus group interview technique was used for post-survey analysis, 'to validate and to further expand on the information gathered from the questionnaires' (Kaske and Sanders 1983, p. 1, cited in Markey 1992, p. 90). Markey says that: 'In the project's final report, subjects' remarks in focused group interviews validated and explained reasons why the survey respondents held particular beliefs and feelings about online catalogs' (p. 90).

Advantages and disadvantages of focus groups

Like other techniques for collecting qualitative data, for example, participant observation (of the traditional kind) and individual interviews, focus groups have strengths and weaknesses. Very often a particular strength is, in another respect, a weakness. Here the advantages are listed first and then matched, as far as possible, with the corresponding number, in the list of disadvantages below.

Advantages

1. Focus groups tap into the human tendency to develop attitudes and perceptions relating to concepts, products, services, or programs in part by interaction with other people (Krueger 1994, p. 10).

   With regard to this point Krueger (1994, p. 11) summarises a discussion by Albrecht (1993) about understanding communication processes in focus groups. He says that surveys and face-to-face interviews assume that individuals form opinions in isolation and really know how they feel. In fact, 'people may need to listen to opinions of others before they form their own personal viewpoints' (Krueger 1994, p. 11). Put another way:

   > ... focus groups allow respondents to react to, and build upon, the responses of other group members. This synergistic effect of the group setting may result in the production of data or ideas that might not have been uncovered in individual interviews (Stewart and Shamdasani 1990, p. 16).

   Krueger (1994, p. 10) also talks about the permissive group environment which is required to achieve the best interaction. It is best to select participants who do not know each other personally, are unlikely to see each other again, but are alike in some ways. This is likely to result in candid portraits of participants' perceptions, which do not emerge so readily in other forms of questioning. The interviewer creates a permissive environment by not making judgments about responses or communicating approval or disapproval through body language, and through encouraging alternative explanations. Krueger notes the fact that long distance travellers (on buses, planes and trains) will often disclose a lot about themselves because they sense they are alike, the situation is non-threatening, and they are likely never to see each other again (Krueger 1994, p. 13).

   Along with other writers, Krueger (1994) warns that the rule for selecting focus groups is commonality in background (although not opinions). Markey's (1992) OCLC study heeded Morgan's (1988, p. 10) view that when respondents are mixed '... the probability is high that the discussion will degenerate in either of two ways: a refusal to share experiences and opinions across categories, or uncontrollable conflict'. Variables that need to be considered include age, education, ethnicity, socio-economic status. A USA research group, Greenberg Quinlan Research, describes their research groups as being particularly powerful for the reason that the company insists absolutely on cultural and demographic homogeneity. 'GQR focus groups are more elaborate than many others because of our insistence on cultural and demographic homogeneity within a group to produce maximum comfort and freedom of conversation' (Greenberg Quinlan Rosner Research 2002).

2. Because of their reliance on the researcher's focus, focus groups are able to produce concentrated amounts of data on precisely the topic of interest (Morgan 1997, p. 13).

    Researcher control is certainly a strength, when compared with participant observation, of the traditional, full participant kind (Glesne and Peshkin 1992), where the researcher is dependent on what crops up and what views happen to be expressed in the naturalistic environment chosen for the research. However, the researcher's or moderator's control is not as great as in individual interviews where there is closer communication between interviewer and interviewee. Morgan (1997, p. 11) states that:

    > By comparison, focus groups may confront the researcher with a choice between either giving control to the group and possibly hearing less about the topic of interest or taking direct control of the group, and possibly losing the free-flowing discussion that was the original intent of the group interview.

3. Focus groups are quick, cheap, easy to organise, and efficient in gathering large amounts of information.

    When compared with a survey, using a questionnaire mailed to a random sample of respondents, focus groups are inexpensive, easy to organise, and much less time consuming. They also take much less administrative effort than do individual interviews. Morgan (1997, p. 14) cites Fern (1982) as concluding that two eight-person focus groups would produce as many ideas as ten individual interviews. This means that, through focus groups, researchers can increase the sample size in a qualitative study without increasing the cost in time and money (Krueger 1994, p. 36).

4. In a focus group, there is the opportunity for the clarification of responses and for follow up questions. The researcher can also observe body language which may be as informative as the verbal responses.

    This advantage also applies to individual interviews, but is not available with questionnaires or observation.

5. The open responses of a focus group result in large and rich amounts of data in the respondents' own words.

As Stewart and Shamdasani (1990, p. 16) point out, 'the researcher can obtain deeper levels of meaning, make important connections, and identify subtle nuances in expression and meaning'. The equivalent number of individual interviews also have this advantage, but at greater cost and inconvenience.

6. Focus groups provide one of the few research tools available for obtaining data from children or from people who are not fully literate (Stewart and Shamdasani 1990, p. 16).

This advantage also applies to individual interviews.

Disadvantages

1. Some participants may be dominated by others in a group situation and may not express their real views or be easily swayed, by others, to views that they privately do not support.

The guidelines, discussed above, such as regarding commonality of background of participants and the greatest possible degree of anonymity, assist with group dynamics. However, Morgan (1997, p. 15) notes it is clear that '... for some types of participants discussing some types of topics, the presence of a group will affect what they say and how they say it'. It is for this reason that Delphi studies, discussed in Chapter 12, are favoured over focus groups by some researchers.

2. The fact that the group is driven by the researcher's interests means that the moderator can influence the group's reactions and create a bias.

In fact, the researcher can exert a great deal of influence in most qualitative techniques, including participant observation and individual interviewing. It is something of which those who undertake research and who use the results need to be fully aware.

3. Focus groups may be cheap, efficient, and easy to organise, but there are strict limitations on generalisations to a larger population, in comparison with the much more complicated and expensive processes of random sample surveys. Also the logistics of assembling appropriate focus groups, in an environment conducive to conversation, may not be as easy or efficient as undertaking individual interviews.

As Stewart and Shamdasani (1990, p. 17) point out:

> ... persons who are willing to travel to a locale to participate in a one to two hour group discussion may be quite different from the population of interest, at least on some dimension, such as compliance or deference.

The advent of the Internet has made some difference to the logistical problem of assembling a focus group. There are now market research firms which conduct focus groups, using a Web-based 'chat room' (Clearwater Research 1998). Clearwater Research even provides the software if a respondent does not have it:

> The group is conducted just like a traditional focus group. The moderator (at the host site) has control, and follows a specific discussion outline. Comments are typed in by respondents, and the usual banter and follow-up takes place, just like in an in-person group

The advantage is that a group can be brought together from across the country, or around the world at a very low cost. The technology provides immediate transcripts of the discussion at the end of the group.

4. The 'live' and immediate nature of responses may lead a researcher or decision maker to place greater faith in the findings than is actually warranted (Stewart and Shamdasani 1990, p. 17).

This may be the case when the statistical summaries resulting from quantitative methods are compared with the findings of focus groups. (On the other hand, there are others who put more faith in statistics than they do in words.) It could also be that, because of the group involvement, focus groups may unfairly carry more weight than individual interviews.

5. The open-ended nature of responses from focus groups often makes summarisation and interpretation of results difficult.

This can also be a problem with individual interviews, but the interaction of responses in a focus group is an exacerbating factor.

6. Focus groups need to be lead by trained interviewers.

This also applies to an interviewer with an individual respondent, but the moderator of a focus group has a more complicated task in keeping the group of people on track. As Krueger (1994, p. 16) points out:

> the open-ended questioning, the use of techniques such as pauses and probes, and knowing when and how to move into new topic areas requires a degree of expertise typically not possessed by untrained interviewers.

Design of focus groups

A number of major decisions which need to be made when designing research using focus group are discussed below.

The objectives of the research (essential to all research)

It is assumed that the objectives of the research will be generated prior to a decision being made about the appropriate method and techniques to be used. Clear objectives are essential, regardless of the method and techniques chosen.

Who will participate in the groups

Focus groups are usually composed of purposively selected samples. This involves a shift from an emphasis on generalisability to theoretically motivated sampling as developed by Glaser and Strauss (1967), which was discussed briefly in Chapter 13. A prime issue is the importance of homogeneity, as discussed above. Morgan (1997, pp. 35-42) provides a very detailed discussion of the issues involved in selecting participants of focus groups.

The size of the focus groups

Morgan (1997, pp. 42-43) says that small groups (fewer than six people) can be unproductive if participants have a low level of involvement with the topic or some of the participants do not get on well with each other. On the other hand, in smaller groups each participant has more time to talk and the researcher can get a better sense of each participant's reaction. Larger groups (over ten people) are more difficult to manage and require greater skill on the part of the interviewer, especially if participants are highly involved in the topic. Morgan (1997, p. 43) therefore specifies a rule of thumb range of six to ten. Whatever size is selected, it is important to over-recruit as people often fail to turn up.

The types of participants to include

This issue includes the need for reasonable homogeneity and anonymity, as discussed above.

The number of groups

Morgan (1997, p. 43) says that a rule of thumb is that the number of groups conducted on a particular topic should be three to five. This comes from the view that more groups usually do not provide meaningful new insights. This is another way of expressing the goal of 'saturation' in theoretical sampling (Glaser and Strauss 1967). It is the point at which data collection no longer generates new understanding (Morgan 1997, p. 43). (See Morgan (1997, pp. 43-44) for discussion of other factors affecting this decision.)

The interview content and schedule of questions

The first question to determine is the length of the focus group interview. Typically this will be one to two hours. Morgan (1997, p. 47) says that: 'Safe advice would be to set the length at 90 minutes, but tell participants that the discussion will run two hours ...'. In terms of deciding the content of the interview, Morgan sees a difference between unstructured groups, which are particularly useful for exploratory research, and structured groups, which are especially useful when there is a strong, pre-existing agenda for the research. He says that, for an unstructured group, there are probably just two broadly stated topics or questions. With the 'unstructured' approach, comparisons between groups is very difficult. 'In a more structured group, the limit should probably be four or five distinct topics or questions, with preplanned probes under each major topic' (Morgan 1997, p. 47).

With structured groups, it is usual for a list of questions to be developed, which the moderator follows from group to group. This facilitates comparison across groups. Questions need considerable thought, planning, and sequencing. Dichotomous questions and 'why' questions are to be avoided (Krueger 1994, p. 69). It is important to expect to cover only a limited number of questions in any one session. Questions must be phrased simply in language that respondents understand. Pretesting of questions with typical respondents is a good idea.

Stewart and Shamdasani (1990, p. 61) say that there are two general principles to be observed in developing the interview guide and that they not always be compatible:

- that questions should be ordered from the more general to the more specific; and

- that questions should be ordered by their relative importance to the research agenda.

Both Morgan (1997, pp. 47-48) and Stewart and Shamdasani (1990, p. 62) strongly assert that there should be flexibility for the moderator to probe more deeply if the occasion arises.

How the data should be transcribed, analysed and reported

The focus group should be taped and transcribed as close to verbatim as possible. In terms of analysis, Morgan (1997, p. 60) believes that

> neither the individual nor the group constitutes a separable 'unit of analysis'; instead, our analytic efforts must seek a balance that acknowledges the interplay between these 'two levels of analysis'.

Analysis is a complex process. (For more detailed discussion, see Morgan (1997, pp. 58-63); Stewart and Shamdasani (1990, pp. 102-121 and pp. 140-156), as well as the analysis of qualitative data section of Chapter 16.) The reporting of the findings should follow basic procedures for the reporting of findings using other research techniques.

Conclusion

Focus groups are a key technique for collecting qualitative data. There is flexibility in the ways in which they can contribute to research. The researcher should consider the whole range of possible techniques in relation to the research questions before making a decision to go ahead with a focus group. Once that decision has been made, a focus group must be set up and conducted with considerable care, forethought and planning, if maximum benefit is to be gained.

Discussion questions

- What factors should be considered in deciding whether to use a focus group rather than another type of technique for the collection of qualitative data?

- What are the major considerations to keep in mind in designing a focus group?

- In what general ways can focus groups contribute to research in the fields of information management and systems?

- Think of specific examples where focus groups might contribute to the data collected in projects in the fields of information management and systems?

Further readings

Markey, Karen Drabenstott. (1992). Focused group interviews. In *Qualitative research in information management*, eds. Jack D. Glazier and Ronald R. Powell. Libraries Unlimited: Englewood, Co, pp. 85-104.

Widdows, Richard, Hensler, Tia A. and Wyncott, Marlaya H. (1991). The focus group interview: A method for assessing users' evaluation of library service. *College and Research Libraries*, **52**, July, pp. 352-359.

References for Chapter 15

Albrecht, Terrance L. (1993). Understanding communication processes in focus groups. In *Successful focus groups,* ed. David L. Morgan. Sage: Newbury Park, Ca., pp. 51-64, cited in Krueger, Richard A. (1994). *Focus groups: A practical guide for research.* Sage: Thousand Oaks, Ca.

Clearwater Research Inc. (1998). Marketing research: Focus groups on the Web. (online). http://www.clearwater-research.com/clearwater/whatwedo/

Fern, E.F. (1982). The use of focus groups for idea generation: The effects of group size, acquaintanceship, and moderator on response quantity and quality. *Journal of Marketing*, **19**, pp. 1-13, cited in Morgan, David L. (1997). *Focus groups as qualitative research.* 2nd edn. Sage: Thousand Oaks, Ca. (1st edn. 1988.)

Glaser, Barney G. and Strauss, Anselm L. (1967). *The discovery of grounded theory: Strategies of qualitative research.* Aldine de Gruyter: New York.

Glesne, C. and Peshkin, A. (1992). *Becoming qualitative researchers: An introduction.* Longman: New York.

Greenberg Quinlan Rosner Research. (2002). Corporations: Reputation and issue management. (online). http://www.greenbergresearch.com/corporations/products.html

Hart, Elizabeth. (1995). The role of focus groups with other performance measurement methods. In *Proceedings of the First Northumbria International Conference on Performance Measurement in Libraries and Information Services,* 31 August- 4 September, ed. Pat Wressell. Information North: Newcastle upon Tyne.

Kaske, Neal K. and Sanders, Nancy P. (1983). *A comprehensive study of online public access catalogs: An overview and application of findings.* (OCLC Research Report Series No. OCLC/OPR/RR-83/4). OCLC: Dublin, Ohio, cited in Markey, Karen Drabenstott. (1992). Focused group interviews. In *Qualitative research in information management*, eds. Jack D. Glazier and Ronald R. Powell. Libraries Unlimited: Englewood, Co., p. 90.

Krueger, Richard A. (1994). *Focus groups: A practical guide for applied research.* Sage: Thousand Oaks, Ca.

Markey, Karen Drabenstott. (1992). Focused group interviews. In *Qualitative research in information management*, eds. Jack D. Glazier and Ronald R. Powell. Libraries Unlimited: Englewood, Co., pp. 85-104.

Morgan, David L. (1997). *Focus groups as qualitative research.* 2nd edn. Sage: Newbury Park, Ca. (1st edn. 1988.)

Reviere, Rebecca (ed.). (1996). *Needs assessment: A creative and practical guide for social scientists.* Taylor and Francis: Washington, DC.

Shanks, Graeme and O'Donnell, Peter. (1997). Focus group on data warehousing. Unpublished paper. Department of Information Systems, Monash University: Clayton, Vic.

Stewart David W. and Shamdasani, Prem N. (1990). *Focus groups: Theory and practice.* Sage: Newbury Park, Ca.

Widdows, Richard, Hensler, Tia A. and Wyncott, Marlaya H. (1991). The focus group interview: A method for assessing users' evaluation of library service. *College and Research Libraries*, **52**, July, pp. 352-359.

CHAPTER 16
Ethnographic techniques
Amanda Bow

Objectives

At the end of this chapter you will be able to:

• understand what ethnography and participant observation are;

• understand the multiple techniques which can be used in ethnography;

• know when to use the various techniques; and

• do an ethnographic study.

Introduction

In recent times, as academic disciplines have merged and borrowed extensively from each other, the distinctions between certain methods have blurred. This is certainly the case for ethnography. Malin (1994) indicates that:

> ethnographic research is alternatively labelled: fieldwork, qualitative research, grounded research, participant observation, descriptive studies, phenomenology, case study, and interpretive research (Malin 1994, p. 9).

Ethnography is probably most closely linked with participant observation. Definitions of ethnography and participant observation are very similar. Chapter 10 describes ethnography in terms of studying people in their every day contexts and utilising the medium of the text to describe and theorise on the nature of the topic under study. Minichiello et al. (1990, p. 18) describe participant observation as 'studying people by participating in social interactions with them in order to observe and understand them'.

Participant observation has always been the major research technique used by ethnographers. Originally participant observation meant that the researcher must become an integral and fully active member of the community being studied. The emphasis was on *observing*, at first hand, the interactions of the group under study in the natural setting. Participant observation has now become much more flexible and often includes a 'set' of techniques. It still provides a major way in which ethnography is undertaken. This chapter takes the approach that ethnographic techniques can usually be equated with participant observation.

What is ethnography?

Chapter 10 provides a detailed discussion of theoretical and historical perspectives about ethnography. In summary, ethnography is very often about studying culture, including subcultures or groups (for example, managers) within a setting (for example, a workplace) in an attempt to understand certain aspects of their interaction and behaviour (for example, the ways in which managers gather and disseminate information). When we talk about 'studying culture' in this way, we are not referring to an ethnic culture or high or popular culture. Instead, culture is defined as 'the ensemble of social processes by which meanings are produced, circulated and exchanged' (Thwaites, Davis and Mules 1994, p. 1). Thwaites, Davis and Mules go on to say that 'meanings come about in and through social relations, those among people, groups, classes, institutions, structures and things' (Thwaites, Davis and Mules 1994, p. 2). Meanings are produced, circulated throughout society and exchanged and are therefore never fixed.

For instance Anderson (1995) notes that an anthropologist visiting Japan just before Christmas saw Santa Claus nailed to a cross in a large department store. This is a fairly unsubtle example, but it serves to illustrate that the Japanese have a different understanding of the meanings of Christmas and religious symbols than do Christian countries. Another simple example might be that the meanings of a pizza are produced by the large pizza chains, the smaller single owner pizza shops, the people who work in the pizza shops, the advertising of pizzas, the people who eat them (where they eat them, and with whom they eat them), and the consumerist society we live in. So the meanings of a pizza are many: food, product, employment, a family outing, a night at home watching television with your friends, and a pleasurable dining experience at an Italian cafe. This perspective on culture is commonly associated with the interpretivist paradigm 'which portrays a world in which reality is socially constructed, complex, and everchanging' (Glesne and Peshkin 1992, p. 4). As such, ethnography is used to gain an understanding of how various people within a culture, subculture, group or setting go about constructing the world around them, that is, how they make sense of the world around them.

Mellon (1990) argues that naturalistic inquiry (such as ethnography) is useful in library and information science, because information is something that always involves people. In order to be able to respond effectively to people's needs, it is important to know how they think and act in relation to information.

Prus (1997) says the aims of ethnography, are the following:

- to permeate the social world of 'the other' (the insiders);

- to achieve intimate familiarity with the other's lived experiences;

- to carefully and fully gather and record information about that life world; and

- to convey to others (outsiders) the life-worlds of the other (insiders) in ways that are both comprehensible to the outsiders yet as closely as possible approximate to the experiences of the insiders (Prus 1997, p. 192).

According to Prus (1997) therefore, the aim of this kind of research is to understand someone else's (the other's/insider's) experience of the world in order to translate that understanding into knowledge that is comprehensible to those who have not experienced the other's experience. For instance, librarians may have some inkling about how students go about negotiating the library, but it is not until a researcher studies students and translates that study into knowledge which is comprehensible to librarians, although still reflecting the experiences of students, that librarians have an 'insider's' (that is, student's) perspective on library usage.

Prus (1997, p. 192) also mentions another important goal of ethnography: 'the development of analytical concepts'. Put another way, ethnography should be about creating theories of how people interpret and create their environments.

The variety of ways of doing participant observation

Participant observation is one of the most flexible techniques or set of techniques for doing research. There is no single way to do participant observation, although many texts read as though there is only one set procedure. Participant observation not only potentially combines a number of techniques, such as interviewing, focus groups, observation, and questionnaires, but also has the flexibility to emphasise some techniques over others, and to leave some techniques out altogether – depending on the requirements and constraints of the research itself, such as the time, money and resources which are available.

Glesne and Peshkin (1992, pp. 16-17) describe participant observation as ranging across a continuum from mostly observation to mostly participation. (See Figure 16.1 for a diagrammatic presentation of this concept). At one end of the continuum is the 'observer' who participates very little in the activities of the setting. The 'observer as participant' (next on the continuum) is primarily an observer but is involved in some limited participation or interaction with participants. The 'participant as observer' participates and interacts quite extensively with the participants, and observation is only one of many forms of researching. The 'full participant' is a full member of the group being studied as well as a researcher. The 'full participant' is likely to be a member of the group already, or would join the group after the research had started (for example, gaining employment in the office, or joining the local gym which is to be the focus of the study).

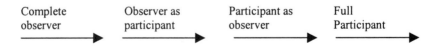

Figure 16.1: Participant observation continuum

Although Glesne and Peshkin's (1992) description of participant observation is more dynamic than most, it still does not capture the breadth and depth of the different kinds of ethnographies which have been done through participant observation. Some of the ways in which participant observation can and has been undertaken are presented below.

The traditional form of participant observation

The traditional form of participant observation is the one which is most commonly talked about in texts on research methods, especially older texts. However, most researchers would have difficulties in aspiring to it due to the practical problems of gaining access to the settings, having the time to do it, or because it is an unsuitable technique for their topic. This closely resembles Glesne and Peshkin's (1992) description of a 'full participant', and originated in the anthropological ethnographies more popular around the beginning and middle of the twentieth century as discussed in Chapter 10. Researchers are encouraged to understand the 'others'' worldviews by experiencing their culture directly, and as a member of the group within its natural setting.

Researchers may have a topic, such as how students negotiate their way through a library system to find material they need. As participant observers in the traditional sense, they will choose a setting and a group of people they are interested in studying and they will participate 'as students' and observe within this setting. What this means is that they will do a lot of hanging around in the library, participating in using the library facilities (to get a feel for how they work), observing students using the system, interacting, and chatting with 'other' students and library staff. They might even attend a few lectures. At the end of this, researchers should have some kind of picture of how students negotiate their way through the library system.

Unobtrusive observation

At the other end of the spectrum, from the traditional form of participant observation, is unobtrusive observation. Kellehear (1993, p. 2) says that unobtrusive methods 'refer to social science methods which do not disturb the social environment'. In other words, researchers do not interact with those they are observing. This is similar to Glesne and Peshkin's 'observer'. In order to do this, unobtrusive observation takes place in public spaces, where the observed do not need to be approached for permission to observe. (This issue is explored further, below.)

According to Kellehear (1993, pp. 117-118), the types of observations that can be made are numerous:

- exterior physical signs (such as clothing, graffiti, street signs, menus, tattoos, hairstyle, houses, calluses, radio transmissions, church services);

- expressive movement (for example bodily movements such as eye, face, limbs, body posture, smiling, frowning);

- physical location (such as the use of settings, the settings themselves);

- language behaviour (for example stuttering, slips of the tongue, general conversational analysis); and/or

- time duration (for example the amount of time the observed spends looking at something or doing something).

An example of when library and information science researchers might use this technique would be if they were interested in understanding and observing how library users use catalogue systems. They could position themselves in a library where they were unnoticed by library users, but could easily observe them using the catalogues.

In the field of information systems, this kind of unobtrusive observation of users of systems can be undertaken. For example, during information systems development and implementation systems, users can be observed carrying out their organisational functions and activities. This will assist in identifying problems in the operation of newly-implemented systems.

Other ways of doing ethnography

The three examples in Box 16.1 reflect three of the many other ways in which researchers can do ethnography. You will notice that these examples do not necessarily fit into Glesne and Peshkin's (1992) participant observation categories.

Box 16.1: Examples of doing ethnography/participant observation

Example 1

Grover and Glazier (1992) set out to study how city managers routinely collect, assimilate and disseminate information. Although the researchers did not participate in the work place of the managers, as in the more traditional form of participant observation, they used a variety of methods. These included interviewing the managers, observing them in the workplace and analysing their documents and correspondence.

Example 2

Williamson, Bow and Wale (1996) examined the barriers that older adults experienced in their access to the Internet in public libraries. One hundred and twenty older adults, across three libraries in Melbourne, Victoria, filled in questionnaires which explored the relationships between how they felt about computers, their current experience of computers and the Internet, their current knowledge about the Internet, and other demographic factors. Of these 120 participants, all of whom were approached initially in the library settings, sixty were recruited to participate in an observation study. This involved participants being observed whilst they attempted to use the Internet. The observers intervened only when participants were unable to proceed alone. They used a standardised table in which to record their observations about the problems the participants were experiencing whilst using the Internet.

This study is closest to Glesne and Peshkin's (1992) 'observer as participant' category. Observers interacted with the participants, but more as guides and interviewers, than as peers. The researchers also spent some time familiarising themselves with the libraries they were studying as well as trying out the Internet in each of the settings used for the research. There is an element of participation within the familiarisation process itself, because the researchers were participating in something participants were also to use. The fact the researchers wanted to study a behaviour that did not exist (they wanted to study older adults using the Internet in public libraries – something very few were known to do at that time), meant that they could not do the traditional kind of participant observation study. Instead, they recruited participants from their natural setting (the library) to participate in an activity they did not normally do, in order to understand the barriers to undertaking that activity.

The study revealed a number of problems for older people in using the Internet. For example, some of the Internet's functions did not make immediate sense to new users; some of the fonts were too small or too faint for people with vision impairment to see properly (Williamson, Bow and Wale 1996). It appeared that unfamiliarity and fear of the Internet were the main reason for older adults not using it. After the study, 85% of the respondents indicated they would use the Internet again.

Box 16.1 (cont.): Examples of doing ethnography/participant observation

Example 3

Gillard, Wale and Bow (1994) did an ethnography of telephone use at home, without actually participating or observing. To participate and observe over a period of time within a setting, usually requires the researcher to become a member of the group being studied or, at least to be present in the setting for a period of time. When the setting of the study is the home, this becomes difficult, as it is usually a private space in which couples, families or friends carry out personal relationships and routines, which they do not necessarily want to share with strangers. Whilst observing in the home may be possible (and does occasionally occur in research, within short spaces of time), participating as a family member is impossible. The researcher can never be a member of the family, and is sure to change the dynamics of the family they are studying. Therefore, the solution to this problem is to interview respondents in a way which will reveal data similar to those which might be collected if the researcher were actually participating in, and observing, the activities of the participants. This means that the researcher needs to ask questions about attitudes and opinions, and also questions about what people do. They need to learn as much as possible about the context of the participants' lives as possible, and preferably to interview them in their home or work environment.

When to undertake an ethnography

Before researchers begin to think about the appropriate method and technique(s) for their study, they should follow the guidelines presented in Chapter 3 on writing a statement of problem and major research questions, sub-problems or specific questions, the literature review and theoretical framework. While it is not unusual for researchers to think about the methods and techniques they might use as they are sorting through these issues, it *is* unusual to think 'I'm going to do an ethnography, what am I going to do it on?' However, often researchers have a philosophical reason for choosing a particular method and technique, and this is likely to determine, broadly, the way in which they go about studying the topic they are interested in. (For example, they may have a preference for qualitative approaches over quantitative ones.)

A researcher's particular topic and research questions may mean that qualitative research, such as an ethnography, is not going to provide the best means of studying the topic. Return to the advice provided in Chapter 2 on which types of questions best lend themselves to quantitative and qualitative research approaches. If your interest is to learn about certain characteristics, behaviours, or opinions of your research participants in depth, then ethnography may be a good choice. Remember that there are also other methods, for example, case study (Chapter 6) and action research (Chapter 9) which also allow in-depth exploration of issues and participation of the researcher.

Gaining permission to enter the field

Before researchers go any further with their research, they need to establish that the subculture, group or setting in which they are interested is actually going to be available to them. There are some ethical issues to consider in gaining access to a setting or group. The following are a few guidelines about the ethics involved in gaining access to a setting for ethnography.

Research ethics is a field which is constantly changing, and its boundaries are at times quite fuzzy. What might be acceptable research behaviour one year, may be unacceptable the next. It is therefore best to be on the safe side, for the sake of the participants and researchers. Universities, and some other organisations, have ethics procedures with which staff and students must comply.

The main ethical issue in gaining access to a setting is obtaining the consent of the participants. Since there is no general guideline which covers all situations, researchers must judge the situation they find themselves in. Kellehear (1993) points out that in certain situations, such as in a bar or at a football stadium, the number of people is so large, and the turnover is so high, that gaining consent is impossible. If researchers are studying people who work in an office, then there is clearly a group of people from whom they can ask consent. Ultimately, though, they need to get the consent of the organisation first, before the consent of the employees. In some cases, researchers only get the permission of the organisation, and not the employees themselves. This is usually the case if organisations are very large, and researchers are studying the whole organisation, or a large part of it. In the case of studying people in organisations who are under the age of eighteen or have guardians (such as some intellectually disabled and some elderly persons), in most cases, researchers will have to gain the permission of the organisation, and the parents or guardians.

Kellehear (1993) suggests that the crux of the issue is privacy: that is, people expect and have a right to privacy. It is unlikely that people expect privacy in public spaces, for example, people do not expect privacy when they are walking down the street. However, people do expect privacy in public spaces when they are involved in private acts, such as going to the toilet.

A general guideline might be that if a person is in a setting in which they would not expect to have other people observing them, then researchers need to gain their consent in order to go ahead with the research. Sometimes it may be in the interest of the research topic that people in private places or participating in private acts, do not know that they are being observed. If this is the case, then researchers must realise that the rights of their participants are to be considered above the researchers' need to research the topic – and the topic must be changed or discarded.

Planning the research

It is important for researchers to have some idea of how they are going to go about doing the research before they actually enter the field. They need to think about the techniques they might use, develop those they can before they begin the research and write a time-line. The plan and details of the research are likely to change over the course of the research, but it is important to have a starting place from which to work.

Time in the field

The amount of time spent in the field is dependent on the amount of time available to do the research, and how much the researcher wants to achieve. Many authors who talk about doing ethnography say that the researcher must be in the field for a considerable time to gain the trust of the people they are studying. However, trust is not necessarily something that comes with time. Sometimes researchers will always be outsiders (for example, if they are studying an ethnic group or a religion other than their own) and will never gain the full trust of the people they are studying. At other times, trust is given immediately. However, it is not usual that everyone within a setting will openly trust researchers.

Researchers are actively involved in creating research, and therefore knowledge, and their role in the process (including gaining trust) is as important as the information they gain. Not gaining trust is not necessarily a tragedy. If total trust has not been gained, then this is an interesting point to reflect upon in the reporting of the research: Why was trust not gained? Were issues such as gender, age, culture, or time barriers to gaining trust? How will this affect the interpretation which is made of this group?

Some of the techniques researchers can plan to in their ethnography are presented below.

Document analysis

If there is a need to gain an understanding of the official policies of the setting researchers are studying, this can often be achieved by reading the documents which are produced by the organisation or setting. For example, company policies, promotional material, and external correspondence, are some of the documents which may provide researchers with valuable insight into an organisation. This kind of material is also likely to give researchers demographic information (such as age and gender) of clients and employees. Internal correspondence and unofficial documents can also provide insight into an organisation.

Interviewing

In ethnography you will most likely use a combination of semi-formal and informal interviewing (also known as unstructured interviewing). Informal or unstructured interviewing usually involves exploratory interviews, which do not have set questions. The semi-formal interview is useful to elicit information which the researcher has thought about prior to the interview, and usually the questions have been worded carefully. The semi-formal interview has set questions, but allows the researcher to be flexible in the interview situation, by asking questions which are not written, and by allowing the questions to be asked in an order that follows the line of thought of the individual respondent. See Chapter 14 for a more in-depth explanation of interviews and how to go about doing them. For ideas on how to construct interview questions, the section on questionnaire design in the same chapter provides some basic, useful guidelines.

Questionnaires

Questionnaires are useful if researchers want to gain general information which is easily quantified, like age and gender, and what people own or use. This kind of information is easier and less time consuming for everyone involved, if it is gathered through a questionnaire rather than an interview. Questionnaires can also be used to measure the number of people who share certain opinions or values. However it is suggested that qualitative research should be carried out first, before attempting to quantify this kind of information. For information on how to construct questionnaires, see Chapter 14.

Observation

Lastly, observing what people do is also a useful technique for understanding their behaviour and what is going on in a setting. Kellehear (1993) suggests that when studying material culture (artifacts/physical structures), one should think about the following issues:

- what does this say about users/creators?

- what role does design play in this?

- how are these shapes/forms part of similar objects or processes in the same era?

- how is the object appropriated/personalised?

- what range of social meanings is possible for this object and its relations? and

- how 'fixed' might meaning/s be for this particular object? (Kellehear 1993, p. 112)

There are four main observation styles: ad libitum, focal, scan and behaviour (Martin and Bateson 1986, cited in Kellehear 1993, p. 132). 'Ad libitum' is impressionistic and non-systematic and particularly useful when researchers are new to the situation or topic they are studying. 'Focal' involves 'choosing an individual or group of persons and recording all their behaviour or physical characteristics over a specific period of time' (Kellehear 1993, p. 132). 'Scan' involves quickly scanning a whole group or individual at regular intervals and then recording the information, which is usually the presence or absence of certain activities. 'Behaviour' involves choosing a particular behaviour and recording who does it, and when it is displayed.

Kellehear (1993, pp. 131-132) says that once one of these observation styles has been chosen, the researcher must then decide whether they will record the information continuously, intermittently, or periodically. Recording continuously means that researchers are recording the information as they see it in a continuous fashion, that is, without stopping. Researchers can record intermittently, for example at ten minute intervals. If researchers choose to record after the observation, the information they record allows them to know if an activity occurred, but not how often. Recording periodically means that researchers make their notes about an observation after it has occurred, away from the actual setting itself. This is most often favoured by researchers when they are participating in the activity they are observing, and it would make them look odd to the other participants if they were to take notes. Stacks and Hocking (1992, p. 163) suggest researchers use a combination of immediate and delayed note-taking.

If researchers choose to use a more structured way of doing their observation (for example the Williamson, Bow and Wale (1996) study), some form of table in which to record observations is usually quite useful.

Entering the field

At one point or another the researcher needs to take a deep breath and actually enter the field. A lot of what is written on ethnography suggests that researchers should find 'key informants' amongst those they are studying. Key informants are people who have power and knowledge about the setting. They lend the researcher credibility, and therefore a certain amount of trust, and they usually know a lot about the group or setting. However, a key informant cannot give the researcher the perspectives of others in the group, and the researcher will often find that the views of the key informant do not necessarily agree with the views of the others in the group/setting. It is normal that each person will have a slightly or completely different opinion from each other. (Remember: 'multiple, constructed realities'.) Each person's same or different viewpoint creates the 'reality' of the setting, and the researcher should not try to force consensus on the group. It is therefore important to gain the viewpoints of a cross-section of those studied. If this is not possible then, in recording the results, it should be made clear who was included and excluded in the research process. For example, if the boss of the organisation made it impossible for the researcher to gain access to a certain group of employees, or if the males of a group made access to the females difficult, the researcher has a responsibility to talk about the implications this has for the research.

Collecting the data: In the field

Once researchers have entered the field and started to collect data, a careful record needs to be made. This is because researchers are about to be swamped with information, and they need a way to cope with it. The best way of doing that is to be detailed and systematic.

Some practical hints are: to use a diary to record thoughts; remember to date everything; tape interviews; record some things on video (unless it is inappropriate or will scare people away from doing what they normally do); keep detailed notes of observations; and file everything so it can be easily found. Data collection and analysis should be undertaken with rigour.

Analysis

Analysis is not something that only happens once the researcher has finished collecting the data. It is occurring on an unconscious level as the researcher goes about doing the research, and it should also happen at a conscious level. A detailed account of how to do qualitative analysis can be found in Chapter 17.

Presenting the findings

There is a fairly standard way of presenting findings which is based on the way traditional ethnographers have presented their findings in the past. In some cases, academic journals will not publish the findings unless they are in this format. Kellehear (1993) suggests that the typical approach includes:

Literature review – which discusses previous studies and theories related to the topic of the research, and evaluates them. It identifies the gaps and omissions in previous work and locates the current study within this framework. It also often provides an historical overview of the topic. (See Chapter 3 for more detail about the literature review.)

Background to the study – this describes the physical, demographic, geographic and historical aspects of the setting under study. It also describes how the researchers entered the field, the methods and techniques they used, and the ethical dilemmas they encountered.

Ethnographic description – this focuses on the lives of those under study. This description is often centred on pertinent themes that arose whilst the analysis of data was taking place.

Discussion – this section develops theories about what has occurred in the field. It also takes issue with the previous literature and research in the area (Kellehear 1993, p. 23).

Reports of ethnographies may also have a section on a theoretical framework (See Chapter 3 for a description.) However with interpretivist research, grounded theory – which emerges from the data – is the type of theory which is usually developed. Instead of 'background to the study' there might be a section called 'methods' which includes all the same information, except for a description of entry into the field; and the 'ethnographic description' might also be called 'results'. Therefore there is some flexibility within this traditional format.

Increasingly there is an outlet in academic journals for presenting the findings of ethnographic studies in new and novel ways. This has included presentations that have read like novels and poetry. Much of this has come about due to criticism of the traditional ethnographic forms of writing which present their findings in a positivist manner, that is, as if they are the scientific truth, and as if the researchers were absent during the development, collection and analysis of the research (Van Maanen 1988, p. 197).

Ethnographic writers, such as Mitchell and Charmaz (1998), present one of the alternative ways of thinking about how to write ethnographies. They use some common sense approaches that are perhaps more familiar to journalists and writers of fiction, than to academics. They suggest that the opening paragraph or the opening chapter of a book should pull the reader into the story. It should provide a context and imply what might follow. This can be done by relating a concrete experience, an anecdote, or an excerpt from an interview. The aim is to hear 'through use of language, imagery, rhythm, order and authentic voice ... a whole human being who lived the story, rather than an anonymous report of it' (Mitchell and Charmaz 1998, p. 236).

Mitchell and Charmaz (1998, p. 238) also believe that the writer should attempt to re-create the experiential mood as this 'keeps the reader engaged, unifies the scene and tightens the story'. This involves being quite descriptive and including the 'story' of the researchers and their part in the research. They warn that researchers can not recount everything that happened. They can only create 'a painting rather than a photograph' (Mitchell and Charmaz (1998, p. 241). 'However crafty and complete our stories are, they can be no more than tentative offerings, possible ways of telling from among many' (Mitchell and Charmaz 1998, p. 243).

Discussion questions

- Apart from those mentioned in this chapter, what kinds of ethical considerations should a researcher think about when doing an ethnography?

- How do theoretical or philosophical views influence the ways in which a researcher might go about doing research?

- Can you think of some research issues and questions which are suited to ethnographic study/participant observation?

- Is it possible to do a positivist ethnography?

Further readings

Glesne, C. and Peshkin, A. (1992). *Becoming qualitative researchers: An introduction*. Longman: New York.

Kellehear, A. (1993). *The unobtrusive researcher: A guide to methods*. Allen and Unwin: St Leonards, NSW.

Mellon, Constance. (1990). *Naturalistic inquiry for library science: Methods and applications for research, evaluation and teaching*. Greenwood Press: New York.

Van Maanen, J. (1988). *Tales of the field: On writing ethnography*. University of Chicago Press: Chicago.

References for Chapter 16

Anderson, W.T. (1995). Introduction: What's going on here? In *The Fontana postmodernism reader*, ed. W.T. Anderson. Fontana Press: London.

Gillard, P., Wale, K. and Bow, A. (1994). *A major line to the outside world: Defining the significance of telecommunications within their social contexts*. Telecommunications Needs Research Group, RMIT: Melbourne.

Glesne, C. and Peshkin, A. (1992). *Becoming qualitative researchers: An introduction*. Longman: New York.

Grover, Robert and Glazier, Jack, D. (1992). Structured participant observation. In *Qualitative research in information management*, eds. Jack D. Glazier and Ronald R. Powell. Libraries Unlimited: Englewood, Co., pp. 61-84.

Kellehear, A. (1993). *The unobtrusive researcher: A guide to methods.* Allen and Unwin: St Leonards, NSW.

Malin, Merridy. (1994). *Quality research in education: A study guide.* Faculty of Education, Northern Territory University: Darwin.

Martin, P. and Bateson, P. (1986). *Measuring behaviour: An introductory guide.* Cambridge University Press: Cambridge, cited in Kellehear, A. (1993). *The unobtrusive researcher: A guide to methods.* Allen and Unwin: St Leonards, NSW.

Mellon, Constance. (1990). *Naturalistic inquiry for library science: Methods and applications for research, evaluation and teaching.* Greenwood Press: New York.

Minichiello, V., Aroni, R., Timewell, E. and Alexander, L. (1990). *In-depth interviewing: Researching people.* Longman Cheshire: Melbourne.

Mitchell, R.G. (Jr.) and Charmaz, K. (1998). Telling tales and writing stories: Postmodernist visions and realist images in ethnographic writing. In *Doing ethnographic research: Fieldwork settings*, ed. S. Grills. Sage: London, pp. 228-247.

Prus, R. (1997). *Subcultural mosaics and intersubjective realities: An ethnographic research agenda for pragmtizing the social sciences.* State University of New York: New York.

Stacks, Don and Hocking, John. (1992). *Essentials of communication research.* Harper Collins: New York.

Thwaites, T., Davis, L. and Mules, W. (1994). *Tools for cultural studies: An introduction.* MacMillan: Melbourne.

Van Maanen, J. (1988). *Tales of the field: On writing ethnography.* University of Chicago Press: Chicago.

Williamson, K., Bow, A. and Wale, K. (1996). Older people, new technologies and libraries. In *Reading the future: Proceedings of the Australian Library and Information Association Biennial Conference.* ALIA: Canberra, pp. 161-170.

Section 4: Data analysis

Introduction

The fourth section, comprising Chapters 17 and 18, deals with data analysis, both quantitative and qualitative, and the evaluation of published research. The latter is a very important skill for professionals who wish to apply research findings in their work place. Thus the book begins with a chapter which discusses the role of research in professional practice and ends by drawing together the criteria for research evaluation for the professional who understands and values that role.

CHAPTER 17
Analysis of quantitative and qualitative data
Kirsty Williamson and Amanda Bow

Objectives

At the end of this chapter you will be able to:

- understand when it is appropriate to use quantitative or qualitative data analysis;

- describe the steps involved in the two different types of analysis;

- understand the concepts of statistical analysis, especially of statistical significance (important in quantitative analysis); and

- describe the major differences in the two sets of processes involved in quantitative and qualitative analysis.

Introduction

Data from fieldwork need to be recorded, analysed and interpreted. The way this happens differs according to whether the research is quantitative or qualitative (described in detail in Chapter 2). The present chapter deals with both types of data analysis. Because the processes involved are complex, it is only possible to give introductory coverage. Further guidance can be found in the references at the end of the chapter.

Quantitative data

Introduction

The major steps involved are the coding of the data; the entry of the data into a suitable computer program; the use of that program to analyse the data; and then the interpretation of that analysis. Most of the references listed in Chapter 14, in relation to questionnaires (for example Alreck and Settle (1995); Australian Bureau of Statistics (1990); Babbie (1992); Bell (1993); Black and Champion (1976); Burns (1990); Busha and Harter (1980); Moser and Kalton (1976); Oppenhein (1966); and Powell (1997)) also discuss the analysis of quantitative data. There are Websites for the major computer data analysis packages, for example: Statistical Package for Social Sciences (SPSS) can be found at: http://www.nyu.edu/acf/pubs/SPSS_win/SPSSwindoc_ToC.html); SAS is at: http://www.eos.ncsu.edu/software/software_index/sas.html); and Minitab is at: http://www.minitab.com/.

Coding the data

The data from most questionnaires are usually too complex to analyse by hand. They require a system by which the responses can be entered into a computer file. 'This system involves translating all responses into numerical codes'. (Australian Bureau of Statistics 1990, p. 69). Codes (which are also called 'values') should be as simple and easy to use as possible. For example, for a question requiring only a YES/NO response, such as that mentioned in Chapter 14 ('Are you a member of the Lamington Library?'), you might use 1 for YES and 2 for NO. You should then use the same codes for all other YES/NO questions.

For each variable involved, these codes have to be entered into a specified and defined column or columns in the computer database. This is necessary so that the computer can immediately identify where particular variables, such as the one concerning the membership of the Lamington Library, are located. With the example, above, only one column is required, to accommodate either a 1, 2, or 0 if there is 'no response'. The computer package can then do such calculations as frequency counts (for example, counts of the numbers of respondents who answered YES to the question, and the number who answered NO), or more complex procedures which will be mentioned later.

The first step is to establish categories for all the data involved. It is best to do this before the data are collected so that the codes can be placed on the questionnaires. This is called pre-coding, the use of which can minimise the number of coding errors and increase reliability. Using numbers rather than boxes, as shown in the opinion question of the 'Questionnaires' section of Chapter 14, is one way of doing this. The numbers circled become the code to be entered into the computer. If boxes are used, the codes can be placed at the edge of the page, in line with the boxes to which they relate. In the latter case, you need to be sure that the number is seen to be clearly aligned with a particular box. The third example in Chapter 14 shows this. The reason why each response has four numbers alongside it, is explained below.

Powell (1997, p. 151) outlines a number of rules, two of which are highlighted here. Firstly, each set of response categories for a particular question on a questionnaire should be exhaustive, which means that every response must fit into one of the categories available. Although the piloting of the questionnaire should ensure that most possible response categories are listed, an 'other' category should always be provided. If, after the data are collected, a number of the 'other' responses are the same, or very similar, one or more additional categories should be established. Powell (1997, p. 151) says: 'It is generally preferable to establish as many categories as possible, and, if necessary, reduce them later'.

Secondly, if respondents are asked to choose only one response category for a particular question, the categories within the set should be mutually exclusive. This means that the categories should be clearly enough defined that it is not possible to place a response in more than one category. An example is the scale question in Chapter 14 where respondents were asked to circle only one number. One number (1 to 5) is entered in the column specified in the database for this variable.

Sometimes, as in the third example in Chapter 14, respondents are asked to tick as many boxes as are applicable. This means that each response category must be coded separately. If you look at the example concerning why respondents use the Lamington Public Library, you will see that it is possible that a respondent might tick a number, or all, of the boxes. For this reason, each response is coded as '1' if the box is ticked or '2' if it is not ticked.

Assuming that the responses to this question were, in fact, mutually exclusive, and only one answer could be selected, you would need to allow two columns even if it was not necessary to accommodate the answers to 'other, please specify'. Since the value '9' is used to indicate where a response is 'not applicable' (see below), the numbers 01 to 10 would be needed to cover the nine response categories for the question. If further categories need to be added, further numbers would be used.

Coding books (manuals or frames)

Especially if this is your first experience of coding and data analysis, you should set up a coding book (manual or frame). Sarantakos (1998) says that a coding book should be used to facilitate accuracy and uniformity in coding when pre-coding is not complete, when open-ended questions are used, when more than one coder is employed, and when large and complicated questionnaires are used (Sarantakos 1998, p. 332).

The structure of the coding book depends on the computer processing software which has been selected. If the software selected is SPSS, a computer package commonly used for data analysis in the social sciences, the following would be appropriate for the coding book:

- a name for each variable (not more than eight characters);

- a description of the variable (that is, a variable label);

- its location in the database; and

- the code assigned to it (which is called the value label).

If the original responses are already numerical, such as test scores or volume counts in a library, they do not need to be assigned new codes unless they need to be re-coded, so that they can be assigned to particular groupings such as 'the top 20% of test scores'. The following shows how a coding book would look for the three questions, included in Chapter 14 and discussed above. It is assumed that the questions are the first three on the questionnaire and that they are sequential. Note that each respondent must have an ID number. If there are 364 respondents in a sample, three columns would be required for the ID numbers: 001 to 364. The data from the questionnaire would therefore begin in the fourth column.

Variable	Column	Variable label	Value
ID	1-3	Respondent ID	001-364
MEMBER	4	Membership of the Lamington Public Library	1=YES 2=NO 0=NR*
SATISFACTION	5	Level of satisfaction with the library	1=very satisfied 2=satisfied 3=undecided 4=dissatisfied 5=very dissatisfied 9=NA** 0=NR
USE1	6	Borrow books	1=YES (tick) 2=NO (no tick) 9=NA 0=NR
USE2	7	Borrow other materials	1=YES (tick) 2=NO (no tick) 9=NA 0=NR

Etc. up to…

* NR = No response
** NA = Not applicable

Variable	Column	Variable label	Value
USE8	13	Use of photocopying facilities	1=YES (tick) 2=NO (no tick) 9=NA 0=NR
USE9	14	To consult print reference materials (for example encyclopedias)	1=YES (tick) 2=NO (no tick) 9=NA 0=NR
USE10	15	To study your own materials	1=YES (tick) 2=NO (no tick) 9=NA 0=NR
USE11	16	To look up genealogical information on the microfiche	1=YES (tick) 2=NO (no tick) 9=NA 0=NR

If you compare the third example in Chapter 14, with the coding manual for that question (above), you will see that several categories had to be added (hypothetically) for the 'other' responses filled by respondents. Categories are only added if sufficient numbers of respondents, for example at least five, have nominated a particular 'other' use. This indicates that, despite the questionnaire having been piloted (once again hypothetically), several relevant categories were missing in the questionnaire. Also note that there is a potential overlap between 'reading newspapers and other materials in the library' and USE9, 'consulting print reference materials in the library'. It depends on how categories are interpreted. This is a good illustration of how difficult it is to include both discrete and exhaustive categories.

There are three further points to note about the coding book, above. Firstly, there are invariably some missing data on some of the questionnaires. Respondents often leave out a response to a particular question – either through carelessness, or because they choose not to answer a particular question. There needs to be a consistent code, for example 0=NR (no response), to indicate this (as shown above). This code is considered to represent 'missing data' and therefore to be a 'missing value'. If a number of questions have not been answered, you may decide to discard the questionnaire entirely and not to use any of the data. If more than about one-third of the questionnaire is incomplete, it would cast doubt on the seriousness of the response, as a whole.

Secondly, it could be that some questions are not applicable to some respondents. For example, if a respondent is not a member of the Lamington Library, the other two questions will be not applicable (NA) to that respondent. There needs to be a consistent code, also considered to be a missing value, to indicate where responses are NA. The number '9' is often used. Whatever number is chosen, it must be used to represent all 'not applicable' responses. For some of the statistical procedures which you may want the computer to undertake, you will need to exclude 'missing values'.

Thirdly, where more than one response may be chosen for a particular question, for example, for the one about why the Lamington Public Library is used, it is a good idea to use the same variable name for each response category, followed by distinguishing numbers – thus USE1 and USE 2, above. As you have seen, this pattern is continued until all response categories are covered. Variable names, however, should not begin with a number.

Data entry and analysis

Once the data have been coded, data entry is simple. Even though the task is mundane, it must be done accurately. You need to understand the requirements of the computer package you have chosen. Once the data are entered, the computer will carry out the analysis you require, for example frequency counts, as mentioned above, cross-tabulations of variables which will be discussed below. Most statistical tests can be generated easily by computer packages, such as SPSS. While the researcher needs some basic knowledge about which are the appropriate tests to apply, and how to analyse the output, computers make the actual calculations easy.

Statistical analysis of data

Statistical analysis is complex. Whole university subjects are devoted to the teaching of it. The following provides some very basic information. There are many simple, introductory books on statistics which can be consulted – see for example Hafner (1997) Rowntree (1981), and Simpson (1988). In evaluating published research, it is important to check that generalisations from the data have been based on a random sample and appropriate statistical tests, even if you do not fully understand the complexities of the tests involved. One concept which quantitative researchers need to understand is that of 'statistical significance'. If a researcher is claiming a relationship between two variables, for example that age makes a difference to frequency of library use, there needs to be a 'statistically significant' difference in library use according to age (and not just a difference which may be due to chance). Evidence of a statistical test which supports this finding needs to be included. (See further discussion, below.)

Levels of measurement

There are four different levels of data which need to be understood, as a basis for statistical analysis.

Nominal data – consist of two or more named categories into which objects, individuals or responses are classified. For example, in the question about reasons for library use (above), a nominal scale would be used for the different categories of use. The simplest nominal scale is dichotomous – having only two values, for example YES/NO; male/female.

Ordinal scale – defines the relative position of objects or individuals with respect to a characteristic, with no implication as to the distance between positions. This type of scale is also referred to as 'rank order'. An example is the scale question, 'satisfaction with the Lamington Public Library' in Chapter 14 (and also referred to above). With this type of scale, one should not assume that each point is equidistant.

Interval scale – provides a ranking of positions, as does the ordinal scale, but the intervals of measurement are equal. The interval scale has a zero point below which scores are given a negative value if they occur, for example a temperature scale. Interval level data are less common than ordinal in the social sciences.

Ratio scale – is comparable to the interval scale except that it has an absolute zero, below which values cannot occur. The ratio scale allows one to compare the magnitude of responses or measurements. For example, frequency of library use (as long as it is in the form of 1, 2, 3, 4, 5, 6, etc. times a month) could be considered to be ratio level data, that is, one could state that one person had used the library twice as often as another. Ratio level data are relatively rare in the social sciences, because few scales have true zero points.

Inferential statistics

These are used to test hypotheses using tests of strength of association, or statistical significance. The latter determines if observed differences between groups are likely to be 'real' differences, or due to chance.

Parametric statistics – require the assumption of a normal population or distribution. They are used with interval level and ratio data. Examples are:

- T-test which determines if the statistical difference between the mean scores of two groups is significant; and

- Pearson's product moment correlation co-efficient – measures the degree of linear association between two variables.

Non-parametric statistics – are considered to be distribution free, that is, they do not require the assumption of a normal population. As they involve weaker assumptions, they are less powerful than the parametric tests and require larger samples to yield the same level of significance. The level of significance is the probability that a result (for example the observed difference between two age groups in the sample and their frequency of library use) has been obtained by chance. It is usually set at 0.05 or 0.01, which means that there is a 5% or 1% probability that chance has caused the result. If the 0.05 level of significance is used you will be saying that, because there is only a 5% probability that your result is due to chance, it is likely (although not certain) that a statistically significant relationship exists between the variables. Note that these statistical tests apply to a *comparison* of variables, rather than just one variable, for example, age levels. It is important to note that statistical analysis of research results can never definitely prove a hypothesis, only support it at certain levels of probability.

Non-parametric tests are used with nominal and ordinal data. Examples are:

- Chi-square test – is useful for determining if a statistically significant relationship exists between two variables, for example, age and frequency of library use.

- Spearman rank order correlation – a non-parametric correlation coefficient that can be calculated for ranked or ordinal level data.

The main point to remember is that generalisations from quantitative research must be based on support from statistical analysis. Informed consumers of research will be vigilant about this. Many successful researchers are not statistical experts, but rather understand when to ask for expert help.

Qualitative analysis

There is a temptation for many researchers to leave the analysis of their data until after they have collected it. This has been the undoing of many good research projects. Sometimes researchers, who may have quite substantial funding from government sources, spend 90% of their resources collecting the data, only to realise they lack the time or money to properly analyse it. A quick and sketchy analysis often follows, which satisfies the funders that the research has been completed, but does little justice to the data or the participants who contributed to the research.

Many forms of qualitative research encourage researchers to analyse data as they collect it (see for example Strauss 1987, p. 8). This helps researchers to stay on top of the large amount of data they are likely to collect, and to stop collecting it when they have enough data to answer their research questions or they begin to have more data than they can analyse.

Put simply, qualitative analysis is the way in which researchers go about making sense of the data they have collected, so that they can communicate their findings to others via reports, books and articles. Rice-Lively (1997, p. 200) says that 'data analysis is the process of bringing order, structure and meaning to the mass of collected data'. In most cases, qualitative analysis is about creating theory. Richards and Richards (1998) talk about qualitative analysis as 'working *up*' from data. 'Working *up*' from the data is most commonly associated with grounded theory, although many other approaches to qualitative analysis strongly identify with it. 'Working up' from the data means that researchers are primarily interested in ensuring that the theory they develop is well grounded in the data they have collected (hence the name 'grounded theory'). Also known as the 'bottom up' approach, researchers begin their analysis within the data, by immersing themselves in it until patterns begin to emerge and theories develop. Geertz (1973) describes qualitative analysis as thick description of culture. Chapter 9, says that 'within this 'thick description', the contradictions, complexity and multiplicity of realities, as they are articulated by the studied and as they are observed and analysed by the ethnographer, are presented'.

There are as many ways of going about making sense of data as there are methods and techniques to produce data. The different qualitative analysis techniques are often aligned with particular methods, theoretical positions, disciplinary areas or topic areas. Examples of the different kinds of qualitative analysis techniques are: conversation analysis, network analysis, biographical analysis, sociolinguistic analysis, dramaturgical analysis, textual analysis, semiotic analysis, sense-making analysis, and content analysis. If you have the time, it is worthwhile canvassing the different types of analysis, as they can add interesting dimensions to the ways in which to think about and interpret data.

How to do qualitative analysis

In recent years researchers involved in qualitative analysis have attempted to articulate how they go about doing it. Unlike quantitative analysis, there are no strict rules which have to be followed. Instead qualitative researchers suggest techniques to help 'make sense of the data', to interpret it.

The following is a guide which researchers may find useful to interpret their data. The important point to remember is that sloppy analysis does not result from not following a set of rules, but from not being thorough, resulting in the final interpretations being inaccurate reflections of the data.

The analysis process can be hastened, as well as enhanced, with the aid of computer technology (Lincoln and Guba 1985, p. 352). Although there are a few programs dedicated to analysing qualitative data, NVivo is one of the more popular and thorough programs. It is by far the most commonly used in Australia. The steps to analysis presented below are best supported by NVivo, although NVivo is not required to do many of them. Other software programs may be adapted to follow some of the steps, and some can be done manually by using filing systems or index cards. This will be explained further.

Analysis can be very tiring and tedious as well as creative and enjoyable. Listed below are steps to analysing data. In order to prevent researchers from becoming tired and bored, it is best to take regular breaks, and to keep the creative juices flowing by being at different stages of analysis with different pieces of data (documents). Researchers should also be aware that the steps do not have to be followed strictly in the order presented. In fact, it is usually more fun to mix up the steps, as long as researchers can keep records of where they are up to, to avoid confusion.

1. Transcribe the data

This simply means to type the notes or interview tapes into a word processor making the information much more accessible and easier to analyse. In some cases, researchers have been known to analyse straight from the tapes. However, this is not recommended as it makes it very difficult to re-check easily what was said, and to categorise the data. Transcribing the data into a word processor also means that researchers can easily use computer software programs such as NVivo. If you are using NVivo or another analysis package, you would put your data into NVivo and print it out after you have finished transcribing it.

2. Read through each transcript in order to familiarise yourself

This step can not be supplanted by any of the other steps, or left out. However it can happen alongside Step 3, the categorising of the data. It is extremely important for researchers to have an overall understanding of an interview or an observation and to be familiar with all aspects of it before they begin to break it apart to look at the specifics.

While reading through each transcript or document, it is always useful to write about overall impressions and to note interesting points. These can be written alongside the data of interest or in a separate document, known as a memo. (Memos will be discussed further, below.)

To make this a little easier to understand, an interview from a study on young people and their uses of the Internet will be used as an example. A researcher may be reading through Annette's interview (see below) and comes upon a passage which seems interesting and worthy of a few comments. Note how each line in the passage from the interview has a number at the end of it. This is done in order to reference the entire interview so that any part of it can be easily located or retrieved. The following example is an excerpt from

Annette's interview. From the numbers on the side, researchers know that they are examining lines 174 to 186 of the interview and that there are at least 173 lines of text before this segment of the interview.

*Annette: Well I figure that it (the Internet) makes an even playing field for women,	174
because if a man comes on to our site and goes 'Yeah bitches', we	175
kick him, and we ban him, and then we harass him, and we know he's not	176
going to come after us with a gun and blow our heads off. Where	177
you can't be that assertive in real life without fear of physical	178
harm. So you've almost got this even playing field which allows you	179
to be whoever and whatever you want. So that can be from the fat girl	180
on the Internet – no-one knows you're fat and so you don't have	181
those judgments placed on you: 'this is what fat people should like	182
and be like, and they shouldn't be flirty', and stuff like that to the	183
black woman, to the Hispanic woman. It's a	184
great playing field, and you can just be who you are without any	185
outside judgment, and without fear of personal safety being breached.	186

A researcher's notes: Annette is very aware of an inequality in society, particularly for women in being able to defend themselves physically when they disagree with men. She talks about the 'real world' as being separate from the Internet. The 'real world' represents danger to women's freedom of expression, and the world of the Internet (the virtual world) represents a space in which they can express themselves without fear of physical threat. Also note that she says that women are also given more freedom because what they say is not re-interpreted by the way they look or their race. She may view this as positive, but it leaves unchallenged the conventional views in society about obesity and race. Would like to explore this more (…)

3. Categorise the data

To make sense of the data, one of the most common techniques suggested is to use categories which allow researchers to 'code and retrieve'. According to Richards and Richards (1998, p. 214), 'the code-and-retrieve process consists of labelling passages of the data according to what they are about or other content of interest in them (coding or indexing), then providing a way of collecting identically labelled passages (retrieving)' Categorising, coding and indexing are often used interchangeably. Categorising helps researchers to think about their data at a more in-depth level, to know how important a particular issue is by the amount of data in a particular category, and to be able to think about the relationships between categories. Categories are usually comprised of a short title, a definition if the title is not self-explanatory, and the data that relate to the category. Initially, categories are likely to be quite broad and messy. As the analysis continues, researchers may break categories into sub-categories in order to be more precise.

Sometimes the result will be multiple categories which are completely different from the original category. Sometimes categories are renamed to better reflect their content.

Data are categorised according to contents, by thinking about and naming the themes which are evident. One way in which to uncover themes is to think about: What is this person saying and what issues are being raised? Are they part of a broader issue?

As an example, the interview excerpt, above, could be broken up into the following categories:

Category	Definition (only mentioned when necessary)
Physical violence	
Internet	
Assertiveness	In this case, retaliation to verbal abuse.
Sexual harassment	In the physical and virtual sense (that is, physical and verbal)
Physical harm	
Prejudice	Includes racism, sexism, prejudice against obesity.
Power	Includes power over others, and lack of power.
Safety	Safety from physical harm.
Being self	To have freedom of expression without prejudice.

One small passage can reveal many different categories, as is evident from the example above. By looking at one small passage, researchers can begin to understand how one woman views gender relations in the 'real' and 'virtual' worlds, and one of the ways in which she views the Internet. Glaser and Strauss (1967) indicate that researchers are likely to develop two types of categories: descriptive and explanatory. Descriptive categories are those which emerge because respondents use them to talk about their own processes and behaviour, whilst explanatory categories tend to be abstract concepts developed by researchers to explain processes and behaviour. For example, 'assertiveness' is a category that Annette uses to talk about the way in which she responds to male verbal abuse. However, 'power' is an analytical category used by the researcher to explain why these issues are important to Annette, and why Annette may be behaving in the way she does.

These categories are only starting categories, that is they are the themes which are evident from a first reading of this particular chunk of data. Glaser and Strauss (1967, pp. 105-109) suggest that as researchers continue to read through the rest of the data, they compare each new piece of data with previously categorised data, in order to ascertain whether the new data fit into one of those categories, or a new one. The more data that is processed, the more researchers can refine their categories.

How researchers keep track of the categories and their data is very much up to individual researchers and their preferences. If they use a computer software program, such as NVivo, categories and their data would be automatically stored, ready for retrieval. Researchers can also use index cards or they can physically file the data in folders which have category labels written on them.

Some researchers fall into the trap of spending all their time categorising the data and then they run out of time to retrieve it. The purpose of categorising your data is to think about and organise it, and to make retrieval very simple. At some stage researchers may want to explore a particular category and the range of different responses from interviewees on that subject. Software for qualitative data analysis is very quick and efficient at retrieval because it stores the references to the data (the line numbers) in each category rather than the data itself. When it retrieves the data from a category, it gives you the text, the line numbers and who said it. If you are using index cards, you may also want to number the lines of your data in order to know precisely which data you have put into which category. Another way of making retrieval simple is to use a word processing package and copy and paste the relevant segments of text into separate documents which are labelled with each category heading. By opening up each document, researchers can easily view all the data from each category.

4. Playing with ideas

Playing with ideas can be done at any stage of the analysis. It is a useful technique for thinking about the data in different ways, which may end in a deeper understanding. Kvale (1996, p. 203) says that 'the most frequent form of interview analysis is probably an ad hoc use of different approaches and techniques for meaning generation'. Three ways in which researchers can play with ideas, is to take a word, phrase or sentence and think about all the possible meanings it could have, what other contexts it could be used in, and opposite meanings. For example, a researcher may decide to play with the following sentence from the above paragraph: 'where you can't be that assertive in real life without fear of physical harm'.

The researcher's notes may look something like the following: The word 'assertive' has become popular, with courses available for people to develop assertive behaviour. Assertiveness is usually seen as a male trait, something that women are lacking. The opposite of assertive is 'subservient'. According to the dictionary 'assert' means 'to put oneself forward boldly and insistently' and 'subservient' means 'serving or acting in a subordinate capacity; subordinate; servile; expressively submissive'. This leads to questions of whether all assertiveness by women results in physical harm, or perhaps the fear of physical harm; what is the difference between being assertive and retaliating; and are women being subservient if they do not respond in kind to male aggressiveness. Also interesting is the interviewee's division between 'real life' and the conversations which occur on the Internet, which are perhaps best labelled as 'virtual'. Why is the 'virtual' not considered as 'real'? Why are these two words presented in opposition to each other, rather than as the 'virtual' constituting a part of the 'real'? Is the difference between 'real' and 'virtual' because of the technology which separates people in the 'virtual'? If this is so, is a telephone conversation 'real' or 'virtual'? The opposite of 'real' is 'fake'. Is there any resonance between the concepts of 'fake' and 'virtual'?

5. Writing memos

A memo is merely a name for a document which is used to write ideas or information about interviews or categories. NVivo allows researchers to tag memos to the interview documents or categories or to have them as separate documents. Researchers can also set aside a book to write their memos in, or us a word processing package. It is useful to write a date next to each entry in a memo to keep a record of how the researcher progressed in their thinking. Whilst it is not essential to write memos, they are a useful tool and can often be the basis for the final report.

6. Conceptually organising the categories

Researchers must have some categories before they can begin to organise them conceptually. However, the analysis does not have to be too far advanced to do this. Conceptually organising categories is something researchers should do continually throughout the analysis. It involves thinking about the relationships between categories, the conceptual similarities and differences and representing the relationships pictorially. There appear to be two main ways of pictorially representing categories: in loose diagrammatic form or via a tree structure. The qualitative data analysis software package NUD.IST supports a tree structure which can present categories in two different ways (See Figures 17.1 and 17.2.)

In the following example, every time interviewees talked about their technical ability the data were coded into a category called 'Technical ability'. Later on, when the researcher realised there were two distinct types of information in this category, it was broken up into two different categories: 'first time' and 'help provided'. 'First time' comprised data from those interviewees who talked about their lack of knowledge the first time they used the Internet. 'Help provided' comprised data from interviewees who talked about the help they got from other people both 'online' and 'offline'. Note that the branching of the categories into subcategories resembles an upside down tree – hence the 'tree structure' label.

(13)	/Technical ability
(13 1)	/Technical ability/first time
(13 2)	/Technical ability/help provided
(13 2 1)	/Technical ability/help provided/online
(13 2 2)	/Technical ability/help provided/offline

Figure 17.1: NUD.IST tree structure 1

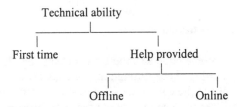

Figure 17.2: NUD.IST tree structure 2

The process of defining categories and conceptually organising them is not in any way linear. Researchers may identify certain text in interviews as talking about technical ability and later break this category into the more precise categories above. Or researchers may identify 'first time', 'help provided', 'online' and 'offline' independently and then later organise them conceptually under the heading 'technical ability'. In most cases 'technical ability' will not actually have any data coded in it, but is used merely as a category which groups other sub-categories conceptually. The actual categorised data is usually found in the lowest sub-categories such as 'first time', 'offline' and 'online'.

Miles and Huberman (1984) also recommend pictorially representing relationships between categories by drawing them freehand on paper or on a software package. This is useful for thinking about your data, for playing with ideas, and can often be incorporated into your final report.

7. Undertake word searches

A useful, but not necessary technique, when doing qualitative analysis, is word searches. Often researchers begin to think that a particular word or phrase is frequently being used by participants. NVivo or a simple word processor can be used to check if this is the case. This is important because sometimes, the interviewer themselves may have used the particular word or phrase rather than the research participants, or researchers may have imagined that the word or phrase was used frequently.

8. Form tentative theories

Once a researcher has gone through the preceding steps they should be at a stage where they have some tentative hunches, ideas or theories about the data. Often these appear in their memos or the researcher may be thinking about them. Researchers should at this stage attempt to write their tentative theories in a form that might resemble the requirements for the formal report.

9. Ask questions and check hunches

Before the final report is completed, researchers must check that their tentative theories are feasible. To do this they need to check through the data for evidence supporting their theories as well as evidence to the contrary. When evidence to the contrary is found the theory does not necessarily need to be thrown out completely, because often it just needs readjusting. For example, a researcher might tentatively propose that all people who use the Internet for the first time experience frustration. On closer inspection they may discover that only three-quarters experience frustration. Rather than casting aside the theory, their quest at this stage is to find out why one-quarter does not experience frustration. This requires reading through the transcripts and/or thinking about the people who did not feel frustration, until the researcher can find an explanation. For example, the researcher might discover that the one-quarter had someone sitting next to them telling them how to use the Internet, or they had more experience using computer software packages than the others. The theory can then be modified to indicate that people tend to be frustrated the first time they use the Internet when they have no-one helping them or when they have had little experience using software packages. This is much more informative than just saying that three-quarters of people who used the Internet experienced frustration.

Conclusion

Whichever style of data analysis is appropriate to you, as a researcher, it is important to remember that the organisation and analysis of your data are only the early steps. The interpretation of that analysis is very important. You must ask yourself: what is the analysis saying? Are my research questions answered by the findings? Is there further analysis needed? It is the researcher's insights and inspirations which are crucial to changing analysed data into a contribution to knowledge and debate.

Discussion questions

*   When would you use quantitative, rather than qualitative data analysis, and vice versa?

*   What are the main differences between the processes of quantitative and qualitative data analysis?

*   What does the concept of statistical significance mean in quantitative analysis? Why is this a key concept?

- What are the implications of the flexibility available to the researcher when undertaking data analysis?

- How can the researcher introduce rigour into qualitative data analysis?

Further readings

Alreck, Pamela L. and Settle, Robert B. (1995). *The survey research handbook: Guidelines and strategies for conducting a survey.* Irwin: Burr Ridge, Il. (Chapter on data analysis, pp. 267-303.)

Miles, Matthew B. and Huberman, Michael A. (1994). *Qualitative data analysis: An expanded sourcebook.* Sage: Thousand Oaks, Ca. (This source book is worth inspection and contains many useful ideas.)

Richards, T. and Richards, L. (1998). Using computers in qualitative research. In *Collecting and interpreting qualitative materials,* eds. Norman K. Denzin and Yvonna S. Lincoln. Sage: London, pp. 211-245.

Sarantakos, Sotirios. (1998). *Social research.* 2nd edn. Macmillan Educational Australia: South Yarra, Vic. (Chapter on data analysis, pp. 98-104.)

References for Chapter 17

Alreck, Pamela L. and Settle, Robert B. (1995). *The survey research handbook: Guidelines and strategies for conducting a survey.* Irwin: Burr Ridge, Il.

Australian Bureau of Statistics. (1990). *An introduction to sample surveys: A user's guide.* Australian Bureau of Statistics: Victoria.

Babbie, Earl .(1992). *The practice of social research.* 6th edn. Wadsworth: Belmont, Ca.

Bell, Judith. (1993). *Doing your research project.* 2nd edn. Open University Press, Buckingham, pp. 75-90.

Black James A. and Champion, Dean J. (1976). *Methods and issues in social research.* Wiley: New York.

Burns, Robert B. (1990). *Introduction to research methods in education.* Longman Cheshire: Melbourne.

Busha, Charles H. and Harter, Stephen P. (1980). *Research methods in librarianship: Techniques and interpretations.* Academic Press: Orlando, NY.

Geertz, C. (1973). *The interpretation of cultures.* Basic: New York.

Glaser, Barney G. and Strauss, Anselm L. (1967). *The discovery of grounded theory: Strategies of qualitative research.* Aldine de Gruyter: New York.

Gorman, G.E. and Clayton, Peter. (1997). *Qualitative research for the information professional: A practical handbook.* Library Association Publishing: London.

Hafner, Arthur W. (1997). *Descriptive statistical techniques for librarians.* American Library Association: Chicago.

Kvale, Steiner. (1996). *Interviews: An introduction to qualitative research interviewing.* Sage: London.

Lincoln, Y. and Guba, E. (1985). *Naturalistic inquiry.* Sage: London.

Miles, Matthew B. and Huberman, Michael A. (1994). *Qualitative data analysis: An expanded sourcebook.* Sage: Thousand Oaks, Ca.

Moser, C.A. and Kalton, G. (1971). *Survey methods in social investigation.* Heinemann: London.

Oppenheim, A.N. (1966). *Questionnaire design and attitude measurement.* Heinemann: London.

Powell, Ronald. (1997). *Basic research methods for librarians.* 3rd edn. Ablex: Norwood, NJ.

Rice-Lively, Mary Lynn. (1994). Analysing qualitative data from information organisations. In Gorman, G.E. and Clayton, Peter. (1997). *Qualitative research for the information professional: A practical handbook.* Library Association Publishing: London, pp. 198-218.

Richards, T. and Richards, L. (1998). Using computers in qualitative research. In *Collecting and interpreting qualitative materials,* eds. Norman K. Denzin and Yvonna S. Lincoln. Sage: London, pp. 211-245.

Rowntree, Derek. (1981). *Statistics without tears: A primer for non-mathemeticians.* Charles Scribner: New York.

Sarantakos, Sotirios. (1998). *Social research.* 2nd edn. Macmillan Educational Australia: South Yarra, Vic.

Simpson, I.S. (1988). *Basic statistics for librarians.* 3rd edn. Library Association: London.

Strauss, A. (1987). *Qualitative analysis for social scientists.* Cambridge University Press: Cambridge.

CHAPTER 18
Evaluation of published research
Kirsty Williamson

Objectives

At the end of this chapter you will be able to:

- describe an effective strategy for reading and evaluating research reports;

- understand the major components of research reports;

- outline the key criteria which should be used to evaluate each of the major components; and

- evaluate a research report, describing its strengths and weaknesses.

Introduction

This chapter provides a summary of many of the points made in earlier chapters of this book. It deals systematically with the evaluation of published research, bringing together points made in relation to specific research components. Many readers of this book may not aspire to be researchers themselves. One of the principal aims of the book is to assist readers to be informed consumers of research which can assist them in their professional practice. This chapter is particularly directed at these readers.

Chapter 1 presents many reasons why research is important to professional practice. In terms of the skills of research evaluation, the key point is the link between the application of research results and improvements in professional practice. It is important that professionals be discerning in this application – a skill that comes from the ability to understand and evaluate published research.

By evaluating a research report, readers can check the quality of the various aspects of the study under consideration. As Hittleman and Simon (1997, p. 49) state: 'Research reports are pictures of research. They are representations of what researchers have done and how they wish to present their research procedures to the public'. Research reports, apart from the research itself, can vary in quality. In fact, Hittleman and Simon also say:

> Four pictures of research are possible: (a) good research methodology, well reported; (b) good research methodology, poorly reported; (c) poor research methodology, well reported; and poor research methodology, poorly reported (Hittleman and Simon 1997, p. 49).

It is one of the tasks in the evaluation process to attempt to discern the standard of the report writing, as well as quality of the various research components.

Many of the general social sciences, educational and information management research methods texts are useful for evaluation, for example, Burns (1990), Busha and Harter (1980), Gorman and Clayton (1997), Powell (1997). Two particular references in the educational research area are very useful: Borg, Gall and Gall (1993), and Hittleman and Simon (1997). For evaluation of information systems research, see Nunamaker, Chen and Purdin (1990-1991), Miles and Huberman (1994), and Weber (1987).

Strategy for reading and evaluating research reports

It is a good idea to work out a plan for reading and evaluating research reports. One suggestion is to use a two-staged approach. In the first stage, the reader skims the report with the aim of gaining an initial understanding of the contents, particularly to see if the report is written in standard form. Careful reading of the abstract, if there is one, is important at this stage. Also, at this stage, you should gain an impression of the clarity of the writing. Is the report well written and easy to understand?

The second stage is to carry out a detailed analysis of each of the report's major components. Apart from considering the criteria listed below for each part, you should consider the standard of the writing, section by section. Are some parts of the report more clearly written than others? Does the level of detail vary, giving an uneven picture of the research process and the findings?

Major components of a research report

The most common components of research reports (regardless of the form of the publication) are:

- the abstract;

- the introduction;

- the research questions, or objectives (and hypotheses, if appropriate);

- the literature review (and theoretical framework);

- the research design (sample, method and techniques);

- the research findings; and

- the conclusions and recommendations.

Each of the major components of a research report are listed and discussed below, in terms of evaluation. While reports differ somewhat in structure and in the components they include, there is still considerable consistency.

The abstract

Most research reports have an abstract. Abstracts need to be brief and clearly written, but also include major aspects of the research: purpose, respondents/participants/subjects, research design (including method and techniques), findings. The evaluator needs to check both content and style.

The introductory section

Research reports should introduce the topic of the research. This section should include an overview of the topic, providing background information and also discussing the significance of the topic. Definitions may be included in the introduction, but may also be part of the literature review and theoretical framework.

The introduction is also the section where information about the researcher or researchers is likely to be found. You should be aware of any affiliations of researchers which might lead to bias, or any emotionally charged words which may indicated a vested interest on the part of the researchers (Borg, Gall and Gall 1993).

Questions you should ask about the introduction include:

- does it make clear to you what the research is about?

- does it provide a succinct overview of the topic?

- is it interesting and engaging? Are you inspired to read further?

- does it provide a convincing justification of why the research needed to be undertaken? and

- is there any evidence of possible bias – in language or in the affiliation of the authors in relation to the research topic?

Research questions

Research questions, or objectives, which have been covered in detail in Chapter 3, usually form part of the introductory section. If you are evaluating research, the first consideration is whether the report at hand, be it a journal article or a longer research report, makes clear to you the purpose of the research. All researchers face the need to develop clear, well focused research questions. This is easier said than done, even if researchers begin with clear notions of their research aims.

As Chapter 3 points out, one of the first tasks of researchers about to undertake a study, is to write a clear statement of the problem, or major questions. This should be done in full grammatical sentences, not just as phrases. The final version of these questions, used to undertake the study, should be included in the report. One of the key tasks of the evaluator is to check that the research has a clear focus through careful scrutiny of the research questions.

There is some flexibility in the ways in which research questions can be presented. As Chapter 3 points out, the research questions for a qualitative study are usually stated more broadly than those for a quantitative study, where the relationship between variables is often important. Also researchers vary in the terminology they use. For example, some researchers may refer to a broad aim or aims and then their more specific objectives; others may talk about major questions and sub-questions.

Make sure you check the clarity of the research questions and whether they cover the major aspects of the research, as undertaken. When you finish reading the report, you should be able to see if the researcher has, in fact, answered the research questions through the research. There should be a clear relationship between the research questions, the literature review, the findings of the research and the conclusions.

Hypotheses

Hypotheses of the 'operational' kind (defined in Chapter 3) are used frequently in positivist studies and can assist in establishing a clear focus for the research. As stated in Chapter 3, each hypothesis should be closely related to at least one of the research sub-questions. In other words, there should be a close link between research questions and hypotheses. As an evaluator, it is important to check that this link is there. The following are the criteria you should use to check operational hypotheses (also included in Chapter 3). Good hypotheses should:

- be stated in correct terminology;

- be as brief and clear as possible;

- state an expected relationship or difference between two or more variables;

- be testable; and

- be grounded in past knowledge, gained from the literature review or from theory.

The testing of hypotheses in positivist research needs to be undertaken with rigour, if generalisations about a population are to based on them. Samples should be randomly selected, as described in Chapter 13, and statistical tests need to be undertaken. (See Chapter 17.)

As Chapter 3 points out, for some interpretivist studies, researchers develop propositions which are similar to research hypotheses. They do not require such precise wording, nor the rigorous testing associated with operational hypotheses. They, nevertheless, can help to provide a similar kind of clarification as operational hypotheses give to a quantitative study. Historians also sometimes use hypotheses of the 'research' kind. (See Chapter 3.) If propositions or hypotheses are used in qualitative research, you must check that they are used to provide clarity and focus, and not as a basis for generalisations about a population.

The literature review (and theoretical framework)

The extent of this section of a research report is determined by whether the publication is a journal article, a conference paper, or a research report. The first two impose space limitations on authors in terms of a literature review. You can only expect the most relevant studies to be cited and briefly described. You need to check that key studies are cited. If important studies that disagree with the researchers' findings are omitted, bias may be the reason (Borg, Gall and Gall 1993, p. 91).

Other questions to consider, especially if you are evaluating a full research report:

- are you made aware of the researchers' theoretical framework?

- are key concepts of the study defined and explained?

- is the literature review arranged under headings related to the research questions?

- do the researchers critically analyse the relevant literature? Do they examine the quality of the research discussed?

- do the researchers conclude by indicating the gaps in the literature and pointing out why further research is needed? and

- is the referencing accurate and comprehensive?

Research design

The major components of research design are usually the sample, the method and techniques.

The sample

As Chapter 13 points out, sampling differs according to whether a study is quantitative or qualitative. If the study you are evaluating is quantitative and makes generalisations about a population, you need to ask the following questions:

- was a 'population' used for the study? If not, was the sample randomly selected?

- is the sample an appropriate size?

- is the response rate adequate? and

- are the generalisations valid in relation to all of the above?

(See Chapter 13 for detailed explanations of these points.)

In relation to sampling for qualitative research, the main points to check are firstly, that the sample includes representatives of all the important sub-groups which should be considered if the study is to answer the research questions; and secondly that the limitations to the generalisations which can be drawn from a non-probability sample have been respected.

Method

As you know, there is a range of methods which can be used for research. In the following section, criteria for the evaluation of each of the methods dealt with in this book are listed.

Please note that only the key specific points for each method are included. For all methods, you need to consider the aspects already covered in this chapter.

Survey

There are three major considerations when you are evaluating a survey.

- The first is the way the sample was selected. When a sample is used to represent 'a population' in a survey, it must be randomly selected if generalisations are to be made to that population. See Chapter 5 and, more specifically, Chapter 13 for a detailed discussion of 'sampling'. If a sample is not randomly selected, or if there is a low response rate, then researchers are not free to generalise to the population from which the sample was selected. This does not necessarily mean that the research has not made a contribution. It is fine to speculate about reasons why the findings are likely to be widely applicable, but the limitations need to be made clear.

- The second key point is how well the data collection instruments, usually a self-administered questionnaire or interview schedule, are designed. Self-administered questionnaires are discussed in Chapter 14 and the key criteria in evaluating them are included below.

- Finally, the quality of data analysis is also important. This is discussed in Chapter 17, and summarised below.

Case study

The fact that case studies come in many different forms makes it difficult to be specific about the criteria for evaluation. A number of points should be considered with regard to multi-site case studies.

- Whether case study is a suitable method to investigate the particular research questions under consideration.

- The overall design of the case studies. With multi-site case studies, has there been an attempt to include a variety of sites in the research?

- The range and variety of techniques used. Do the techniques enable the triangulation of data, which is a key strategy for achieving rigour and verification?

- The standard of the techniques used. The criteria discussed for techniques, below, and in other chapters should be applied.

- The quality of the analysis of data. The kind of the analysis depends on the particular techniques used. (Chapter 17 deals with data analysis.)

- The ways in which the findings and conclusions are handled, keeping in mind the limitations on generalisations beyond the cases under consideration.

Experimental design

Key points to consider when evaluating experimental research are:

- the type of design, and whether it is appropriate to the research questions;

- how well 'other' independent variables are controlled;

- issues of internal and external validity;

- the method by which subjects have been assigned to groups; and

- the rigour of the data analysis (the types and extent of statistical tests applied, and the clarity with which they are described).

(See Chapter 7 for details about experimental design.)

Systems Research

For references on evaluation of information systems research, see Miles and Huberman (1994), Nunamaker, Chen and Purdin (1990-1991), and Weber (1987). Burstein and Gregor (1999) include the following criteria in their discussion of evaluation of systems development research.

- The study must be significant, either theoretically, practically or both. In other words it should be making an important contribution to the field.

- The research must indicate internal validity. This includes checking the credibility of the arguments and the accuracy of predictions and conclusions.

- The research must indicate external validity. This includes the extent to which the study is generalisable and the basis on which generalisations can be made. This is related to the degree of objectivity of the researchers and the extent to which the study is confirmable.

- Also related to the above criterion is the degree of reliability/dependability/auditability. Is the process used consistent, reasonably stable over time and across researchers and methods?

Action Research

In evaluating action research, it is important to keep in mind:

- the purpose of the research and whether 'action research' is the appropriate method;

- the overall design of the action research – are the techniques chosen suitable for solving the problem or problems?

- the standard of the techniques used – the criteria discussed for techniques, below, and in other chapters should be applied;

- the degree and quality of reflection as the cyclical process took place – there should be evidence of this in the written report;

- the quality of the analysis of data – the kind of the analysis depends on the particular techniques used (Chapter 17 deals with data analysis); and

- the level of involvement of the key stakeholders in the research.

Ethnography/participant observation

As Chapters 10 and 16 point out, ethnographies/participant observations come in many different forms. More recently the ethnographic approach has become one of the most flexible ways of doing research. In its modern guise, it has similarities to case study, although it is usually undertaken in only one site. For this reason, most of the evaluative criteria listed for case study are also relevant to ethnography/participant observation. Where ethnographers use grounded theory, you would also need to consider the quality of that aspect. Also, for ethnography, you should particularly check that researchers have been open to their settings and participants. This is an important requirement of interpretivist research.

Historical research

In carrying out an evaluation of historical research, check the extent to which your historian has applied the criteria to the available evidence. Chapter 11 indicates that historians need the skills of: the detective, the sceptic, the attributor, the verifier or clarifier, the disentangler and the storyteller or explainer. A good historian should demonstrate these skills. Above all, good historians do not assume that the facts speak for themselves. They must interrogate the evidence and tell a story about it.

Delphi Studies

In evaluating a Delphi study you should consider:

- whether a Delphi study is a suitable method to investigate the particular research questions under consideration;

- the composition of the panel – in relation to the research questions – is the panel well balanced, given the issues to be discussed?

- the quality of the research instruments used – usually there will be a questionnaire, which is used for each round;

- the quality of the analysis of data from each 'round';

- the quality of the feedback provided to the panel – has the researcher used graphical representation, as well as a comprehensive account of the reasons for answers?

- is there any evidence that the researcher has put his or her own emphasis on the results when providing feedback – this is important, given that only the researcher sees all the responses to the questionnaires;

- the extent to which consensus has been reached – has the researcher 'allowed' the panel to have divergent views? and

- the ways in which the findings and conclusions are handled, keeping in mind that there are limitations on generalisations, as with other qualitative research.

Techniques

There is also a range of techniques available to the researcher. Most are used in more than one method and, for this reason, have been treated in a separate section in this book. As with the methods, above, evaluative criteria are summarised for each technique. Sampling, which is categorised as a technique in this book, has been discussed above.

Self-administered questionnaires

Major questions to ask include:

- is a self-administered questionnaire the appropriate instrument to use to answer the research questions?

- are the forms attractively and clearly presented?

- are questions clear, unambiguous, unbiased, and logically organised?

- are clear instructions given at the beginning of the questionnaire and wherever needed throughout?

- was the questionnaire piloted with typical respondents? and

- was data analysis considered in relation to the design of the questionnaire?

(See Chapter 14 for comprehensive discussion of questionnaire design.)

Interviews

Structured interviews can be used as an alternative to the self-administered questionnaire. If the former are used – and there is the intention to compare findings across respondents – evaluative criteria include:

- the clarity of the questions;

- the indication that questions were asked of each respondent in a consistent way and that appropriate prompts were used consistently;

- the indication that interviewers who were acceptable to the respondents were chosen;

- evidence that interviewers were trained to minimise interviewer variability;

- evidence that the interview schedule was piloted; and

- an indication that data analysis was considered in relation to the design of the interview schedule.

With unstructured or semi-structured interviews, the aim is to explore the views of each interviewee in depth. Evaluative criteria include:

- selection of appropriate interviewers;

- training of interviewers – in this case to be skilled in drawing out participants and following up leads;

- the process of recording interviews; and

- the rigour of data analysis.

(See Chapter 14 for further information on interviews and Chapter 17 for data analysis.)

Focus groups

In evaluating the use of focus groups, you should consider the following points.

- The appropriateness of the use of focus groups to the objectives of the research (or the research questions). Would a different technique, for example the interview, have been more appropriate?

- The number of focus groups, the number of participants in each group, and the appropriateness of the participants. Were the issues considered from enough points of view, given that each focus group needs to be fairly homogeneous in composition?

- The quality of the interviewing. Were the questions asked appropriate and sufficiently wide-ranging to do justice to the research questions? Here you need to keep in mind that other techniques may have been used for parts of the research. Was the moderator skilled and experienced?

- The rigour of the data analysis and the quality of the reporting.

(Chapter 15 provides further details.)

Observation

It is difficult to speak simplistically of 'observation' in the modern research environment, as Chapter 16 attests. Nevertheless, there are studies where an observation schedule is needed. If an observation schedule has been used in a study you are evaluating, you need to decide on issues such as its appropriateness in relation to the research questions, its comprehensiveness, and its rigour. It is difficult to be more precise. In many cases, observation schedules need to be piloted in the same way as self-administered questionnaires and interview schedules.

Data analysis

With *quantitative data,* the major steps are the coding of the data; the entry of the data into a suitable computer program; the use of that program to analyse the data; and then the interpretation of that analysis. Research reports do not usually provide details of the coding process. Usually there will simply be a statement that the data were coded for analysis by a particular computer package, such as SPSS. However, a research report of high standard will give details of the statistical analysis.

It is important to note that you do not usually have to be a statistical expert to judge whether the statistical analysis which has been undertaken for a quantitative study is adequate. If the analysis seems very complex, you may need to consult a statistical expert. Otherwise, you should note the following:

- Whether differences which are claimed between groups in a sample are said to be statistically significant. You need to note if the writer of the report you are evaluating talks about differences between groups, for example education levels in relation to library use, being significant at the 0.05 or 0.01 level. This will indicate whether appropriate tests have been carried out. (Detailed explanation of this is provided in Chapter 17.)

- If other statistical descriptions are given, for example of correlations, once again you would attempt to discern if there is sufficient detail given to indicate that tests were carried out.

- The main point to remember is that generalisations from quantitative research must be based on support from statistical analysis. For example, if differences between groups are not shown to be statistically significant, then generalisation about that difference should not be made. Informed consumers of research will be vigilant about this.

- The interpretations of the data made by the researcher. Has the researcher made a contribution to knowledge through the interpretation of the findings, as well as through linking them to previous knowledge in the field?

It is difficult to give the criteria for evaluating *qualitative data analysis* as there is a lot of variation in the way qualitative data analysis is undertaken. Computer packages can be used, of which the best known is probably NUD.IST. If a researcher has a good memory and the data are not too voluminous, good qualitative data analysis can be done without the use of a computer package. Suggestions of what might be considered in evaluating qualitative data analysis are as follows:

- has the researcher appeared to make good sense of the data collected and been able to convey to the reader the main themes of the findings, in a logical way so as to answer the research questions?

- does the data analysis appear to be rigorous? and

- the interpretation of the analysis is very important. Has the researcher been able to make a theoretical contribution through creative analysis of the data? As is stated in Chapter 16, it is the researcher's insights and inspirations which are crucial to changing analysed data into a contribution to knowledge and debate.

Research findings

Clarity in the presentation of research findings is essential, regardless of the style of research. With quantitative research a major issue is whether the findings are based on appropriate statistical tests. A related question is whether the hypotheses are handled in acceptable ways – that is supported, rather than proved, on the basis of the results of appropriate statistical tests. With qualitative research, the illustrative material is important, such as quotes from participants. The general points to be checked:

- are findings clearly and logically presented?

- if tables are used, are they clear and consistent in presentation? Do they make a contribution to this section of the research, or are they superfluous?

- would some of the description be improved by the use of more tables or diagrams? and

- do the findings answer the research questions?

Conclusions and recommendations

At this stage you should check, once again, how well the major components of the research report are linked: research questions, literature review, choice of appropriate method and techniques, findings and conclusions. With regard to the conclusions and recommendations, the following should be checked:

- that the conclusions and recommendations are clearly related to the findings;

- that the researcher has not over-concluded – in other words, that unwarranted conclusions and generalisations have not been made. In the case of generalisations, you need to consider the population and the sample. If the research is quantitative, generalisations should be based on statistical analysis, as discussed in Chapter 17 (and noted above); and

- that the research questions have been answered.

Conclusion

Apart from the detailed analysis of a research report, set out in this chapter, an overview of the strengths and weaknesses of the research is a good way of concluding an evaluation. This overview should select only the points which are considered worthy of being highlighted.

This chapter has been presented very much in summary form and is further summarised in the checklist of questions for evaluating research reports in Box 18.1 below. It is not possible to be comprehensive when attempting to cover the evaluation of research reports which use a range of methods and techniques. The reader needs to refer back to other chapters and references. There are many other published checklists to aid the evaluation of research (for example Hittleman and Simon 1997, p. 117, and Busha and Harter 1980, p. 28).

Box 18.1: Questions for evaluating research reports

Abstract

Is information about the major aspects of the research – purpose, respondents/participants/ subjects, research design (including method and techniques), findings – included? Is the abstract brief and clearly written?

Introduction

Does it make clear to you what the research is about? Does it provide a succinct overview of the topic? Is it interesting and engaging? Does it provide a convincing justification of why the research needed to be undertaken? Is there any evidence of possible bias?

Research questions (and hypotheses, if appropriate)

Are research questions clear and well focused? Do they cover the major aspects of the research as undertaken? If hypotheses are included, are they appropriate to the type of study undertaken? Do they state an expected relationship or difference between two or more variables? Are they concise, stated in correct terminology, and testable?

Box 18.1 (cont.) : Questions for evaluating research reports

Literature review (and theoretical framework)

Are key concepts of the study explained? Is the literature review arranged under headings related to the research questions? Do the researchers critically analyse the relevant literature and examine the quality of the research discussed? Do the researchers indicate the gaps in the literature and point out why further research is needed? Is the referencing accurate and comprehensive?

Research design

Sample: Are the target population, sampling procedures, and the sample itself clearly described? Is the sample an appropriate size? Is the response rate adequate? Is the sample appropriate to the type of study?

Method: Is the method appropriate to the study and clearly described? Are specific criteria (according to each research method) met?

Techniques: Are techniques appropriate to the design and clearly described? Is information about the development of the instruments included? Have instruments been piloted?

Data analysis: Is data analysis appropriate to the research design and clearly described? If a quantitative research design has been used, are statistical tests clearly described and statistical significance levels indicated?

Research findings or results

Presentation: Are findings clearly and logically presented? If tables are used, are they clear and consistent in presentation? Do they make a contribution to this section of the research, or are they superfluous? Would some of the description be improved by the use of more tables or diagrams? Do the findings answer the research questions?

Quantitative research: Are the findings based on appropriate statistical tests? Are the hypotheses handled in acceptable ways, for example 'supported', rather than 'proved'?

Qualitative research: Are findings supported by illustrative quotes from participants? How convincing are the findings?

Conclusions and recommendations

Are the conclusions and recommendations clearly related to the findings? Does the researcher over-conclude? Have the research questions been answered? (At this stage you should check, once again, how well the major components of the research report are linked: research questions, literature review, choice of appropriate method and techniques, findings and conclusions.)

Overview

What are the main strengths of this research?
What are the main deficiencies of this research?

Discussion questions

- To what extent do you think that the style and quality of the writing in a research report should be taken into account when undertaking an evaluation?

- Apart from the approach suggested in the chapter, can you think of other strategies which might be successful for reading and evaluating research reports?

- What might be the differences between evaluating a full research report, compared with a presentation in journal article form?

- Are there major differences of approach needed for the evaluation of quantitative and qualitative research reports?

References for Chapter 18

Borg, Walter R., Gall, Joyce P. and Gall, Meredith D. (1993). *Applying educational research: A practical guide*. 3rd edn. Longman: White Plains, NY.

Burns, Robert B. (1990). *Introduction to research methods in education*. Longman: Melbourne.

Burstein, Frada and Gregor, Shirley. (1999). The systems development or engineering approach to research in information systems: An action research perspective. In *Proceedings of the 10th Australasian Conference on Information Systems (ACIS'99)*, Victoria University of Wellington, New Zealand, 1-3 December 1999. (In press).

Busha, Charles H. and Harter, Stephen P. (1980). *Research methods in librarianship: Techniques and interpretations*. Academic Press: Orlando, NY.

Gorman, G.E. and Clayton, Peter. (1997). *Qualitative research for the information professional: A practical handbook*. Library Association Publishing: London.

Hittleman, Daniel R. and Simon, Alan J. (1997). *Interpreting educational research. An introduction for consumers of research*. Prentice Hall: Upper Saddle River, NJ.

Miles, Matthew B. and Huberman, Michael A. (1994). *Qualitative data analysis: An expanded sourcebook*. Sage: Thousand Oaks, Ca.

Nunamaker, J., Chen, M. and Purdin, T. (1990-1991). Systems development in information systems research. *Journal of Management Information Systems,* **7** (3), pp. 89-106.

Powell, Ronald. (1997). *Basic research methods for librarians.* 3rd edn. Ablex Publishing: Norwood, NJ.

Weber, R. (1987). Toward a theory of artifacts: A paradigmatic base for information systems research. *Journal of Information Systems*, **Spring**, pp. 3-19.

POSTSCRIPT
Seven questions for information management and systems researchers
Don Schauder

Information management and systems research: A tough mission

It may seem strange that in a book about research in information management and systems not much time has been spent discussing the phenomenon of information. Rather the book has introduced a set of ideas and techniques that can help information management and systems professionals to undertake the kind of research that extends collective understanding of information and the way it operates in the world.

In large part the approaches and techniques covered in the book can be seen as generic for the humanities and social sciences, and indeed for any field of rigorous inquiry. In successive chapters of the book, these approaches and techniques have been linked to information management and systems research and reflective practice by presenting examples of research that has been undertaken. Even though this postscript is in some respects a re-statement of ideas presented in earlier chapters it seems appropriate, in closing, to highlight some of the special challenges of information as a focus of research endeavour.

Information, at the level of abstraction that generally concerns information management and systems researchers and practitioners, begins and ends with knowledge in the minds of people – hence its intimate connection with the burgeoning field of knowledge management. Specifically, information management and systems research is about how people gain, share, and preserve knowledge through selectively encoding it as information which can be transmitted, stored and retrieved through appropriate information systems. Any conceivable system of signs – including languages (natural and computer), mathematical notations, graphical or musical representations and even realia – can be used for such transmission and storage. The process by which people share knowledge is communication, and information can be understood as the content of communication within specific contexts.

In 1927 the mechanistic world-view of atomic physics was changed forever when Heisenberg enunciated the 'uncertainty principle', namely that the techniques available to measure the position and momentum of particles themselves affected the values of those variables (Berry 1988). Similarly, the impact of the observer on the observed and vice versa

– what Giddens has called 'the double hermeneutic' (Giddens 1996, pp. 75-76) – is an issue for all social sciences, but for information management and systems it is especially acute.

Why so? Because the very purpose of the family of information technology disciplines to which information management and systems belongs, is to discover ways of using technology to 'improve' communication. Whether or not the interventions of information technology improve or merely change information flows and resources within information communities, it is difficult – at the beginning of the twenty-first century – to conceive of an information management and systems research praxis that is 'pure', that does not have the potential for changing the situation under study, however slightly. This is even true of historical research in information management and systems where the way the past is interpreted can alter attitudes to issues in the present. The spirit of information management and systems research tends to be 'applied', rather than 'pure'.

Moreover, information management and systems research is no more exempt than any other social action from what Giddens (1996, p. 100) calls 'duality of structure', where all human action – however humble or 'everyday' – in some way changes the structure of the social environment which both supports and constrains such action.

It is entirely legitimate for an information management and systems researcher to choose a focus nearer the 'pure' end of the spectrum, and indeed all information management and systems research projects are in some degree hybrids of pure and applied. The point is that the researcher needs to be self-aware of how far the project comprises detached observation, and how far it constitutes intervention.

In the television series *Star Trek* (1999) there is the principle of the 'prime directive'. The directive states that crew members, in their explorations of space, should not take actions that will distort the development of alien societies with whom they come into contact. This seemingly worthy principle is arguably an impossible expectation for any social action, and perhaps especially for information management and systems research because such research concentrates on communication – one of the fundamental processes that make societies what they are. Intervention is an issue that must be consciously confronted in good information management and systems research, and clearly reflected in the research design.

The question therefore that the researcher needs to ask is:

- *To what extent is my research an intervention?*

In the likely event that some form of intervention is occurring, ethical considerations need to be at the forefront of the researcher's mind. Important issues to address are not only 'What good can this research do?' but also 'What harm can it do, and to whom?' Changes to an existing pattern of information flows and resources almost inevitably bring with them changes in power relationships. So another key question is:

- *How can I ensure that good, not harm, will flow from my research?*

Seeing, observing and modelling

Central to the idea of research is to find ways of **seeing**. The very word *theory* derives from the Greek, to see or behold – theatre comes from the same root (Skeat 1887, p. 503). The great theoretical traditions of positivism and interpretivism are alternative ways of seeing. Researchers need to be self-aware of their theoretical positioning, and to make this explicit to all stakeholders in the research.

Research needs to involve both theoretical perspectives and sufficient specific observation to address the research question. In short, the researcher must model.

If the issues of involvement and detachment took us to the Star Trek prime directive, then the notion of modelling takes us to the holodeck, that remarkable venue on the starship where any kind of physical reality can be simulated at a level which, for practical purposes, is indistinguishable from the original.

It is yet another manifestation of the toughness or complexity of information management and systems research that *what* is studied – information phenomena – are in essence the same as *how* they are studied – the 'tools' used to study them. Both are constituted of processes of modelling.

What information management and systems researchers study is how people selectively take parts of their 'knowledge' – the memories and thoughts that exist in their minds – and *encode* these as representations through 'live' (for example, conversation) or 'recorded' (for example, a written letter) information media so that others can decode them and add them, again selectively, to their own knowledge. In other words they create a model or representation of some aspect of their knowledge.

How information management and systems researchers study such phenomena is that they in turn use information models to explicate the communicative modelling processes they are observing!

In both everyday life and research, such externalised modelling of knowledge may also be used to communicate with oneself – for example writing in a diary or notebook – in order to 'refresh' one's memory or knowledge at a later date. In daily life people create information models for all sorts of reasons. These include:

- reminding (for example, a snapshot of baby in a particular mood);

- proving (for example, a birth certificate as evidence of baby's identity);

- explaining (for example, an x-ray of a baby's broken leg, to explain the injury);

- predicting (for example, trend statistics about the health of babies);

- discovering (for example, a psychological hypothesis about developmental stages in babies);

- deciding (for example, a dietitian's checklist about what you should feed baby);

- entertaining (for example, the movie '*Baby's Day Out*' – baby as pop hero); and

- enculturating (for example, stories of the baby Moses or Jesus).

The modelling undertaken by information management and systems researchers can involve all of the above, except perhaps the last two. As already suggested, the mind-bending part is that what information management and systems researchers are modelling is other people's information modelling!

A research model need not 'look like' what it represents. It can be a series of equations, a conceptual diagram, or an account in words. Good examples are entity-relationship diagrams in information systems. Such models, that select and represent only high-priority factors and relations, are called *homomorphic*. On the other hand – in holodeck style – a model can look exactly like what it represents. Such 'total' models are called *isomorphic* (Beer, Strachy, Stone and Torrance 1988).

All models reflect a system. They map the elements of the system. Some information models are static and do not change, while others are dynamic and change with feedback. Some are concrete and can be experienced through the senses (like a pilot-training simulator), while others are abstract and can only be perceived by the intellect. Some can be causal (as in system dynamics modelling), while others can be associative or probabilistic (like a Chi-square test). Some can focus on only one or a few factors or relationships (like in simple majority decision-making), while others can involve innumerable factors (like explanations of 'the global information society').

More examples of information models in everyday life include: the local street directory (homomorphic); radio-controlled model aircraft (isomorphic); a printed novel like *Pride and prejudice* (homomorphic, compared to – say – the video version, and also in its selectivity from the universe of social relationships that it represents); schematisations of knowledge such as the Dewey Decimal Classification or the Library of Congress Subject Headings (homomorphic). As with other conceptual categories used in social science, homomorphism and isomorphism need not be mutually exclusive. There are many hybrid categories of model across the spectrum between these two 'pure' types.

What about Elle Macpherson – the supermodel. Is she a model in the sense discussed? Elle on a magazine cover is indeed an abstraction and codification taken from the publicist's knowledge of the 'whole' Elle Macpherson to enculturate or persuade others into certain values about beauty and fashion. In this sense the magazine Elle Macpherson *is* a model (a hybrid homomorphic-isomorphic model) while the whole Elle (at home, away from cameras) is not.

What about an elephant in the zoo? To the extent that this is not an elephant in the natural state, but displayed by the zoo to represent a class or category of animal for explanatory purposes – that live elephant is an information model (isomorphic). Return it to the wild, cease using it for education, research or entertainment, and it is a model no longer.

So in addition to the questions of observation versus intervention, and consequentially of ethical principles in research, further key questions the information management and systems researcher should ask are:

- *Am I clear about my way of seeing – my theoretical perspective or perspectives – and can I explain why I have chosen them?*

- *Am I clear about the 'real world' information modelling phenomenon I am studying, as well as the research modelling approach I am using to study it?*

Arguably there is greater congruence between certain kinds of theorising and certain kinds of modelling. For example the preferred setting for research proceeding from an interpretivist theoretical position is immersion in the information phenomena under consideration, as in action-research. For an action-researcher, the information community in which they participate *becomes* a research model (rather like an elephant selected for study in the wild becomes a model in the context of the research). Positivist theorising and homomorphic modelling fit well together, and so do interpretivist theorising and isomorphic modelling. Once again, powerful hybrid combinations cannot be excluded. However a question that the researcher needs to examine is:

- *Is there harmony between my theoretical perspective and my modelling?*

Two final questions

The great seventeenth century physicist, Newton, was – by reliable accounts – not an easy person to get on with. Contemporaries acknowledged his genius but found him arrogant and difficult. However in reflecting on his own research this intellectual colossus who transformed humankind's understanding of the universe in so many ways, said:

> I do not know what I may appear to the world, but as to myself, I seem to have been only like a boy playing on the seashore and diverting myself in now and then finding a smoother pebble or a prettier shell than ordinary, while the great ocean of truth lay all undiscovered before me (Grigson and Gibbs-Smith 1954, p. 303).

And the nineteenth century poet Tennyson wrote of the desire of his hero Ulysses:

> To follow knowledge like a sinking star,
> Beyond the utmost bound of human thought (Tennyson 1842).

It was a journey Ulysses could make only in company with his peers.

Information management and systems researchers are privileged to have information as their subject of study – information, the very phenomenon that makes possible the sharing and transmission of knowledge. From the smallest localised group, to collective action on a global scale, the vast and intricate ecology of information flows, resources and systems make possible the patterns of human interdependence that we call society. It is an awesome terrain. Yet while information management and systems researchers must go forward with confidence in their research approaches and techniques they must also ask themselves:

- *Do I sufficiently comprehend and respect the extent and complexity of the field of study in which I am engaged?*

- *As well as confidence in myself, do I have the humility always to stay alert to the ideas of colleagues and to honour their contributions to the advancement of our common research quest?*

References for Postscript

Beer, Stafford, Strachy, Christopher, Stone, Richard and Torrance, John. (1988). Model. In *The Fontana dictionary of modern thought.* Rev. edn., eds. Alan Bullock and Stephen Trobley. Fontana Press: London, p. 537-538.

Berry, Michael. (1988). Uncertainty principle. In *The Fontana dictionary of modern thought*. Rev. edn., eds. Alan Bullock and Stephen Trobley. Fontana Press: London, p. 882.

Giddens, Anthony. (1996). *In defence of sociology: Essays, interpretations and rejoinders*. Polity Press: Cambridge.

Grigson, Geoffrey and Gibbs-Smith, Charles Harvard. (1954). *People*. Waverley Book Company: London.

Skeat, Walter W. (1887). *A concise etymological dictionary of the English language*. 3rd rev. edn. Clarendon Press: Oxford, p. 503.

Star Trek. (1999). (online).
   http://www.startrek.com/

Tennyson, Alfred. (1963). Ulysses. In *The London book of English verse*. 2nd rev. edn. Eyre and Spottiswoode: London, pp. 517-519.

Glossary of terms used in research

This glossary does not include *all* the terms with which readers may be unfamiliar, for example, sampling terms presented in Chapter 13 or definitions of major research methods such as case study. Given that some terms represent complex ideas the definitions included below are intended to provide only a starting point of understanding.

A priori: obtained by deduction without sensory experience *(The Concise Oxford Dictionary,* 1982). See also *Deductive reasoning.*

Constructivist: the qualitative research paradigm which emphasises either the personal, subjective construction of reality and/or the social (or shared) construction of reality produced by humans acting together. See also *Interpretivist* and *Naturalistic inquiry.*

Critical theorists: aim, through the writing of value-laden texts, to liberate groups which are seen to be oppressed, for example women or certain racial groups, and to produce transformations in the social order.

Deductive reasoning: begins with a generalisation and then moves to inferences about particular instances. See also *A priori.*

Diplomatics: body of techniques, theories and principles for analyzing the form, function and genesis of documents, with a particular view to establishing authenticity.

Emic: insider views, which ethnographers/participant observers, particularly, aim to obtain. See also *Etic.*

Empirical: based on observation or experience.

Epistemology: the theory of knowledge; a concern with what constitutes knowledge and how knowledge is formed.

Ethics: a set of moral principles; the rules of conduct recognized in a particular profession or area of human life *(The new shorter Oxford English dictionary* 1993, p. 856).

Ethnography: the study and description of people in their everyday contexts.

Etic: reliance on an outsider perspective, which occurs with most positivist research. See also *Emic.*

Grounded theory: theory which is built from the ground upwards, that is from data observed and collected in the field.

Hermeneutics: concerned with interpretation; 'the view that observation is an interpretive process' (Bradley and Sutton 1993, p. 406).

Historiography: body of techniques, theories and principles of historical research and presentation involving a critical examination, evaluation, and selection of material from primary and secondary sources.

Homomorphic models: minimalist symbolic representations of key factors and relationships.

Hypothesis: an educated guess which predicts the relationship between two or more variables in a research study, for example the relationship between level of education and library use.

Idiographic: 'pertaining to the intensive ... study of an individual case, as a personality or social situation' (*Macquarie dictionary* 1987, p. 867). Antonym of *Nomothetic.*

Inductive reasoning: begins with intense investigation of a particular instance or instances, and concludes with general statements or principles. As used in 'interpretivism', it involves the 'immersion' of the researcher in the field. Data are collected, analysed, and then 'researchers develop concepts, insights and understanding from patterns in the data ...' (Reneker 1993, p. 499). It is also used in 'grounded theory'.

Interpretivist or interpretive: refers to the qualitative research paradigm, interpretivism, which emphasises natural settings and how individual participants perceive events and interactions within those settings. Focus is on inductive reasoning. Styles of research which come under the interpretivist umbrella are naturalistic and constructivist. See also *Constructivist* and *Naturalistic inquiry.*

Isomorphic models: holistic re-creations of phenomena under study, or 'framing' of actual whole phenomena for purposes of research.

Iteration: the interweaving of various elements in the research process, where the development of one influences the other. For example the interweaving of data collection and the elaboration of theory as researchers move backwards and forwards in a qualitative study; the interweaving of the development of research questions and the examination of different bodies of literature.

Likert scale: a rating scale (usually five-point), frequently used in quantitative research, on which respondents to a research study are asked to rate their preferences or the frequencies of their activities.

Method: see *Research method.*

Methodology: 'a set of principles of methods, which in any particular situation have to be reduced to a method uniquely suitable to that particular situation' (Checkland, 1993, p. 161). Not to be confused with 'method' as an instance of methodology.

Narrative analysis: Body of techniques for examining how narrative or rhetorical tropes are used in documents to "tell stories" or advance particular perspectives or arguments.

Naturalistic inquiry: a complex term, which at its simplest level, means the conduct of research in a natural setting. See also *Constructivist* and *Interpretivist*.

Nomothetic: 'pertaining to the search for general laws' (*Macquarie dictionary* 1987, p. 1158). Antonym of *Idiographic*.

Non-probability samples: samples which do not meet the standards of probability samples where the probability or likelihood of the inclusion of each element of the population can be specified.

Norm: establishing a norm (that is, a standard or pattern).

Ontology: the science or study of being. In discussions of philosophies of research, it 'refers to the claims or assumptions that a particular approach to social enquiry makes about the nature of social reality – claims about what exists, what it looks like, what units make it up and how these units interact with each other' (Blaikie 1993, p. 6).

Paradigm: a set of underlying principles which provides a framework for understanding particular phenomena.

Performance measurement: where output measures are used to determine what has been accomplished by specific programs, services or resource availability.

Phenomenology: description and classification of phenomena, embracing 'the host of personal meanings that are derived from the context of direct experiencing' (Burns 1990, p. 9).

Positivist: from the research tradition, positivism, which adheres to the scientific mode of inquiry and emphasises deductive reasoning, measurement and quantitative data.

Probability sampling: the probability or likelihood of the inclusion of each element of the population can be specified. In true probability sampling, each element must have an *equal* and *independent* chance of being included in the sample.

Prototype: a working version or model of an application system (Pratt and Adamski, 1991, p. 807).

Qualitative data: data in the form of words. (Note that the description of qualitative 'research', rather than 'data', is complex. It is discussed in detail in various chapters of the book.)

Quantitative data: data in the form of numbers. (Note that the description of quantitative 'research', rather than 'data', is complex. It is discussed in detail in various chapters of the book.)

Random sample: each element in the population has an equal and independent opportunity of being selected in the sample.

Relativism: the notion that there is no absolute truth. Truth is contingent on the observer, and the time and place of the observation.

Reliability: is concerned with obtaining consistent, stable research results with replication.

Research method: provides a design for undertaking research, which is underpinned with theoretical explanation of its value and use. Techniques for data gathering and sample selection are usually included as part of this design. (Note that this is the definition employed in this book. Others may adopt different perspectives.)

Research technique: technique means literally 'method of execution' (*Webster's New International Dictionary of the English Language* 1934). In research, techniques are mainly used to collect data.

Symbolic interactionism: a sociological theory which emphasises the individual as a creative, thinking entity, capable of choosing behaviour rather than simply reacting to large-scale forces, as implied by functionalist theories.

Taxonomy: (scientific) classification.

Technique: see *Research technique.*

Theoretical sample: a sample intended to reflect all the major categories of people relevant to the research.

Theory: a viewpoint or perspective which is explanatory. A social science theory is 'a systematic explanation for the observed facts and laws that relate to a specific aspect of life' (Babbie, 1989, p. 46).

Triangulation: the use of two or more methods or techniques to investigate the same research question, or the collecting of '...information from several sources about the same event or behavior' (Hittleman and Simon 1992, p.196).

Validity: is concerned with accuracy. It is a very complex term. Validity in measurement refers to the extent to which a research instrument measures what it is designed to measure.

Variable: something which varies. In a research study examples of possible variables are age, level of education, frequency of library use (for example of respondents in a survey).

References for Glossary

Babbie, Earl. (1989). *The practice of social research.* 5th edn. Wadsworth: Belmont, Ca.

Blaikie, Norman. (1993). *Approaches to social enquiry.* Polity Press: Cambridge.

Bradley, Jana and Sutton, Brett. (1993). Reframing the paradigm debate. *Library Quarterly,* **63** (4), pp.405-410.

Burns, Robert B. (1990.) *Introduction to research methods in education.* Longman Cheshire: Melbourne.

Checkland, Peter. (1993). *Systems thinking, systems practice.* John Wiley & Sons: England.

The concise Oxford dictionary. (1982). 7th edn. J.B. Sykes (ed.). Oxford University Press: Oxford.

Gilliland-Swetland, Anne. (1999). Archival research: A "new" issue for graduate education. Working Meeting of Graduate Archival Educators, 24 August 1999, Pittsburgh. (online). http://www2.sis.pitt.edu/~gaeconf/

Hittleman, Daniel R. and Simon, Alan J. (1992). *Interpreting educational research: An introduction for consumers of research.* Merrill: New York.

The Macquarie dictionary. (1987). 2nd rev. edn. Macquarie Library: Chatswood, NSW.

The new shorter Oxford English dictionary. (1993). Lesley Brown (ed.). Clarendon Press: Oxford.

Pratt, Philip J. and Adamski, Joseph, J. (1991). *Database systems: Management and design.* 2nd edn. Boyd & Fraser: United States.

Reneker, Maxine H. (1993). A qualitative study of information seeking among members of an academic community: Methodological issues and problems. *Library Quarterly,* **63** (4), pp. 487-507.

Webster's new international dictionary of the English language. (1934). C&C Miriam: Springfield, Ma.

Notes on contributors

Amanda Bow is a full-time post-graduate student at RMIT University in Melbourne, working on a thesis which is based on a qualitative study of Australian film audiences, as well as a part-time freelance researcher. She has worked with a number of research organisations, such as QSR (Qualitative Solutions for Research), CIRCIT (Centre for International Research in Communication and Information Technologies) and ITNR (Information and Telecommunications Needs Research). Her work has involved studying consumers and audiences, within the telecommunications and media industries, and, more recently, in online environments.

Dr Frada Burstein is Associate Professor in the School of Information Management and Systems, Monash University. She is an experienced researcher in decision support and knowledge management and systems, with more than 18 years of professional experience in these areas both nationally and internationally. She has been chief investigator for a number of projects researching and implementing systems for delivery of information through various media, and has published more than 100 conference and journal papers based on results of this research. In the School of Information Management and Systems, Associate Professor Burstein has initiated research and teaching in the area of knowledge management. She is currently Director of the Knowledge Management Academic Program and the Monash Knowledge Management Laboratory.

Dr Peta Darke is a Senior Lecturer in the School of Information Management and Systems at Monash University. She holds a PhD in information systems from Monash University. Her research interests include requirements definition, data warehousing and data mining, data quality, and quality in conceptual modelling. Her research has been published in a number of information systems journals.

Professor Ross Harvey is the inaugural Professor of Library and Information Management at Charles Sturt University, taking up his appointment in June 1999. He has held academic positions in Australia (Curtin University of Technology and Monash University), Singapore and New Zealand. His current research is in the areas of preservation of library and archival materials, organisation of information in libraries and archives, and newspaper history. From 1992 to 1995 he was responsible for administering a $450,000 ARC research grant for the 'Australia's Book Heritage Resources' project. He has edited the Bibliographical Society of Australia and New Zealand *Bulletin*, *New Zealand Libraries*, and *Singapore Libraries*, and was a joint general editor of the History of Print Culture in New Zealand Project.

Dr Graeme Johanson is Director of Graduate Studies, School of Information Management and Systems, Monash University. He has published historical works on public health, the politics of conscription, publishing and the book trade, and recently reviewed the patterns of use of resources by scholars in the humanities and social sciences, and the emerging virtual library in Australia. He has worked with researchers and supervised them in a variety of disciplines on a range of different projects.

Professor Sue McKemmish is Head of the School of Information Management and Systems at Monash University. She has been a recordkeeping educator and researcher at Monash University since 1990. As Director of the Enterprise Information Research Group and the Records Continuum Research Group, and Research Associate of the Distributed Systems Technology Centre, she is involved in a wide range of collaborative, multidisciplinary research projects relating to electronic recordkeeping, archival descriptive standards, descriptive metadata, records in distributed enterprises, and enterprise context analysis. Before joining Monash, she worked for 15 years as a recordkeeping professional.

Dr Majola J. H. Oosthuizen received the degrees B.Sc and B.Eng in aeronautical engineering from the University of Stellenbosch, South Africa (1975), and a Graduate Diploma in Business Technology (1988), a Masters in Computing (1995) and a PhD (1999) from Monash University. His research interest is in business strategy development, and in improving commercial strategy-making processes through human facilitation and information systems. He has worked in the aerospace industry in Germany and in the mining, manufacturing and information systems industries in Australia. His current work involves business strategy development in the e-commerce industry.

Solveiga K. Saule is at present studying for a Diploma of Education at the University of Melbourne. She worked as a research associate for the Information and Telecommunications Needs Research (ITNR) group for 18 months from mid-1997 until the end of 1998, and more recently worked on a user needs analysis for a Monash project undertaken for the International Olympic Committee, in which ITNR was involved. In 1999 and 2000 she worked with an international development organisation. Her areas of expertise are qualitative research and evaluation; participation and gender; HIV/AIDS, gender, and poverty.

Professor Don Schauder is Professor of Information Management and Director of Industry and Professional Affairs in the School of Information Management and Systems, Monash University. He is also Associate Dean (Research) of the Monash Faculty of Information Technology, and Chair of the research group, Information & Telecommunication Needs Research, as well as of the Centre for Community Networking Research. He has been Director of several libraries, most recently RMIT University Library. As one of the pioneers of electronic publishing in Australia, he founded INFORMIT Electronic Publishing (now part of RMIT Publishing). He was co-founder of VICNET: Victoria's

Network, based at the State Library of Victoria and has served on information policy committees under successive State Governments, including the Information Society Committee of the Premier's Taskforce on Multimedia and the Library Board of Victoria. His teaching and research focus on the creation and development of information products and services that benefit individuals, organisations and society.

Dr Graeme Shanks is Deputy Head and Associate Professor in the Department of Information Systems at the University of Melbourne. He holds a PhD in Information Systems from Monash University. Before becoming an academic, Graeme worked for a number of private and government organizations as a programmer, systems analyst and project leader. His research interests include information quality, implementation and impact of enterprise systems, and conceptual modelling. He has published his research in *Information Systems Journal, Journal of Strategic Information Systems, Journal of Information Technology, Information and Management, Requirements Engineering, Australian Computer Journal,* and *Australian Journal of Information Systems.*

Kerry Tanner is a Senior Lecturer in the School of Information Management and Systems at Monash University. She is undertaking PhD studies in the in the area of knowledge management in the School. Initially she taught teacher librarians in the Education Department of Victoria, and subsequently at Melbourne State College. She has a Master of Librarianship from the University of NSW and has lectured in the field of library studies and information management since 1972, from 1979 to 1999 as a Lecturer and Senior Lecturer in information management at RMIT.

Dr Kirsty Williamson is Director of Information and Telecommunications Needs Research (ITNR), a joint venture of School of Information Management and Systems, Monash University and School of Information Studies, Charles Sturt University. She is an internationally recognised researcher on information-seeking behaviour and telecommunications use, particularly using an interpretivist approach. She was awarded a three-year scholarship by the Telstra Fund for Social and Policy Research for her PhD research, which was entitled *Older Adults: Information, Communication and Telecommunications.* This PhD study has been internationally recognised, with a project based on it currently being undertaken in Kansas, USA. She has received considerable funding from industry, The Australian Research Council and Monash University, which has enabled her to undertake a considerable amount of research and to publish widely. Her current research interests focus particularly on information and telecommunications needs of older people and people with disabilities, information needs of breast cancer patients, and information provision in public libraries.

Index

social ideals and research, 69-70
social science theory, 58
social sciences research, 25, 27, 39, 159-160, 177, 189
sources triangulation, 36
Spearman rank order correlation, 292
specific questions *see* sub-questions
SPIRT Recordkeeping Metadata Project, 40
Spivak, G.C., 183, 184, 186
Sproull, N.L., 209
SPSS *see* Statistical Package for Social Sciences
Stacks, D. & Hocking, J., 275
standardised interviews *see* structured interviews
Stanfield, J., 178, 183
State Records Authority of New South Wales, 40
statement of research problem, 50-51
statement of research questions, 50-51
static group comparison, 97-99, 140
statistic (sampling), 226
statistical analysis, 41, 290-292
Statistical Package for Social Sciences, 286, 287, 290
statistical probability testing, 126
stereotypes, 184
Stewart, D.W. & Shamdasani, P.N., 169, 251, 254, 256, 258, 259, 261-262
Stieg, M.F., 196
storage of data, 117
stratified sampling, 99, 228-230
structuration theory, 40
structured interviews, 39, 242
subjectivity, 184, 185, 186-187, 188
sub-questions, 51-53
supervision of research, 73
suppression of evidence, 198
surveys, 27, 36, 39, 41, 89-107,
   disk-in-mail, 103
   electronic, 103-106
   email, 104-105
   explanatory, 97-100
   evaluation, 311

   faxed, 103
   health, 99
   newsgroup-based, 105-106
   survey instruments, 92, 235
   telephone, 101-102
   Web-based, 105
Sutton, B., 30, 31, 32, 34
symbolic interactionism, 30, 334
system building, 152-153, 154
system development, 147-155
system evaluation, 152-153
systematic sampling, 230-231
systems research *see* information systems research

Talbot, M., 196
Tam, K.Y., 41
tape recording, 243
taxonomy, 334
technological solutions for libraries, 13
telecommunication needs of older adults, 9, 60
telecommunications behaviour, 35
teleological ethics, 70-71
telephone surveys, 101-102
terminology differences, 38
text analysis, 111
Text Retrieval Conferences *see* TREC
theoretical framework, 10, 58-60, 309-310
theoretical perspective, 325-327
theoretical research *see* basic research
theoretical sampling, 32, 232, 334
theoretical saturation, 232
theory, 58-59
   definition, 334
   in professional practice, 59
   testing, 112, 149, 151
theory building, 6, 7, 17, 31, 34, 53, 58-60, 62, 112, 149-150, 299-300
theses, 63
thick description (ethnography), 178, 183, 186, 293
Thwaites, T., Davis, L. & Mules, W., 266
Tombros, A. & Sanderson, M., 132